FREE SPEECH BEYOND WORDS

Free Speech beyond Words

The Surprising Reach of the First Amendment

Mark V. Tushnet, Alan K. Chen, and Joseph Blocher

NEW YORK UNIVERSITY PRESS
New York

NEW YORK UNIVERSITY PRESS
New York
www.nyupress.org

© 2017 by New York University
All rights reserved

References to Internet websites (URLs) were accurate at the time of writing. Neither the author nor New York University Press is responsible for URLs that may have expired or changed since the manuscript was prepared.

ISBN: 978-1-4798-8028-7

For Library of Congress Cataloging-in-Publication data, please contact the Library of Congress.

New York University Press books are printed on acid-free paper, and their binding materials are chosen for strength and durability. We strive to use environmentally responsible suppliers and materials to the greatest extent possible in publishing our books.

Manufactured in the United States of America

10 9 8 7 6 5 4 3 2 1

Also available as an ebook

To my students

—MVT

To my family and friends, who bring music into my life;
you know who you are

—AKC

To Marin, Ben, and Sam, who make it all meaningful

—JB

CONTENTS

Introduction

The Supreme Court has unanimously held that Jackson Pollock's paintings, Arnold Schoenberg's music, and Lewis Carroll's poem *Jabberwocky* are "unquestionably shielded" by the First Amendment.[1] Nonrepresentational art, instrumental music, and nonsense: all receive constitutional coverage under an amendment protecting "the freedom of *speech*," even though none involves what we typically think of as speech—the use of words to convey meaning.

As a legal matter, the Court's conclusion is clearly correct; but its premises are murky, and they raise difficult questions about the possibilities and limitations of law and expression. Nonrepresentational art, instrumental music, and nonsense do not employ language in any traditional sense and sometimes do not even involve the transmission of articulable ideas. How, then, can they be treated as "speech" for constitutional purposes? What does the difficulty of that question suggest for First Amendment law and theory? And can law resolve such inquiries without relying on aesthetics, ethics, and philosophy?

These are serious challenges for the freedom of speech as it is generally conceived. If the First Amendment is the lodestar of our free speech culture, then it must be able to account for those forms of wordless expression, because they constitute an important type of human communication, both in everyday interaction and in the images, sounds, and actions that make up our cultural and artistic heritage. We express and understand each other through tone and silence, color and structure, rhyme and absurdity.

This book represents a sustained effort to account, constitutionally, for these modes of "speech." We each address one of the categories that the Court confidently declares to be protected: Alan Chen focuses on instrumental music in chapter 1, Mark Tushnet on nonrepresentational art in chapter 2, and Joseph Blocher on nonsense in chapter 3. We employ varying methodologies—Tushnet primarily relies on existing doctrine; Chen and Blocher draw more heavily on aesthetics and analytic philosophy, respectively—and find different justifications for constitutional coverage. But our diverse inquiries reveal and engage overlapping themes and challenges.

I. First Amendment Coverage

As a legal matter, the threshold constitutional question is why the First Amendment should apply *at all* to forms of expression like nonrepresentational art, instrumental music, and nonsense, none of which involve speech in the typical sense. After all, the First Amendment does not even reach all language,[2] let alone all expressive conduct.[3]

Answering the threshold question means charting the boundaries of the First Amendment—a fundamentally different task than exploring its established terrain. The distinction between the two is well captured by what Frederick Schauer has called the coverage/protection distinction.[4] *Coverage* distinguishes those matters to which First Amendment analysis is relevant—handing out a political pamphlet—and those to which it is not, such as discharging polluted water from a factory. *Protection* distinguishes covered material that the government cannot ban or regulate from that which it can. Political speech in a public park, for example, is presumptively *covered* by the First Amendment but can still be banned under particular conditions and therefore might lack *protection* in certain circumstances.

As a doctrinal and scholarly matter, the threshold issue of coverage has traditionally not received nearly as much attention as the intricacies of protection. As Schauer puts it, "the question whether the First Amendment shows up at all is rarely addressed, and the answer is too often simply assumed."[5] Those assumptions dictate results in "easy" cases in both directions, as when we assume without discussion that music, art, and nonsense are covered or that criminal threats and securities offerings are not. This is a serious omission precisely because "questions about the involvement of the . . . Amendment in the first instance are often far more consequential than are the issues surrounding the strength of protection that the . . . Amendment affords the [activities] to which it applies."[6]

The need to understand First Amendment coverage has become all the more acute in recent years because the Supreme Court has demonstrated a sustained interest in the boundaries of free speech. It has decided cases addressing the First Amendment coverage of many unconventional forms of expression, including videos of animal torture,[7] transfers of patient data,[8] and violent video games.[9] In doing so, the justices have also shown an appetite for bright-line rules instead of multifactor balancing tests—when the First Amendment applies, it does so with near-absolute force. This doctrinal development makes the threshold question of coverage even more pressing, because rules tend to collapse the distinction between coverage and protection by extending near-total protection to any speech that receives coverage.

The chapters here offer a new way to look at the question of coverage. Rather than exploring borderline cases, where one might plausibly wonder whether the subject being examined is covered or not, we test the distinction against cases where coverage is intuitively obvious but difficult to justify. Doing so makes it possible to reveal and evaluate not just the limits of First Amendment coverage but the possible *reasons* for it: extensions of existing doctrine, normative visions of free speech, nominalism, conventionalism, or something else entirely. This, in turn, can help make sense of the free speech law we have now and also—as chapter 4 suggests—help answer other questions of the same type.

Explaining the First Amendment's coverage is as difficult as it is fundamental. Consider two appealing and commonly invoked approaches to the matter. One could say that the boundaries of the First Amendment are coterminous with language itself and that "speech" for constitutional purposes consists of words. But as Chen and Tushnet demonstrate in detail in chapters 1 and 2,[10] this kind of "nominalism" is impossible to square with existing (and clearly justified) protection for expressive conduct like flag burning[11] and nude dancing,[12] let alone the Pollocks and Schoenbergs of the world.

One might try to avoid the problem of underinclusion by saying instead that the boundaries of the First Amendment are coextensive not with words per se but with the expression of ideas. In *Miller v. California*, for example, the Court held that "[a]ll ideas having even the slightest redeeming social importance—unorthodox ideas, controversial ideas, even ideas hateful to the prevailing climate of opinion—have the full protection of the [First Amendment's] guaranties."[13] Applying the same logic to the other end of the spectrum, the Court has also indicated that putative speech acts such as fighting words and obscenity fall *outside* the boundaries of the First Amendment in part because they "are no essential part of any exposition of ideas."[14]

But the focus on ideas is also unsatisfactory. Art and music express a great deal, but it would distort them tremendously to say that they must convey "ideas" in order to qualify for constitutional protection. As Chen and Tushnet demonstrate in chapters 1 and 2, art and music can convey a lot, but their power is not tied to the transmission of ideas as such. Blocher shows in chapter 3 that the same can be true even for words that convey no discernible meanings or ideas—such "nonsense" might nonetheless have a strong claim to constitutional coverage. It follows that ideas, like words, are not a reliable guide to the First Amendment's reach.

Given such complications, it is tempting to avoid the question of coverage by transforming it into one of protection. One might simply assume that art, music, and nonsense are covered by the First Amendment but that, in appropriate cases, the government can regulate or ban them—that they are covered but not always protected, in other words. But this, too, is unsatisfactory, as Tushnet points out in chapter 2, because it takes "too much work to solve what should be a fairly easy problem." The whole point of treating the First Amendment as having boundaries is to *avoid* in-depth analysis of cases involving uncovered conduct. If there is no way to have a threshold, then the coverage/protection distinction simply breaks down. This, in turn, illuminates a second theme common to the chapters: the difficulty of providing satisfactory answers to supposedly easy questions.

II. Hard Answers to "Easy" Questions

Ordinarily, constitutional scholars examine hard questions—for example, whether hate speech regulation, pornography bans, or campaign finance rules are consistent with the First Amendment—and, by trying to develop answers, explore and gain a better understanding of the theory and practice of free speech. Here, by contrast, the questions seem easy. It *must* be right that art, music, and nonsense fall within the First Amendment's sphere of coverage.

The very obviousness of these answers probably has led scholars to think that they are *easy* and that exploring the reasons for those answers is not worth the effort. Those judgments are mistaken. Getting to the conclusion about First Amendment coverage is fraught with doctrinal and conceptual difficulties. Those difficulties are worth engaging precisely because they yield interesting and potentially important insights about law and speech.

Asking the easy questions can be surprisingly disturbing, because it reveals that the First Amendment's foundations are less settled than we might suppose or want. The fact that art, music, and nonsense are so hard to justify as objects of the First Amendment demonstrates that some of the results we take for granted are precisely the things that need the most explanation. If First Amendment doctrine and theory cannot explain these results well because these tools were developed in order to address "hard" cases, not easy ones, then their shortcomings must be recognized, and perhaps they must be refashioned. Nowhere is this clearer than with regard to existing First Amendment doctrine.

III. The Limits of Legal Doctrine

Attempts to answer basic questions about art, music, and nonsense using the standard tools of First Amendment doctrine quickly run into problems. Those tools, and their limits, are simple enough to describe.

Consider the fundamental distinction—among the most foundational in all of free speech law[15]—between content-based and content-neutral regulations. Under existing doctrine, a law is content based if it, on its face, regulates speech on the basis of its "content"[16] or if it is justified by reference to the "content" of the regulated speech.[17] Chief Justice John Roberts recently suggested that a regulation is content based "when the conduct triggering coverage . . . consists of communicating a message."[18] Content-based regulations are subject to strict scrutiny, which is frequently fatal. Content-neutral laws, by contrast, are subject to less demanding tests,[19] which the government can usually satisfy. In many First Amendment cases, then, the classification of the challenged regulation as content based or content neutral is outcome dispositive. If it is content neutral, it is constitutional;[20] if it is content based, it is not.[21]

"Buffer zones" around health care facilities provide a particularly salient example of the issue and its importance. In 2000, the Supreme Court considered the constitutionality of a Colorado statute that established a one-hundred-foot radius around the entrances to health care facilities and prohibited persons from coming within eight feet of an unwilling listener for purposes of "oral protest, education, or counseling."[22] Abortion protestors argued that this was a content-based restriction on their speech, but the Court found that the law was content neutral and upheld it. In 2014, the Court was faced with a First Amendment challenge to a somewhat more restrictive buffer zone and again found the law content neutral, although constitutionally defective on other grounds.[23]

Now imagine that, instead of attempting to engage in "oral protest, education, or counseling," the abortion protestors display disturbing nonrepresentational art outside the clinics or play harsh atonal music or shout gibberish. Colorado amends its law to prohibit those actions as well, and the protestors challenge the new law on First Amendment grounds. Are they exercising their right to free speech? Is the revised law content neutral as applied to them?

The standard tools of doctrine described earlier do not provide clear answers. As chapters 1 and 2 suggest, many musicians and artists argue that the form of their work *is* its content. To demand that it have a "message" is to demand that it be something else. It therefore takes some work to say that in this situation "the conduct triggering coverage"—nonrepresentational art, instrumental music, and nonsense—"consists of communicating a message," to take the chief justice's articulation.

Consider, too, the standard test that the Supreme Court has articulated for distinguishing communicative acts from uncovered conduct. In *Spence v. Washington*, the Court held that nonverbal conduct is speech when the actor has "an intent to convey a particularized message" and "in the surrounding circumstances the likelihood was great that the message would be understood by those who viewed it."[24] Instrumental music, nonrepresentational art, and nonsense are unlikely to satisfy either prong of the *Spence* test, let alone both—they might convey no message at all, let alone a "particularized" one, and are very frequently misunderstood in any event. Perhaps that helps explain why the *Spence* test has occasionally been quietly deemphasized and sometimes ignored altogether.[25] Like the content-neutrality inquiry, the questions it asks are ill suited to the job. Nonrepresentational art, instrumental music, and nonsense do not have standard propositional content, and so it is extremely difficult to get even the most basic doctrinal analysis up and running.

IV. The Poverty of First Amendment Theory

When existing doctrinal tools are not up to the task, one option is to go directly to the forge and to craft new ones. For free speech scholars, this typically means turning to the various normative theories that have been proposed to justify and explain the First Amendment itself.

It would take—has taken—many books to canvass the normative theories of the First Amendment that have been proposed over the years. The leading candidates tend to be grouped into three main categories. First are marketplace-of-ideas theories, which suggest that speech must be free so that truth can emerge from open discussion of ideas and competition among them. Second are democratic theories, which hold that speech must be protected to facilitate democratic government. Third are autonomy theories, which connect speech protections to the autonomy of individual speakers. Each of these theories (and their respective values of knowledge, democracy, and autonomy) has implications for what types of speech are entitled to First Amendment coverage. Those who subscribe to a democracy-based theory, for example, tend to accord primary (and sometimes exclusive)[26] protection to political speech.

How do these theories help answer specific questions of First Amendment coverage? One common method of approach is simply to say that acts furthering the relevant value are constitutionally protected. Indeed, it is standard form in scholarly articles—including chapters 1 and 3 here—to canvass the leading theories for this purpose. Thus, for example, if campaign donations help enrich the marketplace of ideas by adding more thoughts to the political milieu or advance the democratic ideal by empowering candidates to challenge incumbents, then they should be considered a form of constitutionally covered free speech (and presumptively protected).

Despite the simplicity and appeal of this theory-based approach, it is not sufficient, as noted in chapters 1 and 3. Chapter 2 likewise demonstrates that scalping tickets is expressive and undoubtedly furthers the autonomy of the scalper (and, perhaps, the marketplace of ideas), and yet no one supposes that it is a freedom protected by the First

Amendment. Perhaps, then, the fact that an act furthers the relevant First Amendment value is a necessary but not sufficient condition for its constitutional protection. Maybe only "speech" acts that further the relevant value can or should be protected. But if that is the case, it simply raises again the question of what acts count as "speech" and why.

One can respond to the awkward fit between those categories of speech and standard First Amendment theories in several different ways. The most obvious options are to finesse or reject the categories as proper objects of the Constitution or else to finesse or reject the theories as inadequate explanations of the Constitution's reach. In this book, we unanimously reject the first option. In keeping with the Supreme Court's confident assertion, we conclude that nonrepresentational art, instrumental music, and nonsense are all within the scope of constitutional coverage, at least sometimes.

As to the second possibility—rejecting First Amendment theory—the chapters differ in their responses to the challenge, but all three find it quite difficult to explain the constitutional coverage of music, art, and nonsense using any master theory of the First Amendment. Any effort to do so raises problems of over- and underbreadth. Consider the first[27] and perhaps still most prominent[28] First Amendment theory: the "marketplace of ideas," which rests on the notion that, if left unregulated, good ideas will eventually win out over bad ones. In U.S. law, the theory is traced to Justice Oliver Wendell Holmes's argument that "the best test of truth is the power of the thought to get itself accepted in the competition of the market."[29] Justice Louis Brandeis similarly argued that "freedom to think as you will and to speak as you think are means indispensable to the discovery and spread of political truth."[30]

But what "truths"—or even "ideas"—are expressed by nonrepresentational art, instrumental music, and nonsense? Scholars have long noted that the cognitive focus of the marketplace theory makes it ill suited to account for such matters.[31] The same is true of other First Amendment theories—in chapters 1 and 2, for example, we find that democratic theories of the First Amendment cannot satisfactorily justify the coverage of nonrepresentational art or instrumental music.

For all three of us, the best explanation arises from cobbling together bits and pieces from a range of approaches to constitutional law. That this sort of theoretical eclecticism or diversity seems necessary with respect to foundational questions in First Amendment law suggests that it might be an appropriate way to think about constitutional problems more generally. In some sense, then, the chapters can be read as contributing to a literature "against First Amendment theory" and even "against constitutional theory" more generally.

V. Looking outside the Law: Theory and Convention

It appears that legal doctrine and even legal theory are unable to provide fully satisfying answers to the kinds of questions with which we started. But precisely because they are legal questions, they are hard to avoid. Generally, a court cannot simply say, "It is too difficult for us to decide whether Jackson Pollock's artwork is 'speech' for First Amendment purposes. It is so ordered." If legal doctrine and theory cannot solve the puzzle, where can judges and scholars turn?

One route is to close the casebooks and go in search of other intellectual tools. The chapters vary in their reliance on these tools. Chapter 2 investigates the First Amendment status of nonrepresentational art while avoiding forays into the philosophy of language or art. The benefits of doing so are considerable, for it permits people with very different (often unarticulated or unexamined) views about deep theories of art to agree on basic constitutional principles—a kind of "overlapping consensus" approach to constitutional law. This approach also avoids reliance on the judiciary's ability to articulate or consciously apply the kinds of intellectually sophisticated theories akin to those offered by professional philosophers, including theorists of art and music. Indeed, as Justice Holmes once put it, judging the value of art is a "dangerous undertaking for persons trained only to the law."[32]

Chapters 1 and 3 make heavier use of theory—aesthetics and analytic philosophy, respectively—in order to explain various legal rules, although neither Chen nor Blocher would necessarily make such theories an explicit part of legal doctrine. They do suggest that extralegal theories can nevertheless be a useful tool in exploring legal results, at least when judges and philosophers confront common questions such as how to impute meaning to images, sounds, or words. This means using philosophy for illumination, not for authority or precedent. Holmes did not need to cite John Stuart Mill and John Milton as authority for his own theory of the "marketplace of ideas,"[33] even though their analogous theories preceded his.[34]

Though we take different routes, Blocher's and Chen's use of theory and Tushnet's skepticism of it end up in some of the same places. Each of us endorses or employs a kind of conventionalism that would focus on art, music, and nonsense as social practices, rather than trying to pin down any easily articulable justification of their meaning or value. Whether this conventionalism is the application of a theory or a rejection of theory, it leads us to face the same basic challenge as the practices we evaluate: to say what cannot be said. And yet those practices often *succeed* in conveying something important—perhaps something ineffable. Beyond the limits of our shared language—beyond words—may well lie important truths and insights. Perhaps any effort to make legal sense of the expressions of those truths must likewise acknowledge the limits of language.

This is a disturbing suggestion for people trained in the law. From the day lawyers start law school, they are inculcated with the view that the very legitimacy of legal decision making rests on its ability to provide *reasons through words*. Judges, no less than lawyers and scholars, go to great lengths not only to announce who has prevailed in a given case but to explain *why*. Indeed, those reasons are considered the "result" that is binding on future cases. If the Supreme Court were simply to say, "The government may not ban Jackson Pollock's paintings, but we will not say why. It is so ordered," lawyers would treat the decision as a form of nonrepresentational performance on par with Pollock's own work.

And yet the obligation to decide persists, even when words fail. Consider Justice Potter Stewart's famous—one might say infamous—statement, "I might never succeed in intelligibly" defining hard-core pornography, and yet "I know it when I see it."[35] Stewart faced, from a judicial perspective, the same problem faced by so many others engaged in art, music, and philosophy—how to express what cannot be said—and his solution was not necessarily much different from theirs.

We might, at least in certain circumstances, have to become comfortable with Stewart's approach[36] and find answers outside of the words and reasons typically thought to be the lifeblood of legal reasoning. Rather than look for a particularized message in an act of "speech," perhaps the best solution is to identify the social practices and conventions that constitute human expression and communication.[37] Indeed, in the same passage in which the Supreme Court declared that Pollock, Schoenberg, and Carroll are "unquestionably shielded," it rejected the notion that free speech is limited to "expressions conveying a 'particularized message'" and went on to hold that a parade qualifies as speech.[38] For First Amendment purposes, the most satisfying explanation for this holding may simply be that the justices know speech when they see it.

Attempts to make constitutional sense of "free speech beyond words" run into the same linguistic barriers as the practices themselves. But as art, music, and nonsense show (rather than say), sometimes things are worth expressing even when they cannot be put into words.

* * *

We began this introduction by endorsing the Court's conclusion that nonrepresentational art, instrumental music, and nonsense are all shielded by the First Amendment, but we have cast doubt on the notion that they are "unquestionably" so. It would, we think, be more accurate to say that they are unquestion*ingly* shielded. And so, in the expectation that the inquiry will ultimately yield something interesting and useful, we take up the question in the following chapters. We approach it in different ways and do not always agree with one another about the answers or even the proper tools, but our tasks are deeply and inevitably intertwined.

Chapter 1 begins with a question: If a picture is worth a thousand words, what about a C#? This chapter critically examines what would seem to be, but is not, an easy free speech question—whether instrumental music falls within the scope of the First Amendment. It comprehensively engages the question of whether there are sound theoretical or doctrinal foundations for treating purely instrumental music as a form of constitutionally protected expression.

In examining these claims, the chapter first surveys existing judicial and scholarly treatments of music as speech to illustrate how our understanding of the expressive value of instrumental music has been undertheorized. It then briefly catalogues historical and contemporary instances of instrumental music censorship, both within the United States and in other nations, by governments and other powerful institutions. The chapter next considers the three dominant theoretical justifications for protection of expression—promotion of democratic self-governance, facilitation of the search for truth, and protection of autonomy through self-realization—and explores the possibilities for and limits of employing any of these three theories to justify protection of instrumental music. As it turns out, these theories do not offer an obvious explanation for why instrumental music should be covered by the First Amendment.

To truly understand how these speech theories might apply, however, the law must first comprehend the nature of instrumental musical expression. Accordingly, the chapter next discusses exactly what it is that instrumental music expresses and how it does so and examines how those conceptualizations fit within the frameworks of the three dominant speech theories. This part concludes with an elaboration of the claim that music is like speech because of its unique power to convey cultural, religious, nationalist, and other social values and to promote emotional expression and experience in its composers, performers, and listeners. Music, then, falls within both the truth-seeking and self-realization justifications for the First Amendment. In contrast, theoretical explanations for free speech grounded in democracy do not map well onto nonlyrical musical expression.

Chapter 2 explores the question of the First Amendment's coverage of nonrepresentational art. That question turns out to be quite difficult to answer in a doctrinal form that preserves other seemingly "unquestionable" results. Every approach one might take to explaining why the First Amendment covers art—that art is communicative, that it contributes to the creation of a culture of self-directed individuals, and others—generates odd anomalies. The exploration does not question the conventional conclusion that the First Amendment covers artwork but rather worries some of the often-unstated assumptions that underlie that conclusion. We will see, for example, that some things one might want to say about the question of whether the First Amendment covers nonrepresentational art lead to the suggestion that James Joyce's *Ulysses* might not be covered, surely a peculiar result. By asking how the conclusion that nonrepresentational art is covered by the First Amendment might be justified, we will come across some unexpected facets of the First Amendment with some implications for other doctrinal areas abutting the First Amendment.

Chapter 3 examines a category of "speech" that has long puzzled philosophers of language but has yet to attract the attention of legal scholars: nonsense. A great deal of everyday expression is, strictly speaking, nonsense. But courts and scholars have done little to consider whether or why such meaningless speech, like nonrepresentational art, falls within "the freedom of speech." If, as many legal scholars suggest, meaning is what separates speech from sound and expression from conduct, then the constitutional case for nonsense is complicated. And because nonsense is so common, the case is also important—artists like Lewis Carroll and Jackson Pollock are not the only putative "speakers" who should be concerned about the outcome.

This chapter explores the relationship between nonsense and the freedom of speech; in doing so, it suggests ways to determine what "meaning" means for First Amendment purposes. The chapter begins by demonstrating the scope and constitutional salience of meaningless speech, showing that nonsense is multifarious, widespread, and sometimes intertwined with traditional First Amendment values like autonomy, the marketplace of ideas, and democracy. The second part argues that exploring nonsense can illuminate the meaning of meaning itself. This, too, is an important task, for although free speech discourse often relies on the concept of meaning to chart the First Amendment's scope, courts and scholars have done relatively little to establish what it entails. Analytic philosophers, meanwhile, have spent the past century doing little else. Their efforts—echoes of which can already be heard in First Amendment doctrine—suggest that free speech doctrine is best served by finding meaning in the way words are *used*, rather than in their relationship to extralinguistic concepts.

Finally, in chapter 4, we suggest ways in which our analysis might be extended to other problems and questions involving extralinguistic communication, such as the constitutional status of dancing and data.

1

Instrumental Music and the First Amendment

After silence, that which comes nearest to expressing the inexpressible is music.
—Aldous Huxley, "The Rest Is Silence"

If a picture is worth a thousand words, what about a C#?[1] Or the flatted
third, fifth, or seventh note in a blues scale? Or a glissando[2] or other run
of musical notes strung together in a particular sequence and rhythm,
such as a Tuvan throat song,[3] the first four notes of Beethoven's Fifth
Symphony,[4] the syncopated piano introduction to Dave Brubeck's "Blue
Rondo à La Turk,"[5] or the trademark guitar riff that opens Jimi Hendrix's "Purple Haze"?[6] The Supreme Court and lower courts have long
accepted that musical expression falls within the category of "speech"
safeguarded by the First Amendment. But no court has ever explained in
any meaningful way why the musical, as opposed to lyrical, component
of such expression is independently covered by the Constitution. There
has been no comprehensive examination of the reasons justifying the
constitutional coverage and protection of the tonal and rhythmic elements that define what we recognize as instrumental music.

The scholarly literature is also surprisingly bereft of comprehensive
discussions of the theoretical or doctrinal foundations for treating purely
instrumental music as expression under the Constitution. Typically, such
music is treated as an aside or is lumped in for discussion with other forms
of nonverbal artistic expression, such as painting and sculpture. Commentators have paid far less attention to the unique elements of pure musical
expression. This chapter attempts to fill that gap by examining, challenging, and defending the conclusion that instrumental music is speech and
is worthy of robust First Amendment protection comparable to the safeguards that are commonplace for most verbal expression. In doing so, it
offers a full theoretical account supporting the idea that instrumental musical expression is constitutionally equivalent to speech.

Instrumental music is a somewhat curious free speech topic. Perhaps it has not received serious attention in First Amendment doctrine and theory because it is inaccurately perceived to be an easy question. Most professional and lay observers probably believe instinctively that instrumental music is constitutionally protected. It is difficult to imagine a functioning democracy in which the state could control the communication of musical notes and rhythms any more than we would tolerate, in most cases, the regulation of pure speech. Moreover, we also cannot imagine circumstances in which such censorship would occur. It seems implausible that the government or other institutional powers would restrict instrumental music or that they would ever have a reason to do so. Yet, as we shall see, they have.

Part 1 of this chapter surveys the slim judicial and scholarly treatments of music as speech to illustrate how our understanding of the expressive value of instrumental music has been undertheorized. Part 1 continues by briefly cataloguing historical and contemporary instances of the censorship of instrumental music. Public school districts in the United States have successfully defeated free speech challenges to their bans on student performances of exclusively instrumental music during school programs because of the music's religious content. Federally licensed broadcasters and private businesses influenced by industry trade groups have prohibited or regulated purely instrumental music. Selective bans on instrumental music have been implemented in democratic states, such as Israel, in totalitarian regimes, such as Nazi Germany and the former Soviet Republic, and in nations with sectarian-dominated governments, such as Iran and the Taliban-controlled Afghanistan.

Though instrumental music is probably widely understood as a form of expression, current theory and doctrine do not offer an easy explanation for why it should fall within the scope of the First Amendment. Part 2 of this chapter surveys the three dominant theoretical justifications for protection of free expression—promotion of democratic self-governance, facilitation of the search for truth, and protection of autonomy through self-realization—and explores the possibilities for and limits of employing any of these three theories to justify protection of instrumental music. Theoretical explanations for free speech grounded in the promotion of democratic self-governance do not map well onto nonlyrical musical expression. Nor is it self-evident that protection of instrumental music is necessary to protect the marketplace of ideas in order to facilitate the search for truth, at least without embracing an unbounded definition of truth. An autonomy-based justification for protection of expression provides what is probably the most intuitive basis for understanding instrumental music as speech. But the autonomy argument for speech is also vulnerable to boundary claims, and a full exploration of the issue at hand must address those claims and precisely articulate what autonomy means in the context of the right to compose, perform, and listen to instrumental music.

The most fundamental challenge of harmonizing instrumental music with the dominant free speech theories is discerning exactly what it is that such music expresses and how it does so. Part 3 explores five possible ways of viewing instrumental music as speech and examines how those conceptualizations might fit within the frameworks of these theories. First, it explores whether the First Amendment might cover instrumental music because of the music's appeal to the cognitive. Instrumental music may evoke or be associated with specific thoughts, ideas, or concepts that provoke cognitive responses or functions in listeners. Music may also be expressive to the degree that it enhances or colors other communicative vehicles in ways that make their messages more effective. A third possibility is that instrumental music does, in fact, have a direct cognitive component that thus far has been unstudied and unappreciated. Ultimately, however, the chapter concludes that none of the cognitive theories are sufficient to support the claim that music is speech.

Next, the chapter examines two different, but compelling, conceptions of instrumental music's communicative value. First, throughout history, the composition, performance, and auditory consumption of musical expression has played an essential role in forming, shaping, maintaining, and distinguishing values of culture, religion, and nationalism through a stunning variety of indigenous music forms and traditions. Simultaneously (perhaps coextensively), music has long been understood as a unique form of emotional expression and experience for its composers, performers, and listeners.

After canvassing the possible ways of understanding how instrumental music communicates, the discussion circles back to examine the implications of each of these communicative possibilities for First

Amendment theory. Ultimately, the chapter argues that the strongest claim for the coverage of instrumental music under the First Amendment can be derived from its dual role in expressing cultural and other social values that might otherwise be at risk of government control and orthodoxy and from its function as a facilitator of emotional expression, experience, and autonomy.[7] These latter two understandings accept the premise that instrumental musical expression is nonrepresentational[8] yet provide compelling support for the claim that in serving these functions, music advances both the truth-seeking and self-realization objectives of free speech theory.

I. The Undertheorization of Instrumental Music as Speech

Although music plays a central role in the social, political, and cultural life of most societies and has been at the center of several important legal disputes, neither the courts nor the academy have carefully studied its foundations as a type of speech that triggers constitutional protection. If instrumental music is not speech, then we never reach the subsequent question of whether it is constitutionally protected. As the following discussion suggests, attention to this issue has been sparse, incomplete, and unsatisfying.[9]

A. The Courts

1. COVERAGE OF NONVERBAL EXPRESSION IN GENERAL

It has long been understood that the protection of the First Amendment, notwithstanding its text privileging the "freedom of speech," is not limited to, and indeed is not defined by, written or oral verbal expression. Some nonverbal communication is covered by the First Amendment; much verbal expression is not.[10] The Supreme Court has found the following nonverbal, communicative acts to be covered by the free speech clause: flag burning,[11] cross burning,[12] participating in a parade,[13] picketing,[14] nude dancing,[15] and wearing a black armband.[16] Instrumental music has also been deemed to be covered, though with very little analysis.

The Court has not been particularly precise about defining when nonverbal communication falls within the First Amendment's coverage.

Among the tests that it (sometimes) uses to discern between communicative acts and uncovered conduct is the one from *Spence v. Washington*. Spence challenged his state law conviction for "improper use" of a flag when he displayed an upside-down American flag on which he had placed large peace symbols made of black tape.[17] The Court underscored that because Spence did not use "printed or spoken words," it was necessary to evaluate the context in which he acted "to determine whether his activity was sufficiently imbued with elements of communication to fall within the scope of the First Amendment."[18] *Spence* held that nonverbal conduct is speech when the speaker has both "[a]n intent to convey a particularized message . . . and in the surrounding circumstances the likelihood was great that the message would be understood by those who viewed it."[19] The Court concluded that Spence's conduct was covered by the First Amendment because he testified that he displayed the flag to express his disagreement with the U.S. military's invasion of Cambodia and his dismay about the shootings of student protestors at Kent State University.

One might infer from *Spence* that the intent and understanding elements of the Court's analysis should determine whether instrumental musical expression and other forms of nonverbal conduct are covered by the First Amendment.[20] But the Court has not rigidly adhered to the *Spence* test. For example, in the first flag-burning case, *Texas v. Johnson*, the Court recognized the burning of an American flag as speech, even though neither the flag burner's intent nor the audience's understanding of his message could be said to be particularized.[21] The protestor's conduct could have conveyed a broad dissatisfaction with the United States as a general matter or any manner of narrower disagreements with the nation's myriad actions and policies. In *National Endowment for the Arts v. Finley*, in which several artists challenged denial of federal funding for their work,[22] the Court assumed the artwork was expressive without even discussing whether such art would convey a specific message that would be understood by viewers. Thus, it is not entirely clear that the particularized message requirement is essential, a point that becomes important when analyzing instrumental music.

Finley also exposes the Court's inconsistent application of *Spence*'s intent requirement. The artists in that case specifically argued that art is often ambiguous in its meaning and not always intended to convey a message.[23] Nonetheless, the Court did not dispute the expressive value of art in rendering its decision.

2. COVERAGE OF INSTRUMENTAL MUSICAL EXPRESSION IN PARTICULAR

Although the Supreme Court has addressed and embraced the constitutional status of musical expression on a handful of occasions, it has never closely examined the premises of its conclusions. Rather than engaging in a careful or thoughtful consideration of music as speech, the Court has instead made superficial assumptions and conveyed lofty, unquestioning platitudes.[24] Perhaps more to the point, it has never broken down musical expression into its essential components—tonal, rhythmic, and lyrical—and independently addressed whether each of them is covered by the First Amendment. Indeed, the phrase "instrumental music" has never appeared in a Supreme Court opinion. Any thoughtful analysis of this question requires the disaggregation of the distinct components of musical expression to help establish a better foundation for understanding why and in what circumstances it ought to be constitutionally protected.

In *Ward v. Rock Against Racism*, the Court examined the First Amendment claims of a nonprofit organization that sponsored an annual event consisting of speeches and the performance of rock music at a band shell in Central Park. Responding to complaints of nearby residents and park users, New York City adopted new regulations that required the organization to use sound equipment and a sound technician provided by the city. The organization's free speech claim was that the city's imposition of these requirements interfered with the performers' expression because the electronic amplification through the equipment affected not only the music's volume but also the way the sounds were mixed. The regulation thus altered the content of the musical performances by dictating the outcome and quality of the sound.[25]

While the Court upheld the city's regulations on the ground that they were reasonable restrictions on the manner of speech in a public forum, it deemed the predicate claim that music is speech under the First Amendment to be self-evident: "Music is one of the oldest forms of human expression. From Plato's discourse in the Republic to the totalitarian state in our own times, rulers have known its capacity to appeal to the intellect and to the emotions, and have censored musical compositions to serve the needs of the state. The Constitution prohibits any like attempts in our own legal order. Music, as a form of expression and communication, is protected under the First Amendment."[26] Nor did the parties even seriously dispute this proposition. However, the Court never specified whether the rock performances at issue were vocal or instrumental and therefore did not unpack and analyze the different components of musical expression. Sound mixing is necessarily about the construction of sound, but it affects not only the quality of the instrumental components of the performances but also the sound and understandability of lyrics. To the extent that the status of instrumental music as speech is in question, *Ward* did not provide a satisfying answer.[27]

In two other cases, *Southeastern Promotions v. Conrad* and *City of Newport v. Fact Concerts, Inc.*, the Court assumed that music was covered by the First Amendment but did not independently consider whether the musical component of the performances was itself expressive. In *Southeastern Promotions*, the Court addressed a prior restraint challenge by a theater company whose application to perform the musical *Hair* at a municipal theater was rejected by city officials on the ground that the play would not be "in the best interest of the community." Although the Court found the city's actions to be an unconstitutional prior restraint, its discussion of live musical drama as speech did not disaggregate the musical components from the lyrics sung by the actors in the play. Rather, as it observed, "[b]y its nature, theater usually is the acting out—or singing out—of the written *word*, and frequently mixes speech with live action or conduct."[28] Thus, the Court's reference to musical expression was limited to its lyrical components. In *Fact Concerts*, the Court also assumed without discussion that music is covered by the First Amendment. Although presented to the Court on the issue of punitive damages, the case essentially involved a concert promoter's challenge to a city's cancellation of a permit for a performance at a jazz festival on the grounds that the musical group Blood, Sweat & Tears was a rock group rather than a jazz group.[29] The Court failed to discuss or distinguish *Spence's* particularized message standard in *Ward*, *Southeastern Promotions*, or *Fact Concerts*.

The closest the Court has come to specifically recognizing instrumental music as speech is in its consideration of whether parades are constitutionally protected forms of expression in *Hurley v. Irish-American Gay, Lesbian and Bisexual Group of Boston*. *Hurley* involved a successful challenge by organizers of a St. Patrick's Day parade to a state public accommodations law that had been held to require them to permit a group of gay, lesbian, and bisexual persons of Irish descent to participate in the organizers' parade. The Court's unanimous opinion in support of the parade organizers' First Amendment rights to exclude the gay, lesbian, and bisexual group from their parade began with a discussion of the speech value of parades. In its analysis, the Court rejected the idea that speech must convey a "particularized message" to be protected by the First Amendment. Such a restrictive interpretation would have meant, the Court observed, that the First Amendment would not "reach the *unquestionably shielded* painting of Jackson Pollock, music of Arnold Schoenberg, or Jabberwocky verse of Lewis Carroll."[30] Schoenberg, a modern classical composer, created mostly instrumental musical works.[31] Again, however, this part of the Court's decision is a conclusion, not an analysis.

For the most part, the lower courts have been equally unedifying. In two recent cases, the federal courts of appeal have addressed First Amendment challenges by high school students who were forbidden to perform instrumental musical pieces because of their religious meaning.[32] One court declared in cursory fashion, "It is clear to us that purely instrumental music—i.e., music with no lyrics—is speech."[33] The entirety of its analysis involved a citation to the Supreme Court's decisions in *Ward* and *Hurley*, as well as a quote from a parenthetical reference to another case that did nothing but cite *Ward* as well. The other court also failed to specifically address whether the instrumental musical performances were covered by the First Amendment.[34]

The most thoughtful lower-court discussion of music actually emerges from a decision about the regulation of nude dancing. In *Miller v. Civil City of South Bend*, later reversed by the Supreme Court in *Barnes v. Glen Theatre, Inc.*, several of the circuit judges' opinions commented in dicta on whether music was speech under the First Amendment. Sitting en banc, the Seventh Circuit in *Miller* invalidated a city ordinance banning public nudity as applied to a commercial establishment where concededly nonobscene nude dancing was performed for entertainment. In doing so, the court rejected the state's and the dissenters' arguments distinguishing art from "entertainment," noting, among other things, "not all music appeals to the *intellect*."[35]

Concurring in the court's decision, Judge Richard Posner observed that the argument that nude dancing is not speech because it does not express ideas or opinions could also support the claim that "nonvocal" (that is, instrumental) music is not speech. Music, he suggested, is covered by the First Amendment even when it does not convey a particular message:

> [E]ven if "thought," "concept," "idea," and "opinion" are broadly defined, these are not what most music conveys; and even if music is regarded as a language, it is not a language for encoding ideas and opinions. Insofar as it is more than beautiful sound patterns, music, like striptease, organizes, conveys, and arouses emotion, though not sexual emotion primarily. If the striptease dancing at the Kitty Kat Lounge is not expression, Mozart's piano concertos and Balanchine's most famous ballets are not expression.[36]

He went on to argue that if music must be propositional to count as speech, it would mean that most instrumental music would receive less protection than nude dancing and that "Beethoven's string quartets are entitled to less protection than *Peter and the Wolf*."[37]

Judge Frank Easterbrook agreed in his dissent that music is a form of art that is protected but argued that it is completely distinguishable from nude dancing in a barroom. In his view, music and other art forms are pure communication, not conduct that is expressive, like flag burning or a strip tease. As he observed,

> People may fairly dispute whether absolute music, such as LaMonte Young's *Well-Tuned Piano*, communicates thoughts, but surely it embodies them (the right place for the major third, etc.); all that we call music is the product of rational human thought and appeals at least in part to the same faculties in others. It has the "capacity to appeal to the intellect," . . . is not "conduct," and is closer to speech (even an emotional harangue is speech) than to smashing a Ming vase or kicking a cat, two other ways to express emotion.[38]

Notwithstanding the judges' fundamental disagreement about the merits of the case, Posner and Easterbrook elaborated more carefully about the conception of music as speech than have any other judicial actors before or since.[39]

B. The Scholarly Literature

Academics have also paid surprisingly little attention to the question of instrumental music as speech. Several excellent scholarly works have tried to define the more general boundaries of art as speech but for the most part have done so without identifying music as a unique form of expression.[40] Nonetheless, these commentaries provide an indispensable starting point, for there is a degree of overlap between the speech value of other art forms and instrumental music. A common thread that connects that work with this book is the agreement that free speech theory and doctrine have not adequately addressed the complex issues associated with artistic expression.

Marci Hamilton and Sheldon Nahmod have presented earlier treatments of art and speech that provide useful foundations for thinking about music. Hamilton argues that art ought to be acknowledged as speech specifically because of its subversive possibilities, offering its "singular capacity to offer the experience of new worlds and therefore new perspectives on the status quo."[41] Thus, art is speech because of its unique ability to be subversive, to "defamiliarize" conventionality, and to promote what she calls its "instrumental, liberty-reinforcing role in a representative democracy."[42]

In contrast, Nahmod argues that it is not fruitful to attempt to derive artistic expression's value through the lens of political speech. Rather, he claims that art should be acknowledged as valuable independent of its role in political discourse, however broadly defined. Drawing on aesthetic theory, and in particular on Plato and Kant, Nahmod suggests that art should be independently valued for its ability to promote the beautiful and the sublime. From his perspective, the flaw in most thinking about art and free speech is the notion that art must convey a specific message or meaning to fall within the three predominant justifications for constitutional protection of expression.[43]

Important insights to the discourse on art and the First Amendment come from Mark Tushnet in chapter 2 in this volume. Tushnet views questions about art's coverage as much more complicated than courts and commentators are inclined to recognize. Though art, like music, seems like an easy case, there are no easy answers.

As we shall see, Tushnet makes a number of critical observations, a couple of which are highlighted here. First, he rejects what he calls the "rationality challenge," which suggests that the question of the First Amendment's coverage of art is not an important one because there will rarely be legitimate governmental reasons to suppress art. On this view, any state regulation of artistic expression would likely be invalidated by a substantive due process challenge because the state's action would not be rational.[44] As Tushnet points out, however, there sometimes may be "legitimate" (though not necessarily compelling) government interests in regulating artwork, such as when highly offensive artwork is displayed publicly.[45]

Indeed, the rationality challenge is a bit of an analytical dodge. It is a sort of legal reverse engineering, working backward from the lack of governmental interest to define something as speech, while offering no independent understanding of why speech is covered by the First Amendment or bears any value at all. There are many government regulations that might lack even a plausible justification, but that does not make the conduct they regulate speech. Such laws may still be unconstitutional because they are arbitrary but not necessarily because the regulated activity is important or valuable.

Tushnet also makes the case that basing coverage determinations on the speaker's intent (as in *Spence*) is both overinclusive (violent conduct intended to convey displeasure with the government is not covered) and underinclusive (many artists produce work that is not intended to convey a specific message). He also suggests that focusing on expression that uses words to define First Amendment coverage is not particularly helpful because there are clearly ways of communicating an identifiable message, even an overt political message, that do not use words, and words do not always even convey meaning (on the latter, see chapter 3 in this volume). This insight is, of course, essential to thinking about instrumental music, which by definition is wordless.

Ultimately, after identifying many of the difficulties in justifying the First Amendment's coverage of art, Tushnet relies on a type of pragmatic reasoning to support the claim. First, he says, we might find art to be covered because it bears a "family resemblance" to political speech. Art may not fulfill all of the conditions we typically associate with speech, but many types of art meet many of the conditions. Second, given that much art fits "enough" of these criteria, he embraces a "rules versus standards" argument, suggesting that a categorical conclusion that all art is covered by the First Amendment is probably superior to a case-by-case analysis of how each art work might constitute speech, a decision that "may well be beyond the capacity of ordinary legal decision makers to do . . . reliably across the range of problems they may encounter" (see chapter 2 in this volume).

In addition to the general scholarship on art and the First Amendment, there has been some academic discussion of government censorship of music because of its *lyrical* content.[46] For example, there was considerable deliberation over government attempts in the early 1990s to forbid the sale of 2 Live Crew's album *As Nasty as They Wanna Be* on the grounds that it was legally obscene. But in that case, the court noted that the case appeared to be the first time an appellate court had been asked to apply the legal standard for obscenity "to a musical composition, which contains both instrumental music *and lyrics*."[47] The lyrical components were clearly the sole basis of the obscenity claim.[48] Accordingly, the scholarly commentary addressed only that question.[49] But legal analysis of government censorship of lyrics, completely disaggregated from the musical content, ought to be no different from evaluating censorship of a book, poem, speech, or leaflet. This is not to say that there are not important social concerns about government efforts to censor songs, just that they do not raise interesting conceptual questions. The 2 Live Crew case may have some bearing on thinking about music as an expression of cultural values to the extent that it implicates concerns over the racial component of the band's musical genre.[50]

With regard to analyzing how First Amendment doctrine and theory apply to purely instrumental music, the only serious effort of any kind thus far has been a student note. David Munkittrick is concerned about the lack of recognition, from the courts or the academy, that instrumental music has not been independently analyzed as a species of expression. He draws on some aesthetic theory and approaches from other disciplines and discusses the basic free speech theories that might apply.[51] As with the scholarly work on artistic expression, his piece provides insight and a valuable starting point. This chapter, however, departs from his work in important ways. First, while Munkittrick acknowledges that "no single First Amendment theory fully explains protection of music as speech,"[52] his work places a stronger emphasis on the role of music in the democratic order than is warranted. Second, this chapter more specifically distinguishes and identifies the different expressive possibilities of instrumental music, which is a necessary predicate to understanding how free speech theory can be mapped onto instrumental music.

C. Instrumental Music Censorship

A logical initial reaction to the lack of either serious judicial or academic treatment of the question of instrumental music as speech might be that it simply does not matter. Beyond a few rare examples, music censorship has occurred relatively infrequently in American society. To the extent that it has arisen, it has focused on the lyrical, rather than musical, component of the expression. The need to examine the grounds for its protection may therefore not be perceived as urgent.

But calls for control and regulation of instrumental music have spanned millennia and have emerged from all parts of the world, from both government entities and other powerful institutions. Plato associated certain forms of music with licentiousness and warned about the negative impact of music on character.[53] In medieval Europe, for many years the Catholic Church banned an interval known as the tritone,[54] an augmented fourth or diminished fifth in the Western musical scale, because its dissonant sound evoked evil. The Church even labeled it the "Devil's Interval."[55] In 1322, Pope John XXII "issued a decree that banned the usage of descant (improvised high melodic lines) in church services."[56] And in a widely known, though perhaps not completely understood, example of "populist censorship" of instrumental work, the 1913 debut of Igor Stravinsky's *The Rite of Spring*[57] was met with a hostile audience reaction that resulted in a major public disturbance. As described by one account, "The altercation, which escalated into a riot that spilled out into the streets (and featured the rare sight of baton-wielding gendarmes thumping the heads of uptown arts patrons), was reportedly sparked by an audience shocked by the musical piece's then unheard of, and therefore extremely *unsettling, rhythms*."[58]

In Nazi Germany, Hitler's regime banned the publication, sale, performance, and broadcast of "Entartete Musik" (degenerate music). Through its Reichsmusikkammer (Reich Chamber of Musical Affairs), the government systematically excluded Jewish performers and composers from nearly all aspects of German musical life. Among the notable composers whose work was banned by the Nazis as degenerate were Stravinsky, Gustav Mahler, and George Gershwin. Jewish composers such as Felix Mendelssohn were specifically targeted for censorship as well, as was jazz music, quite probably because of its association with African Americans. The Nazis also engaged in a form of cultural apartheid, forbidding the performance of works by Jewish composers, except in the context of events sponsored by the Kulturbund (Jewish Cultural League), while at the same time forbidding Jews to perform the work of non-Jewish German composers.[59] Similarly, a long history of music censorship marks several periods of the Soviet regime in the twentieth century, including, most notably, the regulation of the work of Dmitri Shostakovich. The Soviet government censored instrumental music for religious, nationalist, and political reasons. It kept close tabs on music for fear that it would be decadently bourgeois, class hostile, or religious.[60]

Moreover, in contemporary cultures, particularly those with sectarian-dominated government regimes, censorship of instrumental music is common. Though there is wide disagreement about the role of music in Islam, the previously Taliban-controlled Afghanistan and the current Iranian government banned instrumental music because of its association with nonpuritanical values and lifestyles and alcohol or drug use.[61] Similar sectarian-driven animosity from an Islamist rebel group in northern Mali led to the cancellation in 2013 of the Festival au Désert, a world-famous music celebration. As reported by people involved with past festivals, the rebels targeted what they viewed as "Satan's music," including not only Western music but also "local music styles deemed offensive to the standards of Shariah, or Islamic law, that were being imposed on a traditionally tolerant and multicultural society."[62] Among the local genres of music that were censored was music produced by tindé drums, usually performed by female ensembles. Rebels threatened musicians' lives if they performed and destroyed their instruments and equipment. More recently, media have reported that ISIS police officials have punished musicians and smashed their electronic keyboards as "un-Islamic."[63]

Suppression of instrumental music arises in more democratic societies as well. For example, an informal ban on the performance of Richard Wagner's work persisted for decades in Israel. The ban was widely embraced based on claims of Wagner's anti-Semitism and his association with the Nazi regime, though that regime arose well after his death. For many Israeli Jews, Wagner's compositions bore strong associations with the Holocaust.[64] Similarly, after Guinea established independence from France in 1958, its new government took measures to diminish external musical influences and support the music of its own culture. "[E]stablished dance bands and orchestras that specialized in rhythms not native to Guinea were disbanded, and new ensembles were encouraged to make music based on indigenous tradition."[65]

While less widespread or frequent, several examples of governmental or other institutional restrictions on the musical component of expression exist even in the United States. In just the past few years, two public school districts have been sued, albeit unsuccessfully, for restricting purely instrumental musical performances at school programs and ceremonies because of the music's religious affiliations. In *Nurre v. Whitehead*, student musicians claimed, among other things, that the school's ban on their selected performance violated their free speech rights. They had chosen to play an instrumental version of Franz Biebl's *Ave Maria*[66] because "they believed [it] showcased their talent and the culmination of their instrumental work." Nonetheless, fearing that the school district would receive complaints about the religious content of the music and wanting to appear neutral toward religion for both establishment clause and political purposes, officials banned the performance, an action upheld by the Ninth Circuit.[67] In a similar case, *Stratechuk v. Board of Education*, the Third Circuit upheld a ban on the performance of holiday music with religious themes, including instrumental works, at school programs.[68]

Other examples dot the constitutional landscape as well. A successful federal obscenity prosecution in the 1960s targeted two phonograph records, one of which, according to one Supreme Court justice, contained material that was made up "almost entirely of the sounds of percussion instruments" (perhaps the first documented historical ban on aural sex).[69]

Nongovernmental institutions that control forums for musical expression have also played a censoring role. For example, in 1959, federally licensed American radio stations refused to broadcast the purely instrumental Link Wray song "Rumble"[70] on the basis of its title's association with street violence.[71] The BBC banned the broadcast of the instrumental theme song from the Frank Sinatra movie *The Man with the Golden Arm*,[72] because of its connection to a film about drug abuse.[73] And a major retail chain in the Pacific Northwest affixed an "explicit lyrics" warning label similar to the type sponsored by the Recording Industry Association of America (RIAA) to all copies of the Frank Zappa album *Jazz from Hell*,[74] even though the album was composed entirely of instrumental music.[75]

These instances of instrumental music censorship naturally lead to important questions about what exactly is being censored. This inquiry, in turn, leads to a critical examination of the communicative meaning of instrumental music, the subject of part 3.

II. The Uneasy Fit between Instrumental Music and Free Speech Doctrine and Theory

Despite the general assumption that instrumental music is constitutionally protected speech, important and unanswered questions remain. As this part discusses, the dominant utilitarian theories of free speech, which justify protection on the basis of the goal of promoting democratic self-governance and facilitating the search for "truth" by ensuring a free marketplace of all ideas (not just political ones), do not adequately explain constitutional protection for music, except at the broadest levels of abstraction. A partial explanation may emerge under the truth-seeking theory, however, if music is understood as advancing nonideational aspects of truth. Free speech theory based on promoting dignitary interests, such as individual self-realization and autonomy, offers a much better match but makes it difficult to distinguish music from other forms of human liberty protected by the Constitution.[76]

As a quick disclaimer, the aim of this chapter is not to embrace one free speech theory over another or to argue that one is superior as a unifying principle than the others. Rather, its less ambitious goal, accepting that each of these theories provides a plausible theoretical foundation for protecting speech, is to examine how well any of these justifications support the conclusion that instrumental music is and ought to be constitutionally protected.

A. Promoting Democratic Self-Governance

Perhaps the most widely discussed and accepted theory underlying the constitutional protection of speech identifies freedom of expression as a means of promoting a healthy, transparent, and effective democratic system of governance. Earlier scholarly proponents of this theory include Alexander Meiklejohn, whose work argued that the First Amendment is designed "to give to every voting member of the body politic the fullest possible participation in the understanding of those problems with which the citizens of a self-governing society must deal. . . . The primary purpose of the First Amendment is, then, that all the citizens shall, so far as possible, understand the issues which bear upon our common life."[77] Consistent with Meiklejohn's emphasis on promoting democracy, his speech theory in its first iteration distinguished between public discourse, which he viewed as protected by the First Amendment, and private communication, which he deemed as governed by the due process clause.[78] Meiklejohn's narrow focus on democratic self-rule was criticized by, among others, Zechariah Chafee, who pointed out that Meiklejohn's theory meant that the First Amendment did not protect "art and literature." Chafee found it "shocking to deprive these vital matters" of protection under the speech clause.[79]

Meiklejohn's rejoinder to this criticism required him to rethink his original position on artistic expression under the First Amendment. In later work, he took the view that literature and "the arts" fell within the First Amendment's protection because they were included within the forms of communication "from which the voter derives the knowledge, intelligence, sensitivity to human values: the capacity for sane and objective judgment which, so far as possible, a ballot should express."[80] Elaborating on this view, he observed that literature and the arts "are protected because they have a 'social importance' which [he] called a 'governing' importance."[81] But Meiklejohn does not mention music in particular, and it is unclear from his conclusions about the arts whether he would view nonverbal artistic expression, such as instrumental music, as advancing these same values. Indeed, the examples he gave involve verbal media, such as novels, which can be much more directly connected to democracy.[82]

In later work, Robert Bork took a much narrower view of speech and democracy more in line with Meiklejohn's earlier position. He concluded that "[c]onstitutional protection should be accorded only to speech that is explicitly political."[83] "There is no basis," he explained, "for judicial intervention to protect any other form of expression, be it scientific, literary or that variety of expression we call obscene or pornographic."[84] For Bork, this boundary was essential to ensuring that First Amendment law advances the principal objective of "the discovery and spread of political truth."[85] But he rejected the idea that artistic expression facilitated democratic goals.

> I agree that there is an analogy between criticism of official behavior and the publication of a novel like *Ulysses*, for the latter may form attitudes that ultimately affect politics. But it is an analogy, not an identity. Other human activities and experiences also form personality, teach and create attitudes just as much as does the novel, but no one would on that account, I take it, suggest that the first amendment strikes down regulations of economic activity, control of entry into a trade, laws about sexual behavior, marriage and the like. Yet these activities, in their capacity to create attitudes that ultimately impinge upon the political process, are more like literature and science than literature and science are like political speech.[86]

Even more advanced forms of democratic theory arguably do not do the work necessary to support a strong claim for protecting instrumental music. Contemporary theorists embrace the self-governance-promoting foundations of the First Amendment but like Meiklejohn struggle with the dilemma that this theory presents for artistic expression. Robert Post argues for a broader understanding of the democratic self-governance theory that ensures not simply informed decision making about candidates and issues but also protects the process of forming public opinion, "which is understood as a form of communicative action."[87] His theory calls for the protection not of speech per se but of "those speech acts and media of communication that are socially regarded as necessary and proper means of participating in the formation of public opinion," which

Post calls "public discourse."[88] "The function of public discourse is to enable persons to experience the value of self-government."[89] According to Post, self-governance theory is properly understood in relation to its protection of individual autonomy and self-determination in the formation of opinion related to the democratic process.

Post claims that his theory is capacious enough to include protection for artistic expression. He writes, "Public discourse includes all communicative processes deemed necessary for the formation of public opinion. Art and other forms of noncognitive, nonpolitical speech fit comfortably within the scope of public discourse. Public discourse depends upon the maintenance of a public sphere, which is a sociological structure that is a prerequisite to the formation of public opinion."[90] Even with his broad understanding of public opinion, however, it is not obvious how instrumental musical expression is "necessary" to its understanding. Said differently, Post suggests that to be subject to the First Amendment's coverage, artistic expression "need not concern potential policy decisions; it need only contribute to what people think when they communicate to each other in public."[91] Perhaps what he is suggesting is that art must be protected because to fail to do so would undermine the very legitimacy of democratic governance; but that would seem to be true of many other forms of communication, not all of which are protected. And it is not at all clear why music or other forms of nonpropositional expression would contribute to what people "think" when they communicate to each other in public or how that contributes to the public discourse, even broadly defined.[92]

James Weinstein, who also argues for a democracy-promoting First Amendment theory, is more skeptical about the conceptual connection between purely instrumental music and promotion of self-governance. As he observes, "Perhaps its greatest explanatory shortcoming is that a theory based in participatory democracy cannot easily explain the rigorous protection that current doctrine affords non-ideational art such as abstract paintings or symphonic music."[93] Though Weinstein acknowledges the "plausible" democracy-based explanation that "art in general can be a particularly effective means of political persuasion,"[94] that is not always the case with, or even the intention of, musical expression, and his doubts that this adequately explains the rigorous First Amendment protection that artistic speech presumptively enjoys seem well founded.

Similarly, as Seana Shiffrin aptly observes,

Although a case *could* be made that the freedom to compose and to listen to Stravinsky is important to developing the sort of open personal and cultural character necessary for democracy to flourish or that it feeds the "sociological structure that is prerequisite for the formation of public opinion," that justification is strained and bizarrely indirect. In any case, the right of Stravinsky to compose and of audiences to listen (or to cringe in non-comprehension) should not depend upon whether *The Rite of Spring* breeds democrats or fascists, or whether it supports, detracts from, or is superfluous to a democratic culture.[95]

As suggested earlier, Munkittrick's commentary on music and speech relies heavily, though not exclusively, on a democracy-based rationale. On this ground, he argues that the government actually plays a necessary role in promoting musical expression to sustain "a minimum level of diversity in the aesthetic, creative, and emotional decision making that music enables."[96] He goes on to argue that such diversity is essential to ensuring that the democratic functions of music are not impaired. In advancing this view, he suggests that instrumental music is central to political life. But the examples he draws on to illustrate that music can act as "direct political speech" do not involve pure musical expression but the appropriation of music for its performers' specific goals.[97] That is, his arguments are premised more on the association of music with particular events or historical contexts than on the inherent expressive function of the music itself. Associative claims are not really about the music, however; they are derivative of the contexts in which the music is placed and therefore do not support a democratic justification for counting music as speech.

Democratic self-governance theory is typically operationalized, however imperfectly, through doctrinal devices, primarily the Court's articulation of a heavy presumption against regulations that discriminate based on the viewpoint or content of speech.[98] Even if we are to accept the democracy-promoting value of musical expression, it is difficult to imagine how this doctrine would be implemented to evaluate the constitutionality of music regulation. What would the application of viewpoint or content discrimination look like? It is doubtful whether instrumental music, unlike music with lyrics, can ever be said to have a specific view-point.[99] Even if it could, it would not likely be a *political* viewpoint or one that would contribute, directly or indirectly, to the flourishing of democracy. Even if some instrumental music could be said to have an identifiable message or view, strict adherence to democratic justifica-tions for its coverage would exclude large bodies of influential work, such as pieces by the modern composers Edgard (or Edgar) Varèse and Milton Babbitt, whose work most likely was not intended to have a spe-cific message but to disrupt the existing conventions of prior generations of classical music and to challenge its audiences.[100]

This is why Meiklejohn and others have struggled to defend artistic expression under the democratic theory. That is not to say that govern-ments have not attempted to censor instrumental music because of its political associations or, rather, because of their perceptions of its politi-cal meaning. But it would be an odd application of First Amendment doctrine, though perhaps not an entirely inappropriate one, if courts applied strict scrutiny to government suppression of music because of its perceived political content or viewpoint when the composer or per-former had no such intent.

An easier case can be made that different types of instrumental music bear different content and that the government might discriminate based on that content. Content discrimination might come in the form of discrimination against particular genres of music (classical music is okay, rap and hip-hop are not) or matters of taste (allowing perfor-mance of only "good" or "artistic" music but not bad music). Indeed, the *Fact Concerts* case, which involved a challenge to a city's cancellation of a permit to perform because the scheduled band was a rock group rather than a jazz group, is an example of precisely that type of genre discrimination.[101] But again, the implications for democratic self-rule in protecting speech from such restrictions are unclear. The hypothetical regulations here might be viewed as matters of taste, but participation in public discourse has never turned on whether one's musical taste is elegant or tacky. Without taking a broad view of democracy that encom-passes all forms of thought or feeling about all subjects, it is difficult to justify protection of instrumental music under this theory.

In the end, democratic self-governance is at best an incomplete the-ory for protecting instrumental music and at worst simply unhelpful.

That is not to say that democracy-based speech theory is not one of the justifications for constitutional protection of speech. But this chapter argues that promoting democracy is a conditionally sufficient,[102] but not necessary, reason for protecting different forms of expression.

B. Facilitating the Search for Truth

A second dominant theory for protecting speech is the idea that expressive freedom promotes the search for more general truths beyond the world of politics and governing. Derived from the writings of John Milton and John Stuart Mill, this justification is premised on the conception of a broader understanding of truth than is democratic self-governance theory. Most important, Milton's and Mill's conceptions of truth are about the truth of ideas, not historical or factual truth. Thus, Milton argued that freedom in the communication of ideas is essential to promote "discovery" of ideas that might be developed in "religious and civil wisdom."[103] Similarly, Mill claimed that protection of opinion was crucial to liberty because whether the ideas expressed in an opinion are "true" or "false," widely held or marginal, society can only understand truth by a full consideration of all opinions.[104]

Facilitation of the search for truth is most frequently associated with Justice Oliver Wendell Holmes's dissent in *Abrams v. United States*, in which the Court upheld the defendants' convictions under the Espionage Act for conspiring to "unlawfully utter, print, write and publish," among other things, "disloyal, scurrilous and abusive language about the form of government of the United States" and language intended to bring that form of government into "contempt, scorn, contumely, and disrepute."[105] As he wrote, "the best test of truth is the power of the thought to get itself accepted in the competition of the market."[106] Of course, the search for truth substantially overlaps with the promotion of self-governance.[107] However, it has been widely conceived as understanding truth in a more general sense of social enlightenment that is not limited to opinions about government or public policy.

What types of truths might be generated by free speech that are not at least somewhat linked to self-governance or at least are not inherently linked to democracy? Certainly religious or spiritual truths, to the extent that they inform personal and collective understandings of the universe, might fall within this category. In addition, matters of science or morality may fall within a broad understanding of areas in which unregulated discourse is important to produce a better truth through the evolution of ideas. And, as argued later, cultural truths ought to be included as well.

The logical passage to the conclusion that instrumental music is a part of this discourse, however, is still somewhat difficult to navigate. Even these nonpolitical, non-democracy-facilitating areas of inquiry are typically engaged in through propositional verbal expression that appeals to cognitive reasoning. Governmental interference with nonverbal musical expression distorts the marketplace of ideas only if instrumental music conveys or is understood as an idea. But other scholars observe, convincingly, that musical expressions are not part of "ideational" or ideaist way of communicating. Under truth-based theories, the First Amendment might not apply to forms of expression that do not serve to protect the communication and reception of information and ideas. As John Greenman observes, "[W]e can say that 'information' is used to refer to things like sentences, mathematical formulas, musical scores, computer code, and DNA strings. But it is not used to refer to things *like the sound of music* or the way a picture looks. 'Idea,' on the other hand, refers to mostly the same things—sentences, formulas, scores, and so forth—with the added requirement that 'idea' usually connotes a mental phenomenon."[108] Edwin Baker similarly suggests that "all aesthetic experiences, like all experiences generally, can affect who a person is, how she sees the world, and thereby affect her values, politics, and notions of truth. Such explanations for their relevance to the political sphere or to a marketplace of ideas do not, however, distinguish them from, say, hiking in a wilderness area, cooperation in a barn raising, or engaging in a criminal enterprise."[109]

As with the democratic self-governance theory, the search for truth is implemented through general doctrinal rules forbidding viewpoint and other content discrimination. The rationale for prohibiting such discrimination is the prevention of government distortion of the marketplace. Because truth finding is a function of complete and open discourse, any state interference with the landscape of opinion jeopardizes the search for truth.[110] To the extent that the market is one of ideas, information, opinion, or other appeals to cognitive reasoning (even if the objective is not factual truth or political truth but something moral, scientific, literary, and even spiritual), government regulation of instrumental music would not appear to affect the search for truth in any meaningful way. If that is the case, then the truth rationale, without more, is not an adequate explanation for the protection of music as speech. A more complete understanding of how instrumental music may advance certain kinds of truths, however, may cause us to reevaluate this skepticism.

C. Promoting Individual Autonomy and Self-Fulfillment

A third compelling claim for protecting speech is grounded in promoting individual autonomy. Many scholars have articulated the autonomy justifications for freedom of expression, though with varied approaches to defining autonomy. Thomas Scanlon examines the notion of autonomy in terms of the individual's freedom to engage in self-determination. State interference with the ability to experience the universe of competing ideas seriously compromises such autonomy. As Scanlon famously wrote, "An autonomous person cannot accept without independent consideration the judgment of others as to what he should believe or what he should do. He may rely on the judgment of others, but when he does so he must be prepared to advance independent reasons for thinking their judgment likely to be correct, and to weigh the evidential value of their opinion against contrary evidence."[111] A regime under which the government could regulate the free conveyance of such opinions or judgments, therefore, is inconsistent with each person's autonomy to form beliefs about his or her course of thought or action. An important distinction of this version of the autonomy theory, then, is that it emphasizes the value of speech to the individual as much as to the collective interest in a functioning democracy or the societal achievement of truth.

Martin Redish argues for a broader, refined version of this theory, suggesting that the free speech clause serves the value of "individual self-realization." In elaborating on this idea, he explains that self-realization "can be interpreted to refer either to development of the individual's powers and abilities—an individual 'realizes' his or her full potential—or to the individual's control of his or her own destiny through making life-affecting decisions—an individual 'realizes' the goals in life that he or she has set."[112] Redish claims that his theory constitutes a stronger approach to speech protection in part because the objectives of other theories (promoting democracy, the search for truth) are largely subsumed within the promotion of self-realization.

Baker spent much of his life examining and refining autonomy-based theories of free speech. In his later work, he grounded his autonomy theory in the concept of legitimacy. He argues that "a legitimate legal order must fully respect (among other things, e.g. equality) both individual and collective autonomy—both non-political and political speech."[113] He elaborates:

> If the moral value of democracy lies (in part) in its contribution to people's political autonomy in pursuit of their democratically chosen projects— with its implicit premise that it values these people as autonomous— democracy's authority should be limited by this same value. Given this value, democracy (or law) should not, therefore, be authorized to enact laws that disrespect, that are premised on the propriety of denying, a person's autonomy (or, though less relevant here, her equality and maybe her dignity). This conclusion should then guide interpretation of the constitutional guarantee of free speech. It gives equal status to protecting speech as a part of personal, individual self-government and as an aspect of her participation in collective self-government.[114]

Critics of Baker and other autonomy theorists have made several claims. Among them is the concern that autonomy is a justification not only for expressive freedom but also for myriad other types of individual liberty that are clearly not constitutionally protected. As Bork observed, "[D]evelopment of individual faculties and the achievement of pleasure . . . do not distinguish speech from any other human activity. An individual may develop his faculties or derive pleasure from trading on the stock market, following his profession as a river port pilot, working as a barmaid, engaging in sexual activity, playing tennis, rigging prices or in any of thousands of other endeavors."[115] Essentially, this critique suggests that autonomy-based justifications have no limiting principle. But as Baker and others point out, of course, one limiting principle is the First Amendment, which specifically establishes an expression-specific form of liberty, distinctive of other liberties, protected and not.[116] While many other acts may lead to self-realization or fulfillment, they are mostly not expressive or communicative and are covered, if at all, by other aspects of the Constitution.[117]

Shiffrin more recently has articulated a "thinker-based" approach to autonomy and speech. In developing her theory, she identifies eight separate, sometimes overlapping, interests in which the rational thinker should enjoy autonomy: capacity for practical and theoretical thought; apprehending the true; exercising the imagination; becoming a distinct individual; moral agency; responding authentically; living among others; and appropriate recognition and treatment. As she notes, "Speech, and free speech in particular, are necessary conditions of the realization of these interests."[118] Her version of an autonomy theory suggests that each of these values is appropriately advanced by a free speech doctrine, and she explains how they can be used to justify speech that does not fall comfortably under the umbrella of the promotion of democracy or the search for truth:

> Communication of the contents of one's mind primarily through linguistic means, but also through pictorial or even musical representation, uniquely furthers the interest in being known by others. It thereby also makes possible complex forms of social life. Further, it helps to develop some of the capacities prerequisite to moral agency because successful communication demands having a sense of what others are in a position to know and understand. Practicing communication initiates the process of taking others' perspective to understand what others know and are in a position to grasp.[119]

She adds, "Pictorial representations and music (and not merely discourse about them) should also gain foundational protection because they also represent the externalization of mental contents, contents that may not be accurately or well-captured through linguistic means; after all, not all thoughts are discursive or may be fully captured through discursive description."[120]

The Supreme Court has forcefully, though rarely, based free speech claims on autonomy arguments. Perhaps the clearest example of this is in *Stanley v. Georgia*. In *Stanley*, the Court overturned the conviction of a man who was charged with possession of obscene films in the privacy of his own home. The Court embraced the defendant's First Amendment claim that he had the right to determine what material he watched, even if that material could otherwise be regulated or even prohibited. Justice Thurgood Marshall wrote in his opinion for the Court, "If the First Amendment means anything, it means that a State has no business telling a man, sitting alone in his own house, what books he may read or what films he may watch. Our whole constitutional heritage rebels at the thought of giving government the power to control men's minds."[121] Similarly, it is possible to conceptualize a First Amendment analysis of instrumental music under an autonomy-based theory.

As Baker, Redish, and Shiffrin argue, some form of autonomy justification is one of the strongest theoretical foundations for constitutional protection of instrumental music. Shiffrin, in particular, articulates a position that broadens the scope of autonomy in ways that could be used to justify protection of instrumental music, while still maintaining some limiting, if not completely defined, principles that would not result in arguments to protect everything as expression. But there are some unanswered questions that require further elaboration. First, no one has closely examined what it is about instrumental music that advances autonomy values. Part 3 breaks down musical expression into its constituent parts and discusses what makes them distinctly expressive in manners that should be of concern to the First Amendment. Second, music could be said to advance all of the theories of free speech if taken at their broadest level of abstraction. If music is protected, what limiting principles exist to distinguish it from other forms of expressive liberty that might not advance those same values?

III. Understanding Instrumental Music as Speech

If instrumental music can be justified under any of the three dominant theories of free speech protection, its value to the speaker, the audience, and the collective society must be measured in relation to those theories. As with all forms of communication, music can be assessed from the perspective of the speaker (in this case, the composer and the performer) as well as from the perspective of its audience (for music, its listeners). For the composer and performer, music must be understood in terms of its expressive meaning. The value to listeners, in turn, includes how they think about and interpret the music and how it affects their thoughts and emotions—in short, how listeners *experience* music. Each of these values, in turn, may be influenced by the distinct melodic and rhythmic elements of musical expression.

A. What Is Distinctive about Instrumental Musical Expression?

A working definition of music is an important starting point. All musical instruments convey sound by creating vibrations that are transmitted through the air and internally processed by listeners' eardrums.[122] But of course all sound is processed this way, whether it is verbal language, music, or a thunder clap. It seems that every generation stereotypically views the next generation's popular music as so much noise. So what are the distinctive factors that make something music and not noise?[123] The *Oxford English Dictionary* definition of music is "[t]he art or science of combining vocal or instrumental sounds with a view to beauty or coherence of form and expression of emotion."[124] The formal definition is therefore based on some kind of intentionality to make sounds in a manner designed to do more than make noise. But it also, importantly, envisions aesthetic values of beauty and emotion.[125]

1. EXPRESSING THE INEXPRESSIBLE

One possible dilemma in defining the speech value of instrumental music is that it is sometimes said to be capable of conveying expression in a manner that may not be achievable through language (as the Huxley quote in this chapter's epigraph suggests). Indeed, as John Dewey aptly observed, "If all meanings could be adequately expressed by words, the arts of painting and music would not exist. There are values and meanings that can be expressed only by immediately visible and audible qualities, and to ask what they mean in the sense of something that can be put into words is to deny their distinctive existence."[126] Similarly, Greenman writes in his critique of the notion that only speech that conveys information or ideas ought to be protected by the First Amendment, "If instrumental music conveys ideas, then more or less everything must."[127] The challenge is whether these descriptions prove too much. That is, if music expresses something that cannot be reduced to language, then why, if at all, ought it be protected by the freedom of speech? This is one of the questions explored in the remainder of this part.

2. MUSIC COMPARED TO OTHER ARTS

A different, but also reasonable, preliminary question is whether instrumental music is any different from other forms of nonverbal art, such as painting, sculpture, or dancing, though there are also certainly similarities between music and *verbal* forms of artistic expression such as literature and poetry. First, in the case of instrumental music as well as painting and sculpture, the composer, painter, or sculptor may have the intent to communicate a specific idea, emotion, or concept, or he or she may have no intent at all except to create something beautiful, interesting, or entertaining and thereby worth looking at or listening to.

Moreover, some composers have viewed their work as either inspired by or tantamount to visual images. Gunther Schuller's *Seven Studies on Themes of Paul Klee*[128] is a musical homage to Klee's paintings (Klee was also a musician), though some of the movements in the work are more directly representational of the paintings than others. Schuller said, "Each of the seven pieces bears a slightly different relationship to the original Klee picture from which it stems. . . . Some relate to the actual design, shape, or color scheme of the painting, while others take the general mode of the picture or its title as a point of departure."[129] A somewhat different perspective on music as visual is reflected in Varèse's thoughts about his compositional work. Varèse "considered his music to be a form of visual art, . . . 'a merger of the parameters of space and time.'"[130]

Another similarity is that in the case of all three arts, the expression may be open to multiple, varying, and even conflicting interpretations by the audience. This, too, presents something of a challenge for fitting them into speech theory because if there is not an objective, or at least a widely understood, meaning attributable to the expression, it is hard to figure out how it can be classified as speech under the standard doctrine. Consider Shostakovich's Eleventh Symphony,[131] which by his account was meant to memorialize the anniversary of the 1905 democratic uprising against tsarist Russia. Many people have attributed a hidden intent on the composer's part to make a subversive commentary on the Soviet military's suppression of the 1956 Hungarian uprising, but other scholars dispute that Shostakovich had any such motive.[132] If there is no accepted understanding of the message or idea expressed in an artistic work, how would we know when the government was engaging in content or viewpoint discrimination?

An important factor that sets instrumental music apart from painting or sculpture, however, is that music is necessarily dynamic in two ways. All art must begin with its creation. For music, the creation is by the composer, for painting the painter, and for sculpture the sculptor. But once a painting or sculpture is completed (in most cases, setting aside certain forms of interactive or performance art), the conduct is complete. Even if different audiences view and understand the work in myriad ways, the artwork is itself static. A composer creates music, but music involves a second stage of conduct in its performance, which is dynamic. As Dewey described,

> Music, having sounds as its medium, thus necessarily expresses in a concentrated way the shocks and instabilities, the conflicts and resolutions, that are the dramatic changes enacted upon the more enduring background of nature and human life. The tension and the struggle has its gatherings of energy, its discharges, its attacks and defenses, its mighty warrings and its peaceful meetings, its resistances and resolutions, and out of these things music weaves its web. It is thus at the opposite pole from the sculptural. As one expresses the enduring, the stable and universal, so the other expresses stir, agitation, movement, the particulars and contingencies of existences—which, nevertheless, are as ingrained in nature and as typical in experience as are its structural permanences.[133]

But it is not only the dynamism of the specific musical performance that distinguishes instrumental music from other forms of art. In addition, unlike other nonrepresentational art forms, instrumental music is capable of being created, performed, and reperformed and reinterpreted anew on repeated, potentially infinite, occasions.[134] Each performance may convey the expression in a unique manner and be interpreted in a universe of ways. The variation in performance is important because each new performance reproduces the autonomy and cultural protection arguments potentially justifying First Amendment protection.

One could take these latter points to support the idea that music expresses in a different way than painting or sculpture. But dance can also be performed and interpreted by each new dancer and is equally dynamic in both senses.[135] To be sure, while there are strong connections between dance and music (including the fact that most dance is performed to music), there are also differences worth mentioning and factors that distinguish instrumental music from all other art forms. First, music is the only form of art that is communicated entirely through auditory means. There are no visual cues or associations to interpret, no images to look at, no colors, textures, or forms. Second, instrumental music is the only art form that is *always* nonrepresentational. A painting, sculpture, or dance can depict ideas and images in a literal way or an abstract way, opening the door to inquiries about whether only those art forms that convey an understandable message, as the Court suggested in *Spence*, ought to count as speech.[136] The composition and performance of instrumental music can never convey an idea or thought in a literal sense, and no listener can discern a literal meaning from hearing such music. Unlike other art forms, instrumental music can never be propositional and therefore presents the purest form of artistic expression for First Amendment theory purposes. The next section examines the ways in which instrumental music might be considered expressive.

B. The Specific Communicative Aspects of Instrumental Music

From these foundations, a theory of instrumental music as speech must build the case for why such music falls within the purposes of the First Amendment. We have already surveyed the three main theoretical justifications for music as speech—promoting democratic self-governance, advancing the search for truth, and promoting autonomy. If we were considering lyrical or vocal music, the discussion would be simpler because we could examine the lyrics for their content and discuss how the freedom to engage in those verbal expressions advanced any of these three main theories. But separating out the tonal and rhythmic components of musical expression presents significant theoretical (as well as doctrinal) complexities that neither the courts nor legal scholars have adequately addressed.

The following subsections discuss five different possible ways of understanding the communicative component of instrumental music. The first three are "cognitive claims," each of which has power but none of which ultimately can be squared with conventional speech theory in a way that is workable in either a theoretical or a doctrinal sense. The fourth category—music as an expression of cultural, religious, nationalist, or other social values—holds greater promise as a type of communication that the First Amendment ought to cover, even if it cannot be understood to involve particularized messages. The fifth and final category, which considers music as a powerful conveyor of emotional feeling and sensibility, also provides a more solid grounding for understanding instrumental music as speech.

1. THREE COGNITIVE CLAIMS

As the prior free speech theory discussion and the earlier case law survey suggest, an important justification for covering expression under the First Amendment is to promote the conveyance of specific messages, ideas, beliefs, and thoughts. Speech in its most fundamental form is about transmitting these things to others, which requires cognitive engagement. Thus, if instrumental music is "speech," it is important to examine the degree to which it might facilitate cognitive reactions in its listeners. There are three possible ways of thinking about instrumental music and cognition.

a. Instrumental Music as Evocative/Associative of Cognitive Thought

One claim might be that instrumental music, though by definition nonverbal and nonpropositional, nonetheless provokes meaningful cognitive responses in its listeners. Though music might not convey a particular message, it may be ultimately generative of conscious thoughts and ideas in the sense that some music is strongly associated or evocative of specific ideas or themes that are themselves defined by social context. This is the *associative claim.*

For example, a purely instrumental work may have a provocative or controversial title. Though the music itself is targeted by censors, it is not the musical content per se that is objectionable but its association with the work's title. Thus, as described briefly earlier, the song "Rumble," recorded by Link Wray and the Wraymen, was banned by American radio stations in the late 1950s. The explanation provided was that the song was associated with street violence, which broadcasters were presumably afraid would be inspired in those who listened to the song.[137] Again, although the music was purely instrumental, the work became associated with a social problem.

In another incident that may reflect this mode of thinking about instrumental music, Meyer Music Markets, a chain retailer in the Pacific Northwest, created a record labeling program modeled on the controversial efforts of the RIAA. The retail chain then required that its outlets label copies of the Frank Zappa album *Jazz from Hell* with an "explicit lyrics" sticker, even though the album was composed entirely of instrumental music. The retailer's labeling committee apparently assumed that the album must be controversial because Zappa was an outspoken critic of the RIAA and the Parents Music Resource Center, a private advocacy group whose founder, Tipper Gore, had strongly pushed for labeling standards.[138] It is also possible that, like the Link Wray instrumental, Zappa's album was censored because of the title of the album or because of the titles of some of the album's individual instrumental tracks (for example, "G-Spot Tornado").[139] Another example is instrumental music that is censored because of its association with a different art form, such as a motion picture, as in the previously mentioned example of the BBC ban on the broadcast of the purely instrumental theme song from the Frank Sinatra movie *The Man with the Golden Arm* because of the music's connection to a film about heroin addiction.[140]

In other instances, purely instrumental music may have specific communicative qualities that are intended by the performer and widely understood by the intended audience. For example, southern states banned African drumming in early American slave cultures during the late 1700s and early 1800s, because different drumming patterns communicated, and were understood to communicate, specific and concrete messages, such as signaling slave rebellions.[141]

Other music has developed particular meanings within the relevant community. During World War II, anti-German resistance fighters in Belgium adopted the letter *V* as their symbol, representing both the French word for victory (*victoire*) and the Flemish word for freedom (*vrijheid*). Officials at the BBC wanted to use the *V* symbol in their broadcasts to demonstrate support for the resistance fighters, and someone suggested using the Morse code symbol for *V*, which consists of three short signals and a long signal. BBC officials noticed that the famous opening of Beethoven's Fifth Symphony shared the same cadence as the Morse code symbol for *V*, and that became their signal to listeners to alert them to pro-Ally broadcasts.[142]

Yet another example of music that conveys specific ideas or information is music cryptograms. Cryptograms use sequences of musical notes to convey messages by associating certain notes with letters of the alphabet, thus making it possible to hide a verbal message in a musical score.[143] Many classical composers, most famously J. S. Bach, used cryptograms to embed family names and other messages into their compositions.[144] There is even some historical evidence of the use of music cryptograms to carry out espionage or other actions that the speakers hoped to hide from the government.

Each of these is a possible instance of instrumental music being used to communicate in ways we might consider worthy of protection under the First Amendment. Under any of the three major theories—democracy, truth, or autonomy—one could make the case for protection of music because it is associated, directly or indirectly, with particularized messages. The problem with this understanding of music as speech is that if music is really just a code for verbal expression, then it may not actually be the musical component of the expression that is communicative. For example, if an African drum beat or pipe tune is intended by both performer and listener to convey a specific message—one that can be reduced to words, such as "help" or "warning"—then instrumental music in these contexts is really no different from Morse code. It is a series of beats or notes, rather than dots and dashes, that has specific and understood linguistic meanings. The same could be said for cryptograms. In this context, while there would be the easiest justification for categorizing instrumental music as speech, the reasons actually make music here less conceptually interesting because it is not really distinct from traditional speech. That is, the problem with this approach to considering instrumental music as speech is that the very representational associations the music has may in fact take it out of the realm of pure instrumental speech.

Moreover, this form of musical expression arguably already might be covered within an existing doctrinal framework, the law of conduct as speech. In *United States v. O'Brien*, the Court held that one of the factors in determining whether nonverbal conduct may be speech protected by the First Amendment is whether "the governmental interest [in regulating that conduct] is unrelated to the suppression of free expression."[145] Thus, under *O'Brien*, musical expression is conduct that is protected only when the government's interest in regulating it is to address its speech or cognitive component. Under this doctrine, explaining protection of instrumental music that conveys an unambiguous message is a relatively easy task. In the examples just discussed, the governments or other power holders have attempted to regulate instrumental music not because of its musical elements but because of its cognitive message. But *O'Brien* permits the government to regulate the *noncognitive*, nonverbal part of the conduct if it has a sufficient interest. Taking away the message-conveying aspect of the African drumming signals, the conduct is simply the beating of the drum-head surface, which is content-free conduct, like burning a draft card. In fact, *O'Brien*'s analysis would logically lead to the conclusion that the musical component of the expression is *not* protected or at least that the speech and conduct cases do not explain constitutional protection for all instrumental music. For similar reasons, instrumental music that is censored because it is directly associated with an idea, through its title, lyrics, or otherwise, can be viewed as more closely linked to an appeal to an idea or cognitive function and is unhelpful for understanding the purer or harder case.

b. Instrumental Music as Enhancing Other Communicative Messages
A second conceptualization of the cognitive value of instrumental music is that the melodic and rhythmic components of musical expression may sometimes interact in meaningful ways with lyrics or other verbal messages, combining to express something that is both greater than and distinctive from the lyrics alone. This is the *enhancement claim*. Consider a song that is read out loud but with no musical accompaniment. The lyrics would be communicative in their own right. But they might not convey the ideas or information or sentiments in the same way— with the same emphases and dynamic tension—that they might if they were sung with musical accompaniment. Understood in this way, music may influence the lyrical text in a manner similar to the way that visual images sometimes enhance verbal messages. As one commentator notes,

"[A] number of studies have concluded that texts incorporating visual images (sometimes referred to as "visuals") are more effective at influencing people's beliefs than texts containing only words (e.g., a book), sounds (e.g., instrumental music), or even texts combining both words and sounds (e.g., vocal recordings). . . . Sound recordings are the most powerful conveyor of beliefs after visuals."[146] The importance of instrumental music in enhancing lyrical expression is understood only if the musical components are separated out and determined to have a communicative impact independent of or, more accurately, supplementing the vocal elements of a performance.

If music has an identifiable speech-enhancing component that influences verbal expression in an independent, meaningful way, then protection of instrumental music can be justified on the grounds that it promotes self-governance, the search for truth, and self-realization. We might view with skepticism the censorship of an overtly political song whose message is enhanced by its musical elements because of the resulting interference with democratic self-governance. Consider, for example, the difference in inspirational meaning derived from singing a protest song such as "We Shall Overcome" as opposed to simply reading its lyrics out loud.[147] Similarly, a song whose lyrics are directed toward the exposition of nonpolitical ideas or information with similar musical enhancement might be viewed as protected under a truth-searching or autonomy theory.

There is even doctrinal support for the enhancement claim. In *Cohen v. California*, the Supreme Court reviewed the case of a man who was convicted for disturbing the peace when he wore a jacket bearing the words "Fuck the Draft" into a public courthouse. Although the state asserted the power to regulate speech because of its offensive nature, the Court invalidated Cohen's conviction, finding that the profanity that he used to express his clearly political views had speech value because it conveyed the emotional force of his beliefs.[148] In other words, the specific words Cohen chose to communicate his opposition to the government's policy enhanced his message through their emotional impact. "Fuck the Draft" transmits the passion of Cohen's opposition to the draft more powerfully than something more muted, like "That Darned Draft." Although the analogy to *Cohen* is useful, its analysis still focused on the linguistic aspects of the speakers' message.

The limit of the enhancement claim, however, comes from the notion that the musical elements of the speech are inherently tied to verbal expression. If the reason music is expressive is solely derivative through its enhancement of the verbal, it may have little or no independent expressive value. To some degree (though the comparison is not quite complete), it is no different from an amplification device such as a megaphone. And if it has no distinctive substance, it would necessarily be regulated only when it is attached to the verbal message and therefore would be unlikely to need additional First Amendment protection that would not already be afforded to the lyrics. Greenman observes, "One might say that music is protected because it usually complements language, that rulemaking tends to be categorical, and that instrumental music is only protected by dint of its association with vocal music. This is undoubtedly true to some degree. But even so, there must be some principle determining what is communicative other than 'association with language.' People talk during violence, but violence is never communication."[149] Ultimately, the enhancement claim cannot stand alone as a justification to protect instrumental music under the First Amendment.[150]

c. Instrumental Music and Cognition

To this point, the argument has assumed that instrumental music does not directly appeal to or stimulate any sort of cognitive reasoning. Before leaving the topic, however, it is worth considering whether this assumption gives up too easily on a direct cognitive defense, the *pure cognitive claim*. Most theorists would argue that instrumental music is a form of nonpropositional expression, meaning that it does not intend (or does not *always* intend) to convey, nor can it be understood to convey, a particular, identifiable message.[151] While that is undoubtedly the case, that is not tantamount to saying that instrumental music does not stimulate, inspire, suggest, or provoke cognitive processes.

Indeed, some music theorists reject the idea that instrumental music is not representational. For example, as Kendall Walton observes, "'most or even all music will likely have to be considered representational,' for reasons analogous to those brought forward by Richard Wollheim in support of his thesis that both figurative and abstract painting are species of representational art."[152] If this point is valid, however, what exactly is being represented? Berger suggests that the music may be representative of a person or object: "In instrumental music, or in vocal music with independent (*obbligato* is the technical term) instrumental line(s), the instrumental line can sometimes be attributed to a source that resembles to a certain degree a human person or another object we could name, but it can also remain so abstract that we will not be tempted to attribute it to a human or any other kind of recognizable source."[153] One could object to the claimed representational value, here, because of Berger's qualification that such attribution can be made only "sometimes." However, spoken or written words can sometimes also be communicated in ways that do not have representational value, yet we do not dispute their protection under the First Amendment.[154]

Similarly, the formal reliance on language as a precondition of constitutional protection may overemphasize the belief that all language conveys unambiguous ideas or information. Language cannot always convey experiences the way that the arts are capable of doing. Berger argues, "Language's attempt to name the particular is always frustratingly imprecise when compared with a direct experience of the particular, because the name brings the particular under a general concept, associates it with many other particulars, and thus blunts the sharp edges of its particularity. But . . . this tells us something about the nature of language, not of music."[155] In a widely cited letter, Felix Mendelssohn expressed a similar, though counterintuitive, sentiment:

> People complain usually that music is so ambiguous, that it is so doubtful what they should think with it, while words are understood by anyone. But for me it is exactly the other way around. And not just with whole speeches, also with individual words; also these seem to me so ambiguous, so indefinite, so easily misunderstood in comparison with true music. . . . What a piece of music which I love tells me are for me not thoughts that are too indefinite to be grasped in words, but ones too definite. Thus I find in all attempts to express these thoughts in language something right, but also something insufficient . . . because a word does not mean for one what it means for another, because only a song (without words) can tell one the same thing it tells another, can awaken in him the same feeling, a feeling, however, which does not express itself in the same words.[156]

Friedrich Nietzsche similarly observed that "in relation to music, all communication by means of words is of the shameless sort."[157] If we are to accept Mendelssohn's claim, however, we must be willing to embrace a paradox—that instrumental music is both a precise form of expression and, at the same time, not reducible to words. Furthermore, the meaning is apparently, and unapologetically, subjective. For Mendelssohn writes not about all works of music but about works that *he* loves and what they tell him.

In addition, instrumental music could be conceived as conveying cognitive messages not about language but about mathematical patterns, sequences, and harmonies. After all, as others have noted, music was considered to be one of the four mathematical liberal arts, or quadrivium, in ancient Greece.[158]

Another question is whether this cognitive understanding of instrumental music differs from its value as expressive of emotion—or even if it does differ, how it can be conceptualized as expressive in a manner with which the First Amendment ought to be concerned. The emerging interdisciplinary field of music cognition, in which scholars study the connection between musical expression and cognitive function, may lend some insights into this somewhat nonintuitive claim.[159] Even if a connection between instrumental music and cognition were established, however, there may be an important expressive difference between stimulating cognitive *functioning* and communicating an identifiable *message*. In any event, we probably still know far too little about this field to suggest that a legal theory be built on its foundation.

Furthermore, it is unclear which of the predominant speech theories this definition of musical expression fits under. Even if we accept that instrumental music conveys definite thoughts in the sense that Mendelssohn described, without a common understanding of such thoughts, it is impossible to determine either why the expression is valuable or how the state would know that it needs to be suppressed (or, for that matter, how a court would know that it deserves First Amendment protection). Thus, it is difficult to see how this type of cognitive understanding could be justified under a democratic self-governance theory. Perhaps, however, the unspecified cognitive thoughts generated by instrumental music may help a listener to understand certain truths so that the pure cognitive claim is actually supported by the search-for-truth rationale or some versions of it. Just because the state cannot identify the area of inquiry or thought does not mean that its interference with musical expression does not inhibit individuals' ability to reach that truth on their own. And it does not even have to be an abstract or metaphysical truth. Music might lead one to understand truths in a philosophical, cultural, or spiritual sense, if not a political (narrowly defined) one.

Finally, if music stimulates nonspecific cognitive processes in the listener, it is certainly true that autonomy is undermined by the government's prevention of the ability to hear that music. The Court's strong admonition in *Stanley* about the impropriety of the state's role in controlling what we may read or watch surely applies to what we listen to.[160] If this is true for legally obscene movies, so it must be true for the experience of listening to music of one's choice, particularly if that music is understood to have a specific cognitive content. Ultimately, however, the idea of instrumental music as cognitive expression lacks sufficient support at this point to justify its coverage as speech under the First Amendment.

2. INSTRUMENTAL MUSIC AS AN EXPRESSION OF CULTURE, RELIGION, AND OTHER SOCIAL VALUES

Music that is not tied to a specific idea or message can nonetheless be closely associated with cultural, ethnic, religious, and social values. Here, we can identify a distinct expressive value to the instrumental aspects of music and one that can be harmonized with specific First Amendment theories. We can call this the *cultural claim*. There are numerous examples of instrumental music censorship because of these culturally expressive values that provide a context for understanding why constitutional protection might be important.

Instrumental music expresses culture in several ways. First, while most North Americans and Europeans are familiar with the Western twelve-note chromatic scale, music from other cultures is distinctly identifiable by its reliance on other scales that include additional notes that fall in between the tones of those twelve notes.[161] There is, in fact, an extraordinary range of scales embedded in different cultures that convey very distinctive sounds and moods. This is exemplified by the Indian raga, which uses intervals smaller than those in the Western scale, creating a sound that resonates of South Asian culture. Another example involves the African influence on American roots music, particularly the blues, which uses notes such as the so-called blue note, a pitch that falls somewhere between a major and minor third above the chord's root. The blue note is not commonly used in American music that has been heavily influenced by its European antecedents.

Construction of scales and tones can be similarly *counter*cultural, disrupting and challenging convention rather than following familiar patterns. Similar to what we see in other cultures, Western composers and musicians have also experimented with alternative tuning systems, ways of going beyond the twelve-note scale to produce "new" notes and intervals that greatly expand the possibilities of composition, performance, and auditory experience.[162] Indeed, there are even those who argue that the uniform tuning system used by the vast majority of musicians, which sets the note of A in the middle of the treble staff at 440 Hz, is a product of the Nazis and that the "natural" tuning for that note should be set at 432 Hz. Uniformity in tuning may, in fact, be somewhat elusive. As the preeminent music historian Ted Gioia notes, "These conspiracy theorists aren't entirely batty. The tuning of instruments has always been filled with compromises and influenced by competing paradigms. Listeners take for granted the conventional 'well tempered' tuning of modern instruments, but this itself was a controversial innovation in its day—it represented a rejection of the Pythagorean heritage and Renaissance thinking on music. But it also made possible the chromatically-rich compositions of Bach and his successors."[163]

Some forms of singing involve no words but instead use tones and timbres that are indigenous to and distinctive of a particular culture. One commentator observes, "Cultural preferences for particular vocal timbres are, like the entire process of vocalization, essentially intuitive. We learn how a singer's voice should sound by hearing singers, and the preferred timbres of our own musical culture are acquired early and usually taken for granted. The automatic nature of this conditioning is apparent when we hear singing from an unfamiliar culture with aesthetic values different than our own."[164] A paradigmatic example of this phenomenon is Tuvan throat singing, which involves the use of the singer's vocal apparatus to produce a droning sound while simultaneously making audible melodic sounds through the production of overtones. The Tuvans are nomadic herders who live in the mountains of Central Asia.

Their throat singing "both imitates and interacts with the mountainous, riverine landscape of the Tuvan countryside, and the horse-centered lifestyle of the Tuvan people."[165]

Differences in meter are also important and, again, are often specifically identifiable with particular cultures. Thus, rhythmic and polyrhythmic patterns may be distinctively associated with culture. The Black Codes' bans on slave drumming were, at one time, thought to have been an attempt to eliminate African polyrhythms from black music in America.[166] More recently, African rhythms were the source of at least one concern about the emergence of rock-and-roll music in the 1950s, as censors worried that the beats were highly sexualized.[167] There was a pervasive and fairly transparent racial bias embedded in these concerns about the rhythms of rock as well.[168]

In addition, adapting performances of the music of one culture to the instruments, scales, rhythms, and musicality of a very different culture can produce a completely new cross-cultural musical creation that evokes new meaning. An acute example of this phenomenon is the performance of Dave Brubeck's American jazz classic "Take Five" by Pakistan's Sachal Studios Orchestra.[169] This type of musical cross-fertilization is also represented in the mutual influence of African and American music on each other during the emergence of jazz music in the nineteenth and early twentieth centuries. "Anthropologists call this process 'syncretism'—the blending together of cultural elements that previously existed separately."[170] This process also reflects the notion that what probably "feels" like it belongs to a particular culture is at least in part socially constructed.[171]

Preservation of music has long been an essential component of maintaining culture over generations. Gioia observes, "The concept of progress plays a modest role in most ethnic musics. . . . The griots of West Africa aim to preserve their musical tradition as it is handed down to them. This is not a mere aesthetic choice, but a cultural imperative: they are the historians of their society and must maintain the integrity of their precious musical heritage. Such an attitude defines casual experimentation."[172]

Consistent with the understanding that the association between music and culture is strong, the United Nations Educational, Scientific, and Cultural Organization and World Intellectual Property Organization crafted the 1982 *Model Provisions for National Laws on the Protection of Expressions of Folklore against Illicit Exploitation and Other Prejudicial Actions.* These standards define "expressions of folklore" to include "[p]roductions consisting of characteristic elements of the traditional artistic heritage developed and maintained by a community . . . or by individuals reflecting the traditional artistic expectations of such a community, in particular . . . musical expressions, such as folk songs and instrumental music."[173]

Music can also be closely associated with religion, making it a potential target for government regulation. As noted earlier, two recent federal cases involved challenges to public schools' efforts to ban instrumental music because of its religious associations. In both cases, the schools banned student musical performances because they believed that permitting them would raise concerns about the schools' neutrality toward religion, generating complaints from parents and potentially violating the establishment clause. But in neither case did the schools categorically ban the performance or study of religious music. In *Nurre v. Whitehead*, the school expressly permitted performance of religious music at midyear concerts if the purpose of the performance was for the "artistic value" and was performed along with an "equal number of other non-religious works."[174] In *Stratechuk v. Board of Education*, the school district's policy permitted the study of religious music in the curriculum "provided that it achieve[d] specific goals of the written curriculum in various fields of study; that it [was] presented objectively; and that it neither inhibit[ed] nor advance[d] any religious point of view."[175] In these examples, we see government actors connecting even instrumental music with religious belief and their understanding that its expression conveys a message or idea of religious significance that the state did not want to appear to endorse or favor. Interestingly, the schools' policies raise the question of whether musical expression takes on a different meaning depending on the context in which it is performed. As Dewey once asked, "Is the same music nonrepresentative when played in a concert hall and representative when it is part of a sacramental service in a church?"[176]

In some religions, the instruments themselves are used for worship. Batá drums play a central part of the religious practice of Santería, a religion that emerged from the enslavement of the Yoruba people of West Africa who were brought to Cuba, where they began to incorporate some elements of Roman Catholicism into their beliefs.[177] Three batá drums of varying pitches are used in a variety of rituals, including the worship of saints, initiations, and funerals. Although singing is occasionally involved, the specific rhythms and pitches of the drums have important religious significance. To be used in rituals, the drums must be constructed according to strict religious requirements and thereafter consecrated, and the drummers must themselves undergo specific rituals before being able to play.[178]

Conversely, instrumental music can be associated with sacrilege or with conduct or values that are sacrilegious. Indeed, use of the Cuban Santería batá drums in secular contexts and mixed with instruments from other cultures has been considered by some people to be a debasement of the revered sectarian nature of the instruments[179] In many sectarian-dominated government regimes, censorship of instrumental music on these grounds is common. Though scholars of Islamic culture have divergent views about music's role in Islam, the governments of Afghanistan and Iran have outlawed instrumental music because of its purported relationship to lifestyles that conflict with their interpretation of Islamic values.[180] And, of course, religiously based music censorship is by no means limited to Islam, as the Catholic Church's ban on the tritone and descant make clear.[181]

Music not only can reflect or represent existing or past cultures but also may construct and define them. The experience of banned Jewish composers and performers during the Nazi regime reflects their struggle to maintain two important strands of musical influence—they were both Germans and Jews, and both identities were constitutive of their musical culture. The Reichsmusikkammer tried to reconstruct domestic culture by reimagining German music without its important Jewish influences. At the same time, the Kulturbund was its attempt to isolate Jewish musical culture and distinguish and separate it from what was "truly" German.[182] More contemporary examples of music (albeit in these cases lyrical as well as instrumental) as constitutive of culture are communities that have formed around groups such as the Grateful Dead ("Deadheads")[183] and Insane Clown Posse ("Juggalos").[184] Each of these groups self-identifies as its own distinctive subculture.

To the extent that governments might censor instrumental music to destroy or suppress cultural, ethnic, or religious values or identities or as a way of implementing moral or social regulation, they are engaged in a type of content discrimination that is familiar to traditional First Amendment doctrine. With respect to First Amendment theory, viewing instrumental music as an expression of cultural, religious, social, and moral values suggests that at the very least it should be covered under a truth-seeking and autonomy-based theory of freedom of speech. If we view the First Amendment as protecting a diversity of ideas, beliefs, and values about culture, religion, and society, protection of this aspect of musical expression advances the ability to experience cultural diversity as reflected through that music. Still, one might object to the truth-based claim on the ground that even in this context, music is not expressing particular ideas or beliefs, and its suppression does not interfere directly with the individual or the collective desire to achieve truth, assuming we are viewing the achievement of truth as some sort of rational process.

Turning to autonomy-based theories, the cultural claim might lead to the conclusion that autonomy over the formation of one's cultural, religious, or moral identity is advanced by protection against government control over the range of musical expressions of that identity. Identity formation might not be ideational or involve the exercise of judgments and therefore might not fall within Scanlon's concept of autonomy. But it may be an important aspect of self-realization, as conceived of by Redish, and also mesh well with Shiffrin's thinker-based autonomy theory, which acknowledges the value of becoming a distinct individual (cultural and religious affinity) and living among others (distinguishing oneself as well as connecting with others through culture and religion).[185] This understanding of expression also distinguishes instrumental music from other autonomous conduct that we would agree should not be protected, such as engaging in violence, trading stocks, or playing tennis.[186]

The possibility that instrumental music's expression of culture, religion, or values might support a democracy-based theory of free speech has been put to one side until now. However, there is also an argument that instrumental music can convey values of patriotism and nationalism.[187] Instrumental music's ability to create social cohesion may in fact enhance democracy, though not in the traditional discursive way that free speech theorists typically identify. Thus, for example, the marches of John Philip Sousa,[188] Jean Sibelius's *Finlandia*,[189] and countless national anthems could be said to be strongly identified with such values. Government control of instrumental music to instill nationalism or suppress antinationalist values could be construed as a form of viewpoint discrimination that would justify protecting speech even under a narrow version of the democratic self-governance speech theory. However, it is unclear whether music such as Sousa's is inherently nationalistic or patriotic or whether it is actually just a different example of the associative claim. Sousa's compositions, after all, bear patriotic titles, and many of his songs have lyrics. Moreover, even nationalism and patriotism can be conceptualized as cultural values, which would place this example neatly within the cultural claim, along with the notion that protection of nationalistic music advances truth-seeking and autonomy-based speech values.

3. INSTRUMENTAL MUSIC AS EXPRESSION OF EMOTION

A common thread of argument is that instrumental music is communicative because it appeals not to reason but to emotion. Indeed, the Supreme Court has recognized music's capacity to appeal to emotion, albeit without a full explanation of that function.[190] Like many forms of verbal expression, instrumental music has the capacity to inspire, sadden, excite, give joy, anger, confuse, frighten, and lead to other forms of emotional or visceral responses in the listener. This is the *emotional claim*.

Perhaps the most intuitive argument for music's expressive value is its ability to evoke noncognitive responses in listeners, as well as in its composers and performers. That is, completely dissociated from titles, linguistic signals, and other forms of art, instrumental music can be expressive in important ways that elicit emotional and spiritual responses. The emotional claim therefore perhaps presents the cleanest analytical argument for categorizing purely instrumental music as a form of constitutionally protected expression.

This conceptualization of the power of music goes back to at least Plato, who wrote that "[m]usical training is a more potent instrument than any other, because rhythm and harmony find their way into the inward places of the soul, on which they mightily fasten, imparting grace, and making the soul of him who is rightly educated graceful, or of him who is ill-educated ungraceful."[191] Plato, who may have been influenced by Socrates's views on music, believed that "specific scales, rhythms, and instruments can affect human passions in specific ways and thus form character."[192] Aristotle, in turn, believed that "[m]usic . . . directly imitates (that is, represents) the passions or states of the soul . . . when one listens to music that imitates a certain passion, he becomes imbued with the same passion."[193]

All three, however, claimed that precisely because music had the power to instill passion, it also had the potential for dangerous influences on the people. Plato was probably the most wary of the dark side of musical expression, attributing moral decline in ancient Greece to the composition of licentious musical works.[194] He warned that "[a]ny musical innovation is full of danger to the whole State, and ought to be prohibited. . . . [W]hen modes of music change, the fundamental laws of the state always change with them."[195] Similarly, Aristotle wrote of his concern for music's rousing of "ignoble passions."[196]

G. W. F. Hegel also explored musical expression in his lectures on aesthetics, although to a lesser degree than he examined other fine arts. Interestingly, given the modern tendency (generally and under the law) to focus on music's lyrical elements, Hegel's understanding of musical expression emphasized the music and observed that when words accompany music, they are peripheral to the music itself. He wrote, "the text is the servant of the music and it has no other worth than creating for our minds a better idea of what the artist has chosen as the subject of his work."[197] Hegel conceived of instrumental music as originating in "interjection," which he defined as the immediate utterance of feeling or emotion. For him, rhythm, harmony, and melody free the soul to hear its inner movement and be moved by what it hears. More specifically, music, through its conveyance, allows listeners to experience feelings of love, longing, joy, and grief.[198]

Arthur Schopenhauer also examined the emotional component of instrumental music but viewed its evocation of the emotional at a more abstract level. He distinguished the feeling of specific emotions about people, things, or events from general feelings. "[M]usic does not express this or that particular and definite pleasure, this or that affliction, pain, sorrow, horror, gaiety, merriment, or peace of mind, but joy, pain, sorrow, horror, gaiety, merriment, peace of mind *themselves*."[199]

Dewey similarly thought of music as an art that directly stirred emotional responses. "[I]n itself the ear is the emotional sense," he wrote.[200]

He elaborated, "Sounds have the power of direct emotional expression. A sound is itself threatening, whining, soothing, depressing, fierce, tender, soporific, in its own quality."[201] Moreover, it was specifically the *instrumental* elements of musical expression that bore this capacity. "Through the use of instruments, sound is freed from the definiteness it has acquired through association with speech. It thus reverts to its primitive passional quality."[202] "[B]y the use of harmony and melody of tone," he wrote, music "introduces incredibly varied complexities of question, uncertainty, and suspense wherein every tone is ordered in reference to others so that each is a summation of what precedes and a forecast of what is to come."[203]

On this understanding, instrumental music may evoke a surprisingly wide range of deep and varied emotions in its listeners. While this understanding is itself intuitively accepted by many people, it is not an indisputable interpretation of the expressive qualities of music. There is a complex and rich discourse in the field of the philosophy of music that engages this topic as well, though a complete exposition of the competing theories is beyond the scope of this chapter.[204]

Understanding instrumental music as communicating and evoking emotion provides arguments both for and against treating it as speech under the First Amendment. It most likely weighs against arguments from a democratic self-governance perspective, even under broad views of what contributes to democracy. Meiklejohn argued that the arts were constitutionally protected because they are a form of communication that allows voters to derive "knowledge, intelligence, [and] sensitivity to human values,"[205] but it has never been clear in what way the arts in general, or music in particular, facilitate that process in voters. We typically view the formation of political beliefs and ideals as a deliberative and at least quasi-rational process, so it is difficult to see how the protection of a form of expression that appeals exclusively to emotional sensibilities advances the political process. Even under a more nuanced version of the democratic self-governance theory, such as Post's,[206] it is unclear how emotional expression contributes to public discourse.

Some theorists might suggest that communication that appeals purely to passion or emotion has at least some democracy-promoting function. For example, Weinstein acknowledges that there is some power to the argument that pornography should not be excluded from the category of expression because it appeals to passions rather than reason. But he adds that it would be odd to then rely on arguments that passion-eliciting speech should be protected under a rational-thought, reason-based speech theory, which is at the core of most democracy-based arguments.[207] Others, such as Martha Nussbaum, however, suggest that the distinction between emotion and cognitive deliberation is overstated and that emotions such as love and grief are "intelligent responses to the perception of value."[208]

Consideration of the value of speech that is purely or primarily emotional to either the individual or the collective search for truth is more complex. As discussed earlier, most truth-based theories, though they extend the freedom of speech realm well beyond the political, are still largely about truths in opinion or ideas, whether they be political, religious, or philosophical. Even when focused on spiritual truth, these theories tend to be about morality and religiosity (or perhaps culture) rather than more abstract conceptions of the spiritual. So truth theorists tend to underscore the achievement of truth through speech's contribution to cognitive evaluation and assessment. Even a strong claim that instrumental music conveys emotion, then, would not necessarily satisfy the truth-finding justification for its protection.

Autonomy theories appear to present a stronger claim with regard to protecting instrumental music on an account that understands music as expressing the emotional. The power of that claim, however, depends on one's definition of the scope and purpose of autonomy. That is, the limits of autonomy theory to justify the protection of instrumental music as a form of emotional expression are, like other critiques, related to questions about the level of generality at which autonomy is defined. The challenge is to say something more than that protection of instrumental musical expression promotes individual self-realization, fulfillment, and autonomy.[209] What distinguishes instrumental music as a form of autonomous expression turns on what type of autonomy we are trying to protect.

Mill spoke about discovery of *ideas* and protection of *opinion*, both of which fail to encompass the emotional.[210] Scanlon's articulation of autonomy focuses on the protection of the autonomous individual's ability to determine for himself "what he should believe or what he should do."[211] These iterations of autonomy theory suggest that the individual must be able to evaluate and advance independent reasons and weigh the value of others' opinions against countervailing opinions and evidence. Even divorced from democracy and truth finding, this autonomy theory seems based on protecting individuals' ability to reason and form opinions without governmental interference or distortion, which seems cognitive, not emotional.

However, viewing concepts of autonomy from the perspectives of Redish, Baker, and Shiffrin may provide a sounder basis for claiming that emotionally expressive musical speech promotes autonomy in a particularized manner. A notion of emotional autonomy as a path to individual self-realization leads to a robust argument for First Amendment protection for instrumental music. Redish's self-realization is a little harder to link to the emotional claim, as even his broad argument for the autonomous individual seems directed at promoting the individual's ability to make "life-affecting decisions," which implies some sort of deliberative, as opposed to emotional, process.[212] Although Baker argues that an autonomy theory presents the stronger case for protecting what he calls "compositional" music, he never articulates precisely how protection of musical expression contributes to the version of autonomy he embraces. He suggests that "[a] person's autonomy might reasonably be conceived as her capacity to pursue successfully the life she endorses—self-authored at least in the sense that, no matter how her image of a meaningful life originates, she now can endorse that life for reasons that she accepts."[213] If we conceive of that as including the individual's capacity to pursue an autonomous emotional life—through the vehicle of composing, performing, or listening to music that makes him or her feel or not feel sad, excited, angry, exhilarated—then Baker's form of autonomy would support protecting instrumental music on the emotional claim.

This type of autonomy claim is also supported by an increasing body of neuroscience research, which suggests that the emotions elicited by musical expression have direct biological effects on the human brain, including the release of dopamine, a chemical neurotransmitter that produces pleasurable stimulation and causes the body to desire more from the source of stimulation.[214] One can imagine a science-fiction plot in which the state is able to control—through laws, force, and medication—individuals' emotional states in a manner that precludes them from self-realization in more than a decision-making autonomy sense but in the sense of interfering with the core of their very identities. Such totalitarian control would be viewed as unacceptable, even if there were no comparable interference with traditional forms of speech and political deliberation. It is this type of loss of autonomy that Shiffrin's thinker-based approach best addresses. Her references to "apprehending the true" and "imagination" imply protection of emotional autonomy as much as the freedom to deliberate rationally over more concrete aspects of existence. Moreover, "responding authentically" may quite arguably encompass being allowed to live one's life as the emotional person one chooses to be.[215]

C. Speech Theory and Instrumental Music

As we have seen, one of the central challenges to treating instrumental music—which is similar to much but not all other artistic expression—as speech is that music inherently lacks a particularized message or idea. In fact, one of the reasons music can be so uniquely expressive is in this very absence of message. It may well be that speech theorists have made too much of the line between representational and nonrepresentational expression. Words can sometimes be representational (taken for their literal meaning) and can sometimes be nonrepresentational, be symbolic, enhance other speech, bear hidden meaning, or even convey utter nonsense, as discussed in chapter 3. A painting, sculpture, or even dance can be a direct representation or realist depiction of an event or action, or it can be an abstract or even meaningless image, structure, or movement. One solution is to suggest that all forms of art are covered by the First Amendment when they are representational but not when they are nonrepresentational.[216] But this would be normatively unsatisfactory because it would be massively underinclusive to the extent that we find expressive value in nonrepresentational communication. And more importantly, on this view, instrumental music would never be covered because, as we have seen, isolated from its title, lyrics, and associations, it is always nonrepresentational.

As argued earlier, none of the theories about how instrumental music communicates fit comfortably under a First Amendment theory based on promoting democracy. After full consideration of the possible manners in which instrumental music can be expressive, the argument in this chapter comes down to a combination of theories and justifications. Instrumental music can best be understood as speech under the First Amendment both through the recognition that it advances expression of important forms of cultural, religious, nationalist, and other social values *and* to the extent that music has important aesthetic and emotional expressive values, even if in both instances it fails to advance a precise, identifiable message. The cultural claim, as discussed in more detail earlier, suggests that music is an important element of constructing, expressing, or representing values. As a reflection of cultural, religious, and other social values, music serves a cohesive function in that it brings people together in important ways.

This cohesion-building function is clearly illustrated by an anecdote about a performance by the Boston Symphony upon the announcement of President John F. Kennedy's assassination. The conductor, Erich Leinsdorf, after announcing that the president had died, spontaneously changed the program to include the funeral march from the "Eroica," Beethoven's Third Symphony.[217] Recordings of the audience reflect their shocked reaction to the news, followed by their silent contemplation of the performance, which created a cultural experience of shared grieving (though each individual no doubt experienced the moment quite personally, as well).[218]

An interesting example of music bringing people of different cultures together precisely because it lacks words is Sibelius's *Finlandia*. In 1899, in response to increasing Russian control of Finnish society, students organized a rally called the "Press Days," for which Sibelius composed the piece that was later called *Finlandia*. Organizers invited both Finnish and Swedish people to the event, and the music served to connect them precisely because it "transcend[ed] language, class, and political party."[219]

Thus, in music's expression of culture, it serves important social functions by connecting people within and between different communities, and its recognition as a form of speech ensures that government efforts to establish a cultural orthodoxy, like attempts to create a political or religious orthodoxy, are thwarted. Instrumental music is therefore covered because its protection advances what Jed Rubenfeld calls the anti-orthodoxy principle.[220] This argument suggests that it undermines First

Amendment values to allow the government to control cultural (including racial) and other values and to determine which values are worthy, not in a political sense but in a social one.

This reasoning is also consistent with a truth-seeking rationale. As discussed earlier, truth under this theory is not limited to the understanding of ideas but can embrace religious, spiritual, or cultural truths. For there is no one "true" culture or understanding of culture, and the government cannot legitimately define even its own society's culture.[221] Moreover, this definition of truth seeking responds to boundary problems by at least limiting truth seeking to the notion of cultural and social values, not to every conceivable type of truth.

At the same time, instrumental music serves a completely individualizing function and therefore ought to be covered by the First Amendment to the extent that it promotes highly personal expressions and experiences of emotion. Instrumental music allows people to express (through composition, performance, and feeling) and experience (through listening, interpreting, and feeling) as no other medium of communication can. Thus, while music serves a community-building function in terms of cultural expression, it simultaneously advances an autonomy-promoting function in its facilitation of individualized emotional expression and experience. As developed in more detail earlier, music's role in expressing, evoking, and experiencing the emotional could easily be argued to promote self-realization.

The claim that instrumental music serves an important function in constructing and maintaining cultural and other social values and in expressing and experiencing emotion also leads us to another argument for its inclusion as speech under the First Amendment. Thus far, the discussion has focused only on utilitarian or "consequentialist" speech theories, which suggest that speech is protected when it advances specific individual or social interests, such as democracy and autonomy. Another school of First Amendment theorists argues that consequentialist theories are inadequate or incomplete in explaining the right of free speech and that a more sound analytical focus is to closely scrutinize the government's reasons for regulating speech rather than examining what is being regulated. As Larry Alexander writes, "Freedom of expression is implicated whenever an activity is suppressed or penalized for the purpose of preventing a message from being received."[222] Under this theory, free speech "at its core requires regulators to abstain from acting on the basis of their own assessments of a message's truth or value."[223] The idea that a "message" is involved still requires us to make an additional analytical move to include purely instrumental music because, again, such music is always nonpropositional. However, the core of Alexander's argument is essentially that speech ought to be a protected right when the government's reasons for regulating it are based on its belief that the speech is either not true or has no value. Surely, a government ban on instrumental music for the purpose of interfering with, extinguishing, or otherwise adversely affecting cultural, religious, nationalistic (or antinationalistic), or other social values would be illegitimate. Likewise, state regulation of music with the objective of snuffing out emotional expression or experience would fall well outside the parameters of what we would accept as valid government action. Thus, under nonconsequentialist theories of speech, the cultural and emotional claims both also work as justifications for classifying instrumental music as speech under the First Amendment.

Instrumental music is enigmatic. It both brings people together as a community and sets them apart as individuals, and on this paradox, its true value as speech rests. That is not to say that instrumental music has to have a particularized meaning to be covered, only that whatever meanings it conveys are not reducible to any message but rather connect to culture and individuality in ways that are not, in fact, expressible.

Coda

This chapter has demonstrated the complexity involved with understanding instrumental music as a form of speech covered by the First Amendment. The value in such an enterprise is not entirely theoretical. Music continues to be suppressed around the globe by governments and other powerful institutional actors. A more complete understanding of its speech value and function is therefore critical to advancing free speech doctrine.

Instrumental music does not convey a particularized message or idea, does not appeal to reason, and does not transmit thoughts or beliefs in an objectively identifiable form. Nonetheless, instrumental music is a unique way of expressing and experiencing culture and also can be widely understood as an expression of or appeal to the senses in that it has the capacity to convey and evoke joy, sadness, anger, melancholy, and a multitude of other emotional responses. Both of these functions connect to important values of advancing the search for truth and promoting individual self-realization. As such, instrumental music enjoys full status as speech under the First Amendment, even if it does not advance democracy in any direct, meaningful, or understandable manner.

2

Art and the First Amendment

As we noted in the introduction, the paintings of Jackson Pollock are "unquestionably shielded" by the First Amendment, as spelled out in *Hurley v. Irish-American Gay, Lesbian & Bisexual Group of Boston, Inc.*[1] Of course we pretty much knew that already, from the development of the law of obscenity, driven as it was by a need to ensure that the proscription of obscenity not lead to the suppression of depictions that are merely erotic. Beyond authority, though, exactly why are Pollock's paintings covered by the First Amendment?[2] Consider that core First Amendment doctrine places under close scrutiny statutes that regulate speech on the basis of its content and under even closer scrutiny statutes that regulate speech on the basis of the viewpoint it expresses. Yet what—exactly or even roughly—is the content of Pollock's *Blue Poles, No. 11* or the viewpoint it expresses?[3]

This chapter explores the question of the First Amendment's coverage of nonrepresentational art, which proves quite difficult to answer satisfactorily—that is, in a doctrinal form that preserves other seemingly "unquestionable" results.[4] Every approach one might take to explaining why the First Amendment covers art—that art is communicative, that it contributes to the creation of a culture of self-directed individuals, and others addressed here—generates odd anomalies. The exploration does not question the conventional *conclusion* that artworks are covered by the First Amendment but rather worries some of the often-unstated assumptions that underlie that conclusion.[5] We will see, for example, that some things one might want to say about the question of whether the First Amendment covers nonrepresentational art lead to the suggestion that James Joyce's *Ulysses* might not be covered, surely a peculiar result. This chapter does not mean to question *Hurley*'s assertion about Jackson Pollock's paintings. Rather, by asking how that conclusion might be justified, we will come across some unexpected facets of the First Amendment, with some implications for other doctrinal areas abutting the First Amendment.

Part 1 of the chapter raises and briefly addresses some of the most common immediate responses when one questions art's First Amendment coverage, suggesting that the questions are indeed more complicated than immediate responses suggest. Part 2 begins to flesh out the reasons why the immediate responses discussed in part 1 are at least incomplete. It sets out some preliminary questions, such as the distinction between First Amendment coverage and First Amendment protection, and addresses the role of communication in the First Amendment and in artworks. It explains why we cannot finesse the coverage question by displacing it with routine conclusions that artworks are covered but not protected, and it concludes with some cautionary notes about the methodology of First Amendment argument. Part 3 examines why First Amendment theory has taken artworks' coverage for granted, despite the difficulty of fitting such works into general First Amendment theories. Examining why nonrepresentational art is covered by the First Amendment raises deep questions about First Amendment doctrine and leads to the conclusion that general First Amendment theories are unlikely to be particularly helpful in addressing those questions because they are *too* general.

Part 4 takes up the Supreme Court's stated doctrine as relevant to the coverage issue, including an analysis of the cases and, importantly, the inadequacy of textual analysis to resolve the coverage issue. Examining the question of art's coverage in largely doctrinal terms may help us understand questions about the First Amendment's coverage (or absence of coverage) for commercial speech and misleading advertising, for example. In working toward an answer, the chapter attempts to avoid deep philosophical inquiries into the philosophy of language or art, hoping instead to offer answers to some parts of the question that can be accepted by people who disagree about deep theories of language and art.[6] The part also suggests some doctrinal implications of finding artworks covered, particularly with respect to intellectual property law. The chapter's conclusion offers a modest reconstruction of *Hurley*'s observation about the unquestionable coverage of Jackson Pollock's paintings and points out that the chapter's analysis leaves many questions open to further exploration.

I. Some Incomplete Immediate Answers to the Question of First Amendment Coverage for Artworks

Three "easy" answers are typically offered when one raises the question of artworks' First Amendment coverage. The first, and least cogent, is that regulation of artworks on the basis of their "content" is characteristic of totalitarian regimes,[7] as in Nazi Germany's suppression of "degenerate" art and Soviet Russia's promotion of socialist realist art at the expense of abstraction. The ready response to this is that it confuses a symptom of totalitarianism with its causes. Totalitarianism is bad because it does many bad things, not (merely) because it suppresses art on the basis of its content. Many constitutional provisions, including the First Amendment, limit the bad things totalitarian governments try to do, and it is hardly clear that stopping them from suppressing art on the basis of its content has anything to do with stopping them from doing the bad things that make them totalitarian. Or, put another way, if a city council prohibits the display of a Claes Oldenburg sculpture on private property—where the sculpture is visible to the public—because it thought the sculpture was ugly or silly, we are unlikely to find Adolf Hitler or Joseph Stalin lurking in the bushes.[8] A second, seemingly more substantial easy answer is that many activities that are not covered by the First Amendment provoke the imagination, encourage people to think, and the like.[9] Running a small business, for example, does this. The proprietor has to identify a market niche, devise a marketing strategy, and more. Further, people who *observe* small businesses in operation have their imagination provoked. Ticket scalping provides a useful example of such a small business. The public interest in regulating ticket scalping, while sufficient to satisfy modern requirements of economic due process, is thin enough that adding even a slight increment to the required justification because ticket scalping might implicate First Amendment concerns such as provoking the imagination might lead to the conclusion that prohibiting ticket scalping is unconstitutional under the First Amendment.[10]

Pointing in the other direction, the third easy response is that the coverage question is largely inconsequential, because governments in the United States rarely attempt to regulate artworks on the basis of their content. Rather, they seek to apply content-neutral regulations that are

Claes Oldenburg, *Spoonbridge and Cherry*. Copyright 1988 Claes Oldenburg and Coosje van Bruggen.

widely applicable to many activities to artworks that happen to present the same social problems as those other activities. And, in general, the Supreme Court's standards for determining when a generally applicable regulation can be applied to material plainly covered by the First Amendment are rather easy to satisfy. The conclusion is that we can treat artworks as covered by the First Amendment without seriously jeopardizing regulations that serve good social ends—and that, when the Court's standards are not satisfied, we should not be troubled by denying the government the ability to regulate the artwork. A full response to this easy answer will occupy substantial space later, and a shorthand version will have to suffice at this point. We can turn the point around and say that treating artworks as *not* covered by the First Amendment will have few adverse consequences because of the Supreme Court's standards and that it indeed might be a matter of concern that, for example, the First Amendment might be interpreted in a way that places some artworks outside the scope of historic-preservation ordinances. At the least, doing so raises questions about whether the courts should say that the social value of artworks trumps legislative judgments about historic preservation.

The easy answers are unavailing. We must develop a more complex analysis.

II. Preliminaries: Wondering Why the First Amendment Covers Art

A. Coverage versus Protection

First Amendment analysis conventionally distinguishes between the question of whether some activity is *covered* by the First Amendment and the question of whether that activity, if covered, is *protected* by the First Amendment.[11] First Amendment analysis is simply irrelevant to activities not covered by the First Amendment.[12] Consideration of whether a regulation is content based or content neutral, for example, is not appropriate for activities not covered by the First Amendment.[13]

When activities are covered by the First Amendment, in contrast, we have to apply standard First Amendment doctrine to assess the constitutionality of regulations applicable to those activities. Sometimes activities covered by the First Amendment are also protected by it, but sometimes covered activities are unprotected. Assume that nonrepresentational art is covered by the First Amendment. Consider the Oldenburg example described earlier. Perhaps the ban is content based because it is justified with reference to the asserted ugliness or silliness of those sculptures. And if—as most advocates of the view that art is covered by the First Amendment believe—nonrepresentational art is a category that receives something more than low-level protection against content-based regulations, the municipal regulation would be constitutional only if it were justified by quite strong public policies and advanced those policies with a fair degree of precision.[14] If the city fails to come up with justifications of the required strength, the ban is unconstitutional, and the Oldenburg sculptures are both covered and protected by the First Amendment against the municipal ban. In contrast, if the city bans the display of nonrepresentational art in places where drivers might see it, on the ground that drivers puzzled by what they are viewing might be distracted, the regulation is (probably) content neutral and is justified if the city's concern about driver distraction is reasonably well founded and the ban is reasonably well suited to achieving the goal of limiting distractions. The Oldenburg sculptures would then be covered but not protected.

B. Why the Coverage Question Is Puzzling: Communication through Art and Otherwise

Of course nonrepresentational art is "communicative" in some sense, although one of the points about nonrepresentational art is that what it communicates often depends almost entirely on what a viewer takes it to be communicating. Yet many other activities are communicative in that way,[15] and we should be wary of dismissing questions about the First Amendment's coverage of nonrepresentational art because, being communicative, it is "obviously" covered by the First Amendment.

Consider several examples. William Carlos Williams was prescribing how a poet should proceed when he wrote, "No ideas but in things." Poets, he believed, should convey their ideas by the "things" they described.[16] For Williams, then, at least some "things" could convey ideas—the things described in poems. But if those things convey ideas when described in poems, why should we not think that they can convey ideas when encountered in the physical world? Marcel Duchamp's *Fountain* is a thing that he used to convey an idea by placing it in an unexpected context; why might it not be communicative in other contexts? As another example, panhandling communicates something to those who observe a panhandler.[17] Some will say, "See that? It shows how shiftless and irresponsible some people are," others, "See that? It shows how terribly thin our social safety net is."[18]

It is similar with ticket scalping.[19] Some people will see a ticket scalper at work as a demonstration of unregulated capitalism's vibrancy, providing opportunities for entrepreneurial types to start a small business and make a good living, while others will see the same activity as a demonstration of the failure of unregulated capitalism, which allows the "greedy" to exploit the "needy." And, again to state the obvious, the interpretations people give to panhandling and ticket scalping might have effects on the political choices they make.[20]

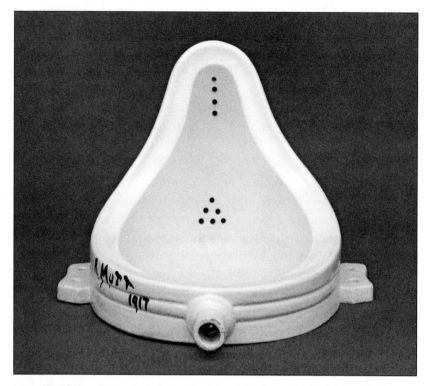

Marcel Duchamp, *Fountain*. © Succession Marcel Duchamp / ADAGP, Paris / Artists Rights Society (ARS), New York, 2015.

C. Applying the Coverage/Protection Distinction: A Case Study

Consider *Kleinman v. City of San Marcos*. Judge Edith H. Jones provided a crisp statement of the facts:

> Appellant Michael Kleinman operates Planet K stores throughout the San Antonio and Austin areas. Planet K stores are funky establishments that sell novelty items and gifts. Kleinman has a tradition of celebrating new store openings with a "car bash," a charity event at which the public pays for the privilege of sledgehammering a car to "a smashed wreck." The wrecks are then filled with dirt, planted with vegetation, and painted. Placed outside each store, the "planters" serve as unique advertising devices.

An Oldsmobile 88 car-planter was created upon the opening of a new Planet K store in San Marcos, Texas. Kleinman arranged to have the smashed car planted with a variety of native cacti and painted with scenes of life in San Marcos. Positioned in front of the store, the distinctive planter is visible to motorists traveling north on Interstate 35. Kleinman did not dictate the content of the illustrations, but he requested that the phrase "make love not war" be incorporated into the design. Two local artists, Scott Wade and John Furly Travis, were commissioned to paint the wreck. At trial, Travis testified that he had no particular message in mind when he painted the car, "just happiness." He intended his images to convey the idea that "you could take a junked vehicle, junk canvas, and create something beautiful out of it." Wade sought to transform "a large gas-guzzling vehicle" into "something that's more respectful of the planet and something that nurtures life as opposed to destroys it." Wade explained that his intent was to describe American car culture and the link between gasoline and the war in Iraq.

The city had an ordinance declaring "junked vehicles" a public nuisance. Such vehicles were "self propelled, inoperable, and . . . wrecked [or] dismantled, . . . [or were] inoperable for more than 45 consecutive days."[21] The city defended the ordinance against Kleinman's First Amendment challenge on the ground that the ordinance was a content-neutral regulation aimed at eliminating "eyesores" and promoting public order. The court of appeals expressed some skepticism about Kleinman's claim—accepted by the city for purposes of litigation—that "this cactus planter" was an artwork. According to the court of appeals, *Hurley*'s discussion of artworks "refer[red] solely to great works of art." The "heavy machinery of the First Amendment" ought not "be deployed in every case involving visual non-speech expression." Before finding that the ordinance survived intermediate First Amendment scrutiny, the court strongly suggested that the ordinance could be applied to the car if it was a "reasonable regulation." "Irrespective of the intentions of its creators or Planet K's owner, the car-planter is a utilitarian device, an advertisement, and ultimately a 'junked vehicle,'" and those "qualities objectively dominate any expressive component of its exterior painting."[22]

Jenna Birchum, *Planet K Car Planter.* Copyright Jenna Birchum.

The dealer's sponsorship of the artwork was probably inspired, perhaps indirectly, by *Cadillac Ranch*, located in Amarillo, Texas, 430 miles from San Marcos. Licensed under Creative Commons Attribution Share Alike 2.0, http://creativecommons.org/licenses/by-sa/2.0/.

Intermediate scrutiny was appropriate if the vehicle were treated as an artwork because the law was "a content-neutral health and safety ordinance," "not intended to regulate 'speech' at all." Applying intermediate scrutiny, the court held that the regulation "protect[ed] the community's health and safety from the problems created by abandoned vehicles left in public view." Junked vehicles were "an attractive nuisance to children" and attracted "[r]odents, pests, and weeds" as well. Junked cars caused "urban blight" and vandalism and depressed property values. Further, the ordinance was "reasonably tailored," because owners of junked vehicles could keep them on their property if the vehicles were enclosed.[23]

Some aspects of *Kleinman* are clearly questionable, particularly the court's effort to distinguish between great works of art and other ("mere"?) artworks.[24] Drawing a line between covered and uncovered "visual non-speech expression" may well be impossible, at least without invoking content-related criteria. Nor is it clear that one can describe something as an "eyesore" without making a content-based judgment,[25] as indeed the apocryphal comment on Jackson Pollock's paintings, that "my six-year-old could do that," suggests.[26]

Those aspects of the court's opinion aside, its perhaps grudging application of intermediate scrutiny seems defensible. The ordinance is a content-neutral regulation of an activity that is not necessarily expressive but happens to be expressive in this case. The doctrinal standard for determining whether the homeowner's First Amendment claim is valid comes from *United States v. O'Brien*: Does the ordinance "further[] an important or substantial governmental interest . . . unrelated to the suppression of free expression" and is "the incidental restriction on alleged First Amendment freedoms . . . no greater than is essential to the furtherance of that interest"?[27] My aim here is not to provide an analysis of those questions but rather to observe that *if* artworks like those displayed by Kleinman are covered by the First Amendment, the conclusion that the ordinance can be applied to them notwithstanding his First Amendment claim amounts to a conclusion that the artwork is covered by the First Amendment but not in this instance protected by it.[28]

My aim in this chapter is to explore the First Amendment's *coverage* of art, leaving aside questions about the circumstances under which art, if covered by the First Amendment, is also protected by it.

D. Why the Question of Coverage Cannot Be Finessed

We might be tempted to finesse the question of coverage by attacking the problem from two different directions, which are labeled here the *rationality* challenge and the *content-neutrality* challenge. If successful, the combination of attacks would make the coverage question uninteresting.

The rationality challenge deals with regulating artworks on the basis of the works' content—their ugliness, for example.[29] The attack asserts that the grounds for such regulations are typically so weak that the artworks would be protected by a substantive due process requirement that exercises of government power must be minimally rational. Yet even a reasonably robust rationality requirement—more robust than the current Court seems likely to apply—will be unable to finesse some seemingly content-based regulations. In my view, a ban on the display of offensive artworks on property visible to the public, for example, would almost certainly satisfy even a robust rationality requirement. In such a case, we would have to decide whether artworks are covered.

Yet calling regulations based on ugliness or the like "content based" might prejudice the inquiry in favor of finding coverage. The reason for regulation is an aesthetic judgment about which people will of course differ. In this, though, the reason for regulation seems indistinguishable from all sorts of morals-based legislation, which in most instances are constitutional simply because they reflect moral judgments. In the absence of *other* reasons for thinking artworks covered by the First Amendment, why should aesthetic judgments be different from moral ones for purposes of constitutional law?

Consider another version of this approach. Sally Mann's photographs of her daughter are undoubtedly disturbing. They induce thoughts—or better, inchoate feelings, a sense of unease—about childhood sexuality. Yet they are not examples of child obscenity under current definitions. Nor could they be criminalized in a statute that was not unconstitutionally overbroad—but in large part the overbreadth would result from the assumption that art is covered by the First Amendment. Suppose a state sought to create a separate offense that *would* criminalize Mann's photographs. We could not avoid the coverage question with the contention that, like every statute legislatures might enact that penalized works of art as such, this one would surely be unconstitutional on rationality grounds. The state interests in ensuring the portrayed child's consent to a depiction that will be permanently available and that might lead the child once grown to be ashamed of what she might then perceive as her immodesty should be sufficient to satisfy the mere-rationality requirement.

Kleinman offers a version of the content-neutrality attack. Here the temptation is to assert that every content-neutral regulation applied to every artwork will survive constitutional scrutiny.[30] The governmental interest will be strong, and the incidental impact on speech will be weak—or so this attack hopes. If so, the distinction between coverage and protection would be irrelevant in practice with respect to content-neutral regulations because artworks, even if covered by the First Amendment, would never be protected by it against content-neutral regulations.

Of course, it is easy to come up with examples of content-neutral regulations that can be applied to artworks without violating the First Amendment. The most obvious cases involve performance artworks that violate ordinary criminal statutes. Performance art that takes the form of defacing public or private property or interacting with unsuspecting and unwilling bystanders in ways that amount to technical assaults, for example, is clearly not protected by the First Amendment because the government interest embodied in general criminal law is substantial and excising all artworks from the coverage of those laws is impracticable.[31] Other plausible examples, though, can place under pressure the conclusion that it will always be unproblematic to apply content-neutral regulations to works of art. Consider for example the application of historic-preservation ordinances or environmental regulations to works by Christo and Jeanne-Claude. With a building owner's permission, those artists wrap buildings in cloth for short periods, thereby altering the facades in a manner that might well be found to be inconsistent with an especially stringent historic-preservation ordinance.[32] The temporary nature of their installations means that the works will have only a modest impact on the interests served by historic-preservation ordinances. Perhaps the interest in historic preservation should prevail over the artistic work, but we should not rule out in advance the possibility that the First Amendment ought to make it unconstitutional to apply such an ordinance to one of these wrappings. Yet by assuming that the

Christo and Jeanne-Claude, *Wrapped Reichstag*. Wolfgang Volz/laif/Redux.

First Amendment test used when content-neutral rules affect covered activity will always allow regulation, that is precisely what this attempt to finesse the issue of coverage does.

Next, consider the application of ordinary consumer-fraud rules to the following hypothetical problem. A museum dedicated to the history of the Middle East advertises an exhibition, *Jerusalem 1947*. A visitor pays the admission fee and is outraged upon discovering that the exhibition consists solely of a large painting titled *Jerusalem 1947*, which consists of a red square with a yellow border in the style of Josef Albers or Mark Rothko, with preliminary drawings. Alleging consumer fraud, the visitor sues for a refund of the admission fee and other damages. Assume that the visitor can satisfy the ordinary requirements for a fraud action, such as reliance (in the example, on the exhibition's title) and a departure from what a reasonable consumer would take the advertisement to assert. The museum defends itself on the ground that the First Amendment defeats the fraud action. If the First Amendment covers nonrepresentational art, the defense is far from frivolous.

Consider as well the problem posed by panhandling and ticket scalping. Undoubtedly we could deal with First Amendment objections to regulations of those activities by finding them covered by the First Amendment but (almost) never protected by it. Yet the covered-but-not-protected argument is too much work to solve what should be a fairly easy problem. In general terms, the "too much work" principle is put in play when one needs a complicated analysis to reach an answer that intuitively seems so obvious that a simple analysis should suffice.[33] Assassination provides a standard example of the "too much work" problem in connection with finding an activity covered but not protected. Another example would be shaming sanctions unauthorized by law, imposed by a community vigilante group, such as "tagging" an offender's car or home with spray-painted squiggles. The fact that the shaming sanction is expressive should not require additional work to explain why the state can permissibly subject the vigilantes' actions to punishment.[34] Were these arguments to arise because we somehow had to figure out a way to deal with odd cases on the margin, we might tolerate them. But here they arise because we have simply assumed without much analysis that artworks are covered by the First Amendment.

We will often, but not always, be able to put the question of coverage aside by finding an artwork unprotected even if covered by the First Amendment. The question of coverage remains independently important.

E. The Inutility of "Intent" as a Standard for Coverage

A common suggestion is that art is covered by the First Amendment because artists intend to communicate or express something, though with nonrepresentational art, determining what they intend to express is notoriously difficult. An "intent" criterion is both over- and under-inclusive. That is not enough to disqualify it, because every individual criterion for identifying what falls within a legal category has that characteristic.[35] But specifying the problems of mismatch yields additional insights into some of the problems of art's coverage under the First Amendment. To begin, many modern sculptors would deny that they "intend" to express anything in their work. Rather, they seek to explore the relation between shape and space, nothing more (or less). Nor is

David Smith, *Untitled.* Art © The Estate of David Smith / Licensed by VAGA, New York, NY.

the abjuration of an intent to express limited to sculptors: artworks "should not mean but be," as Archibald MacLeish put it.[36] Consider the work known colloquially as "Whistler's Mother." Its creator gave it the title *Arrangement in Grey and Black* (with the subtitle *The Artist's Mother* added to satisfy perceived audience demand), to emphasize that his interest lay less in rendering his mother's appearance accurately than in exploring the possibilities of a limited palette of color.[37] Art as form—*being* rather than *meaning*—is not intended to communicate even though it may sometimes do so. A related point is that sometimes artworks are engagements with a tradition. As such, it is not clear that they "mean" anything. Consider here what Picasso's reimagining of Velazquez's *Les Meninas* could mean: "I am a Spanish artist greater than Velazquez"?

Consider next *non*artistic activities intended to express something. The ticket scalper may be a libertarian and indeed may say to purchasers that she is scalping tickets as a way of subverting the regulatory state.[38] Her intent to express her libertarian views through the act of ticket scalping almost certainly should not bring this activity under the First Amendment's coverage. The justifications for bans on ticket scalping might be sufficient to satisfy the demands of modern substantive due process in the economic domain. Placing the libertarian ticket scalper under the First Amendment would seem to require at least a tiny increment in the justification for regulation, and the justifications for bans on ticket scalping might not survive even an extremely modest demand for a bit more justification.[39]

James McNeill Whistler, *Arrangement in Black and White: The Artist's Mother.* © RMN-Grand Palais / Art Resource, NY.

Pablo Picasso, *Las Meninas*. Museu Picasso, Barcelona. Photograph, Gasull Fotografia.

Finally, consider a parent who uses reasonably forceful methods of disciplining his children in public, with the intent to demonstrate—express to those who happen to see it—his view that such methods are better than less coercive "modern" parenting methods. Here too the presence of an intent to express something probably ought not change the analysis we would otherwise use. The parent might be able to raise a modern substantive due process claim resting on family autonomy, but as with the libertarian ticket scalper, the disciplinarian parent should not benefit from some increment in protection because of the intent to express something.

These examples bring the "too much work" principle into play. Confronted with the argument that some criteria for bringing art under the First Amendment would also bring other activities under it, some people respond that those activities *should* be covered but that doing so will pose no particular difficulties because the relevant First Amendment analysis will show that regulating those activities is permissible even when regulating art is not. The "too much work" principle con-

Diego Velázquez, *Las Meninas.* © Madrid, Museo Nacional del Prado.

cedes the possibility but then observes that reaching the presumably acceptable outcome requires too much analytic work (and that if the same outcomes are always reached, bringing the activities under the First Amendment seems pointless). The proposed criteria, that is, are in fact not general ones but are jerry-rigged to achieve the desired result of covering art without providing any incremental protection to those other activities.[40]

F. The Attractions and Perils of Nominalism

Perhaps we can begin to make some progress by a rather nominalist approach: the First Amendment is about speech and the press—about words. Perhaps we should take words, or *word-equivalents*,[41] as the starting point for thinking about nonrepresentational art and the First Amendment. The role of words and word-equivalents is inevitably complex. Treating words as *necessary* for First Amendment coverage will rule out coverage for much nonrepresentational art and leads to results that seem pretty clearly wrong in some instances.[42] Treating words as *sufficient* is more promising yet sometimes will seem to find coverage for the wrong reasons. In addition, we can observe a tendency for judges to treat words as sometimes meaningless. Finally, treating the reproduction of words as something covered by the term *press* in the First Amendment leads to odd results as well. Addressing these questions provides a pathway into a deeper understanding of the problems with which this chapter is primarily concerned.

1. ARE WORDS NECESSARY?

I think it fair to assume that political commentary lies at the First Amendment's heart. The word *commentary* suggests something using words—as of course does the word *speech*. One might think, then, that on strictly textualist grounds words might be a necessary component of material covered by the First Amendment.[43] This will of course leave much outside that coverage—including Jackson Pollock's paintings.

This textualism seems difficult to defend. As the *Oxford English Dictionary* indicates, commentary can take many forms.[44] Wholly apart from the fact that the First Amendment might well cover more than political commentary, some political commentary occurs without words. What matters, it seems, is that a large number of viewers will impute roughly the same political content to an image. Words might not be necessary for First Amendment coverage, but perhaps a reasonably widespread imputation of roughly the same meaning is. This suggests why ticket scalping is outside the First Amendment's coverage: some viewers may indeed impute political meaning when they observe a ticket scalper, but any such imputation will not be widely enough shared to bring the activity within the First Amendment. Yet this approach will still not ex-

Eddie Adams, *Saigon Execution*. AP Photo / Eddie Adams.

plain why *Blue Poles, No. 11* is covered by the First Amendment. It is entirely unclear whether anyone imputes any meaning to it, much less a political meaning, and whatever meanings are imputed are likely to be not widely enough shared to make the painting a word-equivalent.

2. ARE WORDS SUFFICIENT?

Any acceptable account of the First Amendment's coverage would have to ensure that political cartoons fall within the amendment. The images in such cartoons are inextricable from their political content—and yet sometimes the images would not be understandable as political without accompanying words. The image of a severed snake in what may be one of the ten most famous U.S. political cartoons might well be meaningless, or "only" an image, without the caption "Join, or Die." Perhaps we should conclude that the First Amendment covers art that is accompanied by words.[45] That conclusion would not explain why nonrepresentational art—art without accompanying words or word-equivalents—is covered. Even more, though, it is plainly overbroad. Jenny Holzer's installations are made up of words in illuminated neon

"Join, or Die."

"signs." Yet one goes wrong in paying too much attention to the words that flow through the installations.[46] The art lies in the words' visual impact and, perhaps, in the cognitive disjuncture between the visual appearance and the meaning observers find themselves almost compelled to impute to the words they are seeing. If there are reasons for including these works of art within the First Amendment, the fact that they employ words is not one of them.

In addition, a focus on words may be underinclusive as well. Sometimes images without words will convey meaning because the images have been so often associated with specific words that they become the equivalent of words. Think of the donkey and elephant as symbols of the Democratic and Republican Parties. The images have no intrinsic meanings, and surely there are depictions of donkeys and elephants that have no political content. But deployed in political cartoons, the images have propositional content.

Nonconstitutional law already responds to the fact that images can take on meanings independent of words. A purely symbolic image can be protected by trademark law when it acquires a secondary meaning—a regular association in viewers' minds between the image and the product to which it is implicitly but, importantly, not openly attached.[47] Perhaps nonrepresentational art is covered by the First Amendment on similar grounds: even if not word-equivalents and therefore not fairly encompassed within a purely textualist analysis, enough people may impute *some* meanings, and not entirely idiosyncratic ones, to such artworks.[48]

A textualist insistence that words' presence is either sufficient or necessary for First Amendment coverage thus seems mistaken and unable to account for the coverage of nonrepresentational art. Perhaps the textualist analysis can be salvaged on second-best grounds: textualism's insistence that words are both necessary and sufficient for First Amendment coverage is indeed arbitrary with respect to any purposes we might

Jenny Holzer, *Installation for Bilbao*, 1997. Electronic LED sign, nine columns. Site-specific dimensions. Guggenheim Bilbao Museoa. Photo: Guggenheim Bilbao Museoa © FMGB Guggenheim Bilbao Museoa, photo by Erika Barahona Ede.

impute to the Amendment, but it is better than any alternative in defining that coverage. Arbitrary inclusions (e.g., Jenny Holzer's work) and arbitrary exclusions (e.g., Jackson Pollock's) are the inevitable result. Perhaps so, but recall that we began with *Hurley*'s assertion that Jackson Pollock's paintings were unquestionably covered. The textualist analysis cannot accommodate that assertion or the clearly widespread intuition that it is correct.

What is at work in these arguments is a sense—not more than that—that First Amendment coverage turns on treating covered material as somehow equivalent to words. Many of the moves described so far seek to convert nonrepresentational art into word-equivalents. What, though, if even words might be meaningless?

3. CAN WORDS BE MEANINGLESS?

Reading Supreme Court opinions dealing with words that some justices find troubling, one notices an interesting trope: a justice will note the words and assert puzzlement at what they mean or otherwise deprecate the words' communicative effectiveness. Probably the most prominent example is Justice Harry Blackmun's description of Paul Cohen's display of the words "Fuck the Draft" on his jacket as an "absurd and immature antic" and "mainly conduct, and little speech."[49] More recently, the Court called "Bong Hits 4 Jesus" "cryptic." Importantly, the Court noted that the words might be interpreted differently by different people: "It is no doubt offensive to some, perhaps amusing to others. . . . [School] Principal Morse thought the banner would be interpreted by those viewing it as promoting illegal drug use, and that interpretation is plainly a reasonable one."[50] Chapter 3 examines the question of First Amendment coverage for nonsense in more detail. Some observations are appropriate in the present context. Here again multivocality enters the analysis. A "reasonable" imputation of meaning to otherwise meaningless words—or symbols?—is sufficient to trigger First Amendment coverage.[51] Word-equivalents arise when there is enough convergence in viewers' understandings of an activity's meaning for the activity to function as a shorthand for words expressly setting out that meaning.[52] Perhaps some viewers would be puzzled at the meaning of burning a flag, but enough people will impute identical meanings to the act for it to count as a word-equivalent.[53]

"Bong Hits 4 Jesus." © Clay Good / ZUMA Press.

I wonder whether many works of nonrepresentational art are word-equivalents, at least if the threshold for determining sufficient convergence in imputed meaning among viewers is more than just a bit above the ground. Is that threshold satisfied by whatever meanings viewers impute to *Blue Poles, No. 11*? More troubling, perhaps, is this question: is the threshold satisfied by the meanings *readers* give the last line of James Joyce's *Ulysses*?[54] Or is it enough that every reader gives some meaning to the last lines even though there may be no significant convergence among readers on what that meaning is?

4. THE SPECIAL QUESTION OF REPRODUCTIONS

The question about *Ulysses* leads to another possibility. Switch from the speech clause to the press clause, and think in purely textualist terms. Books are covered by the press clause because they are printed by presses. So are books containing pictures, and so, therefore, are books containing depictions of nonrepresentational art.

Robert Smithson, *Spiral Jetty*. Courtesy of James Cohan Gallery, New York and Shanghai.

This gets us something but not nearly enough. Even with respect to words, this invocation of the press clause ends up protecting books but not the manuscripts submitted to publishers. With respect to art, the press clause protects reproductions but not the originals. And this might be consequential if, for example, the government were able to seize the film on which a photograph is imprinted before the film is transmitted for reproduction. Perhaps more interesting, the approach leaves uncovered some of the artworks most likely to be the subject of problematic regulation—site-specific works that might trigger environmental-protection or historic-preservation concerns.

G. Two Additional Paths to Avoid If Possible

1. STIPULATING THAT ART IS COVERED

Finessing the coverage question by moving directly to the protection question is impossible, and dealing with it through a nominalist approach seems troublesome as well. Supreme Court doctrine on other First Amendment issues points out another possibility. That is to "solve" the problem by stipulation—by declaring that nonrepresentational art is categorically included or categorically excluded from the First Amendment's coverage, without further explanation.

The Court has taken this path in two areas bordering on the issue here. After holding that commercial speech was not categorically low value, the Court defined commercial speech as speech that "concern[s] lawful activity and [is] not . . . misleading."[55] If misleading commercial advertisements were covered by the First Amendment, long-standing regulations of false advertising would be brought into question. This may have motivated the Court to exclude such advertisements from its definition of commercial speech.

Why, though, is the government entitled to label some advertisements as misleading and thereby exclude them from the First Amendment's coverage? As the constitutional law of commercial speech has developed, the Court has increasingly emphasized that the government cannot prohibit commercial speech on the paternalistic ground that consumers given information by an advertisement will make imprudent choices. Yet characterizing a facially truthful statement as misleading is just that sort of paternalism, expressing the government's judgment that consumers—assisted by competitors' counteradvertising and various forms of consumer-generated content such as websites with product reviews—will be unable to determine for themselves the information's accuracy or significance. Excluding misleading speech from the category of commercial speech covered by the First Amendment solves a difficult problem by stipulation.

The Court has treated the First Amendment dimensions of copyright similarly. In *Eldred v. Ashcroft*, the Court rejected a First Amendment challenge to the Copyright Extension Act of 1998, holding that it was not different enough from prior copyright extension acts that it had upheld. In discussing the First Amendment claim, the Court alluded to exceptions built into the structure of copyright law itself. Among those exceptions is the fair-use doctrine. The Court concluded that any First Amendment interest in using another person's copyrighted words was "generally adequate[ly] . . . address[ed]" by "copyright's built-in free speech safeguards."[56] Depending on what the Court meant by "generally adequate," this may overstate the ease with which copyright can be accommodated with the First Amendment.

The *Eldred* analysis suggests that banning "unfair" uses as defined in copyright law would not violate the First Amendment as interpreted outside the copyright context—that is, that unfair uses are defined so as to ensure that the high standards required for content-based regulations are satisfied. Yet this conclusion might not be warranted. Two examples suggest why.

The first is *Harper & Row, Publishers v. Nation Enterprises*, which held a magazine liable for infringing a publisher's copyright by embedding approximately 300 words of the most newsworthy portions of Gerald Ford's memoirs in a 2,250-word article published two weeks before the book's official release date.[57] The Court held that this was not fair use. Second, in adopting the present version of the "fair use" rule in 1976, Congress had before it an "agreement" between authors, publishers, and educators setting out guidelines for classroom copying. One apparently unfair use is the planned (nonspontaneous) distribution to a class of copies of a complete short poem, defined as "less than 250 words" and "printed on not more than two pages." "Spontaneous" is defined as a decision to distribute the poem that occurs "so close in time" to "the moment of its use for maximum teaching effectiveness ... that it would be unreasonable to expect a timely reply to a request for permission."[58]

In both examples, the justification for allowing the imposition of liability for unfair use is to ensure that authors and publishers have sufficient incentives to produce copyrightable material in the first place. As *Harper & Row* put it, copyright is "the engine of free expression."[59] It is not clear that ordinary First Amendment standards applicable outside the copyright context would make it permissible to impose liability for the publication of newsworthy material (e.g., a tort action claiming that the publication cast the subject in a false light, or nonspontaneous distribution of complete short poems in an action seeking damages for injury to reputation).[60] One could reasonably question whether the incentive-based justification for imposing liability is sufficiently strong to satisfy standards applicable outside of copyright, such as the "compelling interest" one. Similarly, one could question whether the standards for determining when uses are fair or unfair are sufficiently well defined to satisfy ordinary notice standards applicable in other First Amendment areas. Perhaps more important, the incentive-based justification for imposing liability explains why we are engaged in "restrict[ing] the speech of some elements of our society in order to enhance the relative voice of others," which in other contexts we have been told "is [a practice] wholly foreign to the First Amendment."[61] The tenor of copyright doctrine is that the main aspects of copyright law simply cannot violate the First Amendment—a classic solution by stipulation. Stipulated solutions are not always undesirable. They may sometimes be inevitable, as when the problems posed are so intractable that integrating a doctrinal solution to a particular problem into the general body of First Amendment law is extremely difficult. Choosing such a solution, however, should be a last resort.

2. BALANCING

The same can be said of a second path for avoiding the problems of determining why nonrepresentational art is covered by the First Amendment. That path uses a standard balancing analysis that makes the considerations discussed throughout this chapter all relevant to determining the questions of coverage and protection and that trusts the good sense of legislators, administrators, and judges to arrive at sensible solutions. Some performance artworks would not be covered, and some would be; some that are covered would be protected, and others would not be, depending on the exact contours of the problems presented. A Christo-Jeanne-Claude wrapping might be prohibited if it threatened "too much" environmental damage or if the temporary wrapping of a historic building posed "large enough" risks of permanent damage to the building's exterior but not if the environmental threat or the risk to the building's exterior was "small enough."

Balancing tests are familiar in First Amendment law. They tend to have an air of the disreputable about them because they are thought by many people to give insufficient guidance ex ante to people hoping to engage in activity they believe to be both covered and protected by the First Amendment. For this reason, it is helpful to try to pin down with as much precision as possible doctrinal alternatives to a balancing test, even though in the end we may end up concluding that balancing is the best we can do.

III. First Amendment Theory and the Assumption That Art Is Covered

A. Why We Assume That the First Amendment Covers Art

I suspect that we assume that even nonrepresentational art should be covered by the First Amendment for several reasons. The first is that we think that such art is, in some sense, a "good thing." But of course not all good things receive constitutional protection (chocolate ice cream, for example). And perhaps more interesting, some contemporary artists defend their work on the ground that it is transgressive, meaning that it implicitly rejects prevailing standards for determining what fits with the class of good things—and suggesting that defenders of the status quo might have good reasons, from their own point of view, to regulate or suppress such works.[62]

As suggested earlier, we may also assume that nonrepresentational art is covered by the First Amendment because we find it hard to imagine circumstances under which governments would try to regulate it; the coverage question, we might assume, is otiose. Perhaps nonrepresentational art exists for its own sake (unlike ticket scalping), which is why governments do not try to regulate it. In addition, the answer to the coverage question has implications for other problems. For example, if nonrepresentational art is not covered by the First Amendment, questions about government subsidies for some artworks but not others become relatively easy, and we need not take the First Amendment into account in determining whether one person's reproduction of an artwork violates another's rights under copyright or trademark law. And, of course, the a fortiori argument made in *Hurley* would be unavailable; the case's reasoning would have to be reconstructed. In the other direction, if nonrepresentational art is covered by the First Amendment, we must face some difficult questions about copyright law and the law of trademark tarnishment.

Another reason for thinking that the First Amendment covers art is that we know that the First Amendment is about communication, and we think that art communicates as well. This is a logical fallacy: that the First Amendment covers some things that communicate does not imply that it covers all things that do so. In addition, "communicate," in its use in the First Amendment context, is a transitive verb. Speech covered by the First Amendment communicates *something*. Yet what art communicates is often quite unclear.

B. Problems Fitting Art's Coverage into Prevailing First Amendment Theory

The questions that animate this chapter can be put in this way: Exactly how is nonrepresentational art different—for First Amendment purposes—from panhandling and ticket scalping?[63] And how is nonrepresentational art similar to core examples of political speech clearly covered by the First Amendment?

Alexander Meiklejohn's treatment of art indicates why the first question is interesting and difficult. Meiklejohn offered a general account of freedom of speech as a protection for "those activities of thought and communication by which we 'govern.' . . . Self-government can exist only insofar as the voters acquire the intelligence, integrity, sensitivity, and generous devotion to the general welfare that, in theory, casting a ballot is assumed to express." Yet "there are many forms of thought and expression within the range of human communications from which the voter derives the knowledge, intelligence, sensitivity to human values." These include "[l]iterature and the arts," which "lead the way toward sensitive and informed appreciation and response to the values out of which the riches of the general welfare are created." He continued, "the novel is at present a powerful determinative of our views of what human beings are, how they can be influenced, in which directions they should be influenced by many forces, including, especially, their own judgments and appreciations."[64]

We might wonder whether nonrepresentational art could be described in similar terms. Even if it could, we should note that the characteristics relevant to governance that Meiklejohn identifies in novels also characterize panhandling and ticket scalping. Or, to fill in the steps, governance-relevant views can be shaped by running a small business. We might require that governments provide some reason for requiring that specific businesses be licensed, but we surely do not want to subject licensing requirements to even a modest increment of required justification—of the sort dealt with through the doctrine concerning content-neutral regulations—because running a small business is governance relevant. Finally, governance-relevant learning can occur by reading a novel *or* by observing a panhandler or a ticket scalper.

The widely used metaphor of the marketplace of ideas shows why the second question is interesting and difficult. Archibald MacLeish's assertion that "a poem should not mean but be" suggests that art is not "about" ideas, nor does it "convey" or "express" them.[65] What "idea" does Jackson Pollock's *Blue Poles: No. 11* convey? Even more, what idea does *Ulysses* convey? "Human experience is wondrously various," perhaps. But then, panhandling and ticket scalping convey that idea as well.

The most prominent general "theory" of the First Amendment runs into difficulty in explaining art's coverage. Autonomy-related theories are both promising and problematic. They are promising because artistic expression is, in the Romantic tradition at least, precisely a way in which an artist lives autonomously; they are problematic as a way to distinguish artistic expression from essentially all other human activities, which can be ways in which people live autonomously.[66] Perhaps not panhandling but at least some forms of ticket scalping are autonomous expressions of the self, unless one stipulates that the market is not a domain for self-expression, as some autonomy theorists quite controversially do.

General First Amendment theories that do not invoke either politics or autonomy are hard to come by. Jack Balkin argues that the First Amendment protects a domain in which a democratic culture, not confined to politics, can flourish.[67] Balkin's is a historicist approach to constitutional law,[68] and like all such approaches, it has difficulties connecting the descriptive with the normative. As applied to art, the argument goes something like this: Nonrepresentational art falls within a category—artworks including works of imaginative literature—that today's legal culture takes as contributing to a more general democratic culture. Further, today's legal culture is inclined to use relatively large legal categories—"artworks in general"—rather than smaller ones such as "representational art" or "written literature," for reasons familiar from discussions of the desirability of rules rather than standards. For example, large categories provide better guidance to larger numbers of people and are easier to administer for judges acting under substantial constraints of time and ability.

But precisely because Balkin's argument must describe the legal culture as committed to a specific version of the rules/standards debate, it is vulnerable to the usual normative criticisms of all the positions taken in that debate and to the additional historicist criticism that the existence of widespread controversy over the "right" way to think about the rules/standards question shows that today's legal culture is not in fact committed to the use of large rather than small categories. Both the normative and historicist criticisms of Balkin's position take on special force in dealing with questions, such as that of art's coverage, that test the boundaries of the categories conventionally used.

Similar difficulties attend Robert Post's weakly sociologized account of art's coverage. For Post, art "fit[s] comfortably within the scope of public discourse," which he defines as "all communicative processes deemed necessary for the formation of public opinion,"[69] because it is a "form[] of communication that sociologically we recognize as art."[70] Given the existence of controversies over whether works like *Cadillac Ranch* and Kleinman's planter fall within the category "art," Post's "we" must refer to something like "a well-informed and reasonably well-educated and sophisticated group of people who reflect on the nation's commitment to free expression," rather than, as one might think, "the people as represented in their legislatures." And, again as with Balkin, Post's category is the relative large one of "art in general," rather than "nonrepresentational art" or, perhaps, "art as understood by MacLeish."

IV. First Amendment Doctrine and Art

A. The Supreme Court on Art and the First Amendment

The Supreme Court's references to art in general and to art that does not have propositional content apparent on its surface have been remarkably casual. An early decision, since overruled, held that motion pictures were not covered by free speech principles.[71] According to Justice Joseph McKenna, "The first impulse of the mind is to reject the contention" that "motion pictures and other spectacles" are covered by those principles. He acknowledged that motion pictures "may be mediums of thought," but, he continued, "so are many things . . . [such as] the theater, the circus, and all other shows and spectacles." Making and showing motion pictures was "a business, pure and simple, . . . not to be regarded . . . as part of the press of the country, or *as organs of public opinion.*" As *Joseph Burstyn, Inc. v. Wilson* held, the mere fact that an activity is conducted for profit cannot possibly be the basis for placing it outside the First Amendment's coverage,[72] but Justice McKenna's reference to "organs of public opinion" might have become the basis for serious consideration of the First Amendment's coverage of imaginative literature and nonrepresentational art.

It was not to be. In *Winters v. New York*, Justice Stanley Reed rejected the proposition that "the constitutional protection for a free press applies only to the exposition of ideas," because "[t]he line between the informing and the entertaining is too elusive for the protection of that basic right." He continued, "Everyone is familiar with instances of propaganda through fiction. What is one man's amusement, teaches another's doctrine."[73] Here too we can glimpse the hint of a delineation of the First Amendment's coverage: activities covered by the First Amendment must somehow teach doctrine or otherwise convey ideas even if they are not expositions of ideas. It seems clear, though, that neither Justice Reed nor his colleagues saw that line. Justice Felix Frankfurter, dissenting, observed almost off-handedly that "Keats' poems [and] Donne's sermons" are "under the protection of free speech," not noticing that Donne's sermons differ from Keats's poems precisely in that the sermons are expositions of ideas whereas treating Keats's poems as such expositions drains them of much of their essence.[74]

It would be tedious to compile the passing references to the First Amendment's coverage of undifferentiated categories of "art" and "literature," coupled with mention of the ways in which some forms of art and literature can be, as Justice Reed said, propaganda or vehicles for ideas. The culmination came in the Court's efforts to define obscenity. As the Court understood the problem, obscene materials lay outside the First Amendment's coverage. That made identifying what was obscene critically important. Throughout the Court's efforts to define obscenity, it has simply assumed that material that can be described as sufficiently artistic cannot be obscene.[75] Its assumption has been that art is presumptively covered by the First Amendment. The Court's assumption was probably an unconsidered result of the initial confrontation with works labeled obscene. The celebrated cases, such as that involving *Ulysses*, involved serious written literature, readily enough characterized as covered by the First Amendment if only because the works used words. But, instead of treating the challenged works as (merely) written literature, the courts protected them because of what the courts called the works' "artistic" value. Then they generalized from the category "written works with artistic value" to "all works, whether written or not, with artistic value," without realizing that the elimination of words from the works ought to have triggered some thought about how such works could be described as "speech" or "press."

That assumption underlies the Court's most extended recent confrontation with the relation between the First Amendment and contemporary art. In *National Endowment for the Arts v. Finley,* the Court tied itself into knots trying to figure out how to deal with a seemingly content-based rule for awarding federal subsidies to art.[76] Suppose the NEA decided not to provide a subsidy to Jackson Pollock. The First Amendment aside, no one would worry about the grounds on which Congress decided to award selective subsidies. Yet how could we begin to think about the subsidy's denial by invoking standard First Amendment doctrine about content-based regulations?[77] For reasons the Court has never bothered to explain, the fact that something is denominated "art" changes the constitutional landscape dramatically.

B. Doctrinal Building Blocks

The Supreme Court has given us three building blocks for understanding why nonrepresentational art is covered by the First Amendment. The first is the *Hurley* case in which Justice Souter declared that Jackson Pollock's paintings were unquestionably covered by the Amendment.[78] He found it necessary to make that statement because of the argument made by the respondents, a group of gay Irish Americans who wanted to participate in Boston's St. Patrick's Day parade, which was conducted by a private organization. The Massachusetts Supreme Judicial Court held that the parade was a place of public accommodation under the state's antidiscrimination laws and therefore could not exclude gays because of their sexual orientation. The parade organizers contended that a rule requiring that they make the parade available to gays violated their First Amendment rights. The gay group responded by arguing that a parade as such, even one in which participants carried signs identifying themselves or otherwise making statements, did not convey a message.

Justice Souter replied that parades were for "marchers who are making some sort of collective point, not just to each other but to bystanders along the way." What exactly was the point of the parade? "[A] narrow, succinctly articulable message is not a condition of constitutional protection," which was why Pollock's paintings are covered by the First Amendment. Rather, the parade's organizers had "the autonomy to choose the content of [their] own message," again, even if that content was not readily articulable. But if the organizers could not readily articulate what they meant by picking and choosing among applicants for places in the parade, how can we say that they had any message at all? The answer, Justice Souter wrote, lay in the meaning *observers* would impute to participation: "[T]he parade's overall message is distilled from the individual presentations along the way, and each unit's expression *is perceived by spectators* as part of the whole." Viewers seeing the gay group's banner might mistakenly infer that the parade's organizers had no objections to the "unqualified social acceptance of gays and lesbians."[79]

Hurley implies that the First Amendment's coverage depends on whether observers impute "meaning" to what they see. Note, though, that the "meaning" need not be univocal. Some people viewing the gay group's banner in the parade might take it to indicate the sponsor's indifference to gay sexuality; others might take it to indicate the sponsor's endorsement of gay sexuality (as one among many); yet others might not think it of any significance at all. We might come up with some limits on the multivocality of objects covered by the First Amendment. *Rumsfeld v. FAIR* suggests a "reasonable observer" standard: the reasonable observer must understand that the object on view *is* expressive, though not all observers will agree on what it expresses.[80] Perhaps an object to which only a handful of people impute "meaning" is not covered, and perhaps truly idiosyncratic imputations of meaning could be disregarded.[81] This analysis has two attractive features. It accounts for the intuition that nonrepresentational art is covered, because one feature of such art is that viewers impute "meaning"—indeed, many "meanings"—to it. In addition, it accounts for the fact that the First Amendment's coverage may change when enough people start to understand an object as "art" rather than, for example, immature scribblings.

The second building block is *Cohen v. California*, which identifies the meanings that the First Amendment covers. The case's facts are well-known, as is its central rationale. Cohen carried a jacket with the words "Fuck the Draft" written on its back. He was arrested for engaging in offensive conduct. As Justice John Marshall Harlan carefully explained, the case turned on whether the state "can excise . . . one particular scurrilous epithet from the public discourse." The state argued that doing so did no damage to anyone's ability to assert any proposition. Cohen could continue to assert and write on his jacket, "Down with the Draft," or "Abolish the Draft." But, Justice Harlan replied, those words *meant* something different from "Fuck the Draft": "[M]uch linguistic expression serves a dual communicative function: It conveys not only ideas capable of relatively precise, detached explication, but otherwise inexpressible emotions as well. In fact, words are often chosen as much for their emotive as their cognitive force."[82] Prior to *Hurley*, perhaps this building block might have been limited to cases in which the noncognitive component was attached to some distinctive cognitive one. But *Hurley*'s endorsement of multivocality means that every form of expression has some cognitive content for some viewers or listeners. *Cohen* is thus available as a general building block.

Here, then, is a second reason that the First Amendment covers nonrepresentational art. *Cohen* provides some reasons for rejecting a distinction hinted at in some prior decisions, between activities that convey ideas and those that expound them, and hints even more mutedly at the possibility that the First Amendment covers works that expound but not works that convey ideas. The intuition is that nonfiction works expound ideas while works of imaginative literature (sometimes) only convey them. So it might be thought that nonrepresentational art might convey some ideas, but in general it does not expound them. *Cohen* suggests that the distinction between "conveying" and "expounding," which parallels that distinction, will often be quite thin. Paraphrasing Martin Luther King, Jr.'s "Letter from Birmingham Jail" can restate some of King's ideas, but a paraphrase that strips King's rhetoric from the "Letter" transforms its meaning. It is similar, but perhaps to a greater extent, with poems, representational art, and nonrepresentational art.[83] Absent *Cohen*, doctrine might need to be structured to deal with the question, "Is the loss of meaning from paraphrase or restatement or statement (in the case of nonrepresentational art) small enough to make nonrepresentational art sufficiently similar to expository writing that it should be covered in the same way that such writing is?"

Yet perhaps that is the wrong way to think about the problem of art's coverage. *Cohen* might be taken to reject the idea limned by MacLeish that artworks do not mean at all but rather simply are. For MacLeish, to state what artworks mean is to commit a category mistake, to apply to artworks concepts suitable for something else but unsuitable for them. If so, saying that artworks are covered by the First Amendment would be something like saying that dish detergent is covered by the First Amendment. Despite the force of MacLeish's insight, *Cohen* appears to reject it.

So, *Cohen* suggests, nonrepresentational art has the noncognitive force associated with words.[84] Indeed, nonrepresentational art's multi-vocality might rest on its noncognitive force: representational art, we might think, says something particular; nonrepresentational art "says" many things. "No ideas but in things" takes on another meaning: *only* things convey ideas fully fleshed out, because ideas expressed in words can be polluted by the noncognitive features of their precise mode of expression. Things, in contrast, allow viewers to impute all possible non-cognitive meanings to the ideas the things embody—and to choose for themselves which of those meanings makes the most sense for them.

Parenthetically, for myself, even the claim that representational art says something particular is questionable. For example, portraits are, to my eyes, quite frequently multivocal. See, for example, portraits by Ivan Albright.

But if *Hurley*'s emphasis on defining the First Amendment's coverage with reference to the meanings viewers impute to covered material and *Cohen*'s emphasis on the noncognitive aspects of covered material explain why the Amendment covers nonrepresentational art, the two cases threaten to undermine the distinction between covered and uncovered material. At the least, if enough people come to understand ticket scalping as a performance of opposition to the regulatory state, ticket scalpers might have a First Amendment defense to the prohibition of their activity.

Perhaps more serious, *Hurley* and *Cohen* create what might be thought of as a paradox in copyright law. One standard defense of copyright against First Amendment challenge is that copyright's built-in limitations narrow its scope to the point where the incentive effects of copyright provide a strong enough reason to justify barring people from speaking (by infringing on others' copyrights). One of those built-in

Ivan Albright, *A Face from Georgia*. © The Art Institute of Chicago.

limitations is that copyright protects the expression of ideas but not the ideas themselves. But, given *Hurley* and *Cohen*, it might seem that either nothing is copyrightable or everything is. On the one hand, nothing, because ideas and expression—the cognitive and noncognitive aspects of expression—are inseparable: you can't copyright an expression without copyrighting precisely the idea that it expresses. But tweak the expression a bit—place an emphasis here rather than there—and you have another idea. Further, *Hurley* suggests that if enough viewers see complete copying as an expression around which the "infringer" has placed visible or invisible quotation marks, the quoted material expresses a different idea from the original. On the other hand, everything, because "no ideas but in things" implies that every discrete object is simultaneously an idea and an expression of that idea.

The possibility that explaining why the First Amendment covers nonrepresentational art could create chaos in our understandings of the Amendment is compounded by the Court's third and most recent building block. As noted earlier, one common method of evading questions of the First Amendment's coverage lies in assuming that the regulated material is covered but then observing that the regulation at issue is a general one, not directed at speech. Restrictions on expression are incidental to the general regulation, and the regulation's constitutionality is then said to turn on a relaxed standard of "intermediate scrutiny." The Court's decision in *Holder v. Humanitarian Law Project* throws this analysis into question.

The case involved a federal statutory ban on supplying "material assistance" in the form of "training," "service," and some forms of "expert advice or assistance" to terrorist groups. As construed by the Court, the ban applied to training and the like that took the form of speech and nothing more. The government urged the Court to hold that the statute taken as a whole covered conduct, some of which took the form of speech. According to the government, in such cases the Court should treat the statute as content neutral and apply intermediate scrutiny to determine whether the conduct ban had an impermissible incidental effect on speech. Chief Justice John Roberts's opinion for the Court rejected that analysis, holding that the ban regulated speech on the basis of its content: "Plaintiffs want to speak to [designated terrorist groups] and whether they may do so . . . depends on what they say. If plaintiffs' speech . . . communicates advice derived from 'specialized knowledge' . . . then it is barred," but it would not be prohibited "if it imparts only general or unspecialized knowledge." The government's argument that the statute should receive intermediate scrutiny "because it *generally* functions as a regulation of conduct," the chief justice wrote, "runs headlong into" *Cohen v. California.* A regulation is content based "when the conduct triggering coverage . . . consists of communicating a message."[85]

Taken seriously, that standard would convert many regulations heretofore understood to be content neutral—general regulations of land use, for example—into content-based regulations when the regulated activity "communicates a message." Taken together with *Hurley* and *Cohen, Humanitarian Law Project* implies that any activity that enough people regard as having some meaning, noncognitive as well as cognitive, must survive the highest level of scrutiny, because *Hurley* and *Cohen* tell us that those are the conditions for determining when something communicates a message. San Marcos can regulate the car/cactus planter there only if it can show—as it almost certainly cannot—that its interest in avoiding unsightly displays that diminish property values and attract rodents is extremely strong and cannot be advanced by less restrictive methods, such as requiring fencing, explanatory placards, and exterminators. Perhaps more important, the building blocks taken together rather strongly suggest that bans on misleading advertising are constitutionally suspect, particularly when the misleadingness resides in the advertising's noncognitive aspects.[86]

C. Some Implications

Much of the foregoing probably should be treated as an exploration of First Amendment theory with few practical implications. Direct regulation of artworks as such is rare, and what there is almost always takes the form of content-neutral regulations that readily pass the relevant doctrinal tests. Some questions of copyright and related intellectual property law, though, might be affected by resolving questions about art's coverage under the First Amendment.

Artworks (and music) are not uncommon objects of intellectual property litigation,[87] probably because there is money to be made from reproducing copyrighted works without paying permission fees. As the

Court has observed, copyright law—and associated intellectual property law—has built-in limitations structured to ensure that copyright law does not improperly limit free expression. Among these are fair use, transformative use, and parodic uses. These doctrines would not disappear were we to conclude that artworks were not covered by the First Amendment. Their structure might change, though. Promoting free expression would become a policy goal, not a constitutional imperative, and the doctrines could be developed to accommodate the policy of free expression with other purely copyright-relevant policies. At least around the edges, some uses that would not infringe copyright under a doctrine accommodating copyright policy and the First Amendment might be found infringing under a restructured doctrine: mere policy goals surely ought to play a smaller role than constitutional imperatives when competing policies are accommodated.

More interesting are some implications of finding artworks completely covered by the First Amendment. As just noted, intellectual property law has already accommodated the First Amendment to some degree. Yet full coverage suggests that some reproductions *not* protected by copyright and intellectual property doctrine would be protected by the First Amendment were artworks fully covered. Or, perhaps better, the analytic structure for dealing with intellectual property questions would change. We would ask whether the legal rule sought to be invoked to impose copyright or similar liability is consistent with the First Amendment rather than asking whether the reproduction fits within one of the built-in accommodations.[88]

Consider a trademark dilution ("tarnishment") action. Some visual artists create frames that, in their view, are integral parts of the works themselves. Suppose a museum curator wants to show how different frames affect the way viewers see and appreciate artworks. She finds a work like Georges Seurat's *Evening, Honfleur, 1886* and makes several reproductions of the scene depicted without obtaining permission to do so. She places each reproduction in a different type of frame: an ornate wooden frame, an austere stainless steel one, no frame at all, and the like. The show "works" in the sense that the frames do change the visual experience. The artist who painted the original might well object that precisely because the new frames change the visual experience, the curator has damaged the artwork in a way analogous to trademark dilution.[89]

Georges Seurat, *Evening, Honfleur, 1886* (2'7" × 3'1", oil). Digital Image © The Museum of Modern Art / Licensed by SCALA / Art Resource, NY.

But the fact that the show "works" means that it affects enough viewers to satisfy *Hurley*'s audience-oriented test. As a result, the museum would be able to claim First Amendment coverage for its show. The only relevant question is whether the conditions for imposing liability conform to First Amendment requirements, not whether the show fits within a First Amendment–sensitive statutory scheme of liability.

Or consider someone who buys a Katy Perry CD and makes a large number of copies, which he then packages in a jewel box whose cover art is of a sort associated with heavy metal. *Hurley* suggests that the seller could claim the First Amendment's coverage if he can show that enough listeners or purchasers regarded the combination of cover art and music to convey a message different from Katy Perry's original CD. It is not clear that the combination fits comfortably within any of copyright's accommodations of the First Amendment. The "new" CD is probably not a fair use, nor is it a parody of Perry's work, though the cover art may be a comment on her work. The "too much work" principle suggests that it is better simply to ask directly whether the copier has a First Amendment right to do what he did.

Of course most questions of tarnishment and the like arise in connection with commercial speech. It is easy enough to salvage the tarnishment cause of action from the First Amendment by observing that the First Amendment standard applicable to commercial uses that tarnish another's product is different from, and more tolerant of regulation than, the standard applicable to noncommercial speech. Yet, as noted earlier, the Court has excluded misleading commercial speech from First Amendment coverage by stipulation. That may not be a stable position. Because speech that tarnishes is misleading or at least very like misleading speech, instability in the Court's commercial speech doctrine, coupled with open acknowledgment of art's First Amendment coverage, might end up undermining the tarnishment cause of action.

* * *

This chapter has raised questions about the First Amendment's unquestionable coverage of nonrepresentational art. Yet those questions need not impair the conclusion that such art is indeed covered. Combine a "family resemblance" argument with a "rules versus standards" argument and the questions raised here might receive entirely acceptable answers. The "family resemblance" argument begins with the observation that we need not, and should not, develop a list of necessary and sufficient conditions to determine the First Amendment's coverage. There may be a list of conditions, but we check off only some items on the list to determine that political cartoons are covered, other items to determine that song lyrics are covered, and so on for each candidate for coverage. We find coverage if enough items are checked off. Artworks are sometimes intended to communicate relatively precise messages; they are sometimes the object of suppression because of their assumed political content; they contribute something to the development of a democratic culture; and perhaps more. In short, artworks bear a family resemblance to core political speech.[90]

The "rules versus standards" argument begins with the observation that some artworks fit all the criteria one might develop for coverage, and others fit many. Distinguishing between artworks that satisfy enough of the criteria we might develop and those that do not is possible in theory, but it may well be beyond the capacity of ordinary legal decision makers to do reliably across the range of problems they might encounter. Given that there is "propaganda through fiction" and through some forms of representational art, it is better to have a rule that all artworks are covered.[91]

I have no deep quarrel with these conclusions and so no deep quarrel with Justice Souter's statement in *Hurley* regarding First Amendment coverage for Jackson Pollock's paintings. But this chapter has suggested that the First Amendment's coverage of artworks either may rest on shaky foundations that ought to be shored up or may have implications that ought to be explored more extensively than they have been.

3

Nonsense and the Freedom of Speech

What Meaning Means for the First Amendment

Ludwig Wittgenstein, whose approach to meaning and language changed the course of modern philosophy,[1] once wrote, "Don't *for heavens sake*, be afraid of talking nonsense! But you must pay attention to your nonsense."[2] His exhortation is especially salient for people interested in the scope of the First Amendment, because courts and scholars have often suggested that the Amendment's terrain is defined by meaning,[3] without doing much to show what meaning (or its absence, nonsense) actually *means*. As a result, the concept of meaning operates like a rogue boundary surveyor, erratically charting the First Amendment's territory without judicial or scholarly accountability.

This state of affairs raises a variety of interesting and difficult questions. If meaning establishes the boundaries of the First Amendment, then what are we to make of nonsense—"words or language having no meaning or conveying no intelligible ideas"?[4] If the Supreme Court is right that the Amendment's "constitutional safeguard . . . 'was fashioned to assure unfettered interchange of *ideas* for the bringing about of political and social changes desired by the people,'"[5] then speech lacking such ideas—assuming that it is actually "speech"—would not seem to merit constitutional coverage at all. That would be a jarring conclusion indeed, which might explain why even those who treat meaning as an essential ingredient of speech tend to avoid it. This is perhaps most noticeable in the context of instrumental music and nonrepresentational art—the topics of chapters 1 and 2. As Alan Chen and Mark Tushnet note, the Supreme Court has reassuringly declared these to be "unquestionably shielded" by the First Amendment.[6] But far from being *un*questionable, their shielding in fact raises questions that are, as Tushnet generously puts it chapter 2, "quite difficult to answer satisfactorily."

Part 1 of this chapter demonstrates that the difficulty of these questions is not the only cause for concern and that artists—though they seem to have a special relationship with nonsense[7]—are not the only would-be speakers who should be keenly interested in the answers. This is true even if we focus exclusively on linguistic communication, which by many accounts is presumptively entitled to First Amendment coverage.[8] Sometimes we speak without intending to "mean" anything at all—exclamations, jokes, doggerel verse, and even philosophical illustrations may all be nonsensical.[9] As Wittgenstein himself wrote in the *Tractatus Logico-Philosophicus*, "My propositions are elucidatory in this way: he who understands me finally recognizes them as senseless, when he has climbed out through them, on them, over them."[10] Other times, we are unaware of our own nonsense, either because we wrongly believe our propositions to be meaningful or because we are simply misunderstood.[11] If meaning is a prerequisite for constitutional coverage, and much of what we say is meaningless without our ever knowing it, then the boundaries of the First Amendment are not only narrow but also unknown.

Consider *Morse v. Frederick*, in which the Supreme Court upheld the suspension of a high school student who had unfurled a banner reading "BONG HiTS 4 JESUS" at an off-campus school function.[12] The Court conceded that the banner's purported message "is cryptic. It is no doubt offensive to some, perhaps amusing to others. To still others, it probably means nothing at all."[13] But it concluded that the student's suspension was "consistent with the First Amendment" because the banner "was reasonably viewed as promoting illegal drug use."[14] The student himself said, quite plausibly, that "the words were just nonsense meant to attract television cameras."[15] In dissent, Justice John Paul Stevens similarly concluded that "[t]his is a nonsense message, not advocacy."[16] What if Stevens had commanded the majority? Would the student's comments be unpunishable, or would they not count as speech at all?

Simply to describe the broad scope of nonsense both demonstrates its importance and suggests that meaning is an unreliable guide to the First Amendment's hinterlands.[17] Moreover, meaning's guidance would not necessarily be welcome even if it were accurate, because much nonsensical speech rests solidly on the normative foundations of the First Amendment—the values that the doctrine is designed to protect. Primary among these are the marketplace of ideas, individual autonomy, and democratic participation. Nonsense can and often does further each of them.

Part 1 thus sketches the terrain of nonsensical speech and makes a preliminary case for its protection. In doing so, it uncovers a uniquely convenient entrance to the very depths of the First Amendment, shining light on the idea of meaning itself. Spelunking in this area is hazardous business, and part 2 proceeds with caution. Despite the difficulties, the exploration is worthwhile, for First Amendment theory and doctrine often suggest that meaning is an essential element of constitutionally salient speech without defining what meaning is or where it comes from. In other words, courts and free speech scholars have not explained what meaning *means*.

Analytic philosophers, meanwhile, have made meaning a primary target.[18] Throughout the past century (paralleling almost exactly the life span of the modern First Amendment), they have developed two general methods for charting the boundaries of what can meaningfully be said. Their goal in doing so has been to find the limits of language, thought, and the world,[19] not to generate constitutional doctrine. And yet the tools they have created—which with egregious but necessary oversimplification can be called "representational" meaning and "use" meaning—have been wielded, sometimes awkwardly and perhaps unknowingly, by the Supreme Court justices themselves.[20]

The representational approach finds meaning in the relationship between expression and underlying concepts.[21] Some version of this basic idea underlies the logical positivism associated with thinkers like Bertrand Russell and Wittgenstein in his early writings, among many others. Under the representational approach, speech that fails to represent extralinguistic ideas is simply nonsense and, if meaning is an essential ingredient of constitutionally salient speech, therefore falls outside the realm of the First Amendment. As Russell once put it, "Absorption in language sometimes leads to a neglect of the connexion of language with non-linguistic facts, although it is this connexion that gives meaning to words and significance to sentences."[22]

A representational approach to meaning apparently animates many of the Supreme Court's efforts to chart the boundaries of the freedom of speech, from the oft-repeated aphorism that "[t]he First Amendment . . .

embodies '[o]ur profound national commitment to the free exchange of ideas'"[23] to the *Spence* test, which asks whether "[a]n intent to convey a particularized message was present" and whether "the likelihood was great that the message would be understood by those who viewed it."[24] The representational approach is also central to investigations of nonrepresentational art. Nonrepresentationalism, after all, is problematic for the First Amendment only if representativeness itself is constitutionally relevant.

Despite the intuitive appeal of the representational approach, it is defective as a constitutional principle. Requiring speech acts to represent ideas would exclude nearly all of the potentially valuable nonsense described in part 1, including vast stretches of discourse regarding ethics, aesthetics, and religion.[25] On the representational account, they simply "cannot be expressed,"[26] and thus "the tendency of all men who ever tried to write or talk Ethics or Religion was to run against the boundaries of language. This running against the walls of our cage is perfectly, absolutely hopeless."[27] Fortunately, the First Amendment is not so limited; the boundaries of the freedom of speech are not coextensive with the "walls of our cage."

In part to escape that cage, much of analytic philosophy took what is known as the "linguistic turn."[28] That development, which is closely associated with Wittgenstein's later work, speech-act theory, and ordinary-language philosophy, generally holds that "[t]he bounds of sense, as it were, are all within language, and meaning is nowhere other than in the many activities in which human beings use their various languages."[29] As Wittgenstein explained, "For a *large* class of cases—though not for all—in which we employ the word 'meaning' it can be defined thus: the meaning of a word is its use in the language."[30] Finding the boundaries of meaning, then, depends on identifying the "language games" that "consist[] of language and the actions into which it is woven."[31]

Echoes of a use-meaning approach can already be found in First Amendment discourse and doctrine. The use-meaning approach explains the Court's conclusion that constitutional coverage extends to practices that form a "significant medium for the communication of ideas"[32] and is not "confined to expressions conveying a 'particularized message.'"[33] One can also find the influence of such an approach in First Amendment scholarship, perhaps most prominently and thoughtfully in Robert Post's argument that First Amendment values "do not attach to abstract acts of communication as such, but rather to the social contexts that envelop and give constitutional significance to acts of communication."[34]

The use-meaning approach improves on the representational approach both descriptively and normatively. It accounts for the constitutional value in various forms of nonsense, captures the contextual and socially embedded nature of language, and provides better answers to thorny problems like the constitutional status of art. Under the use-meaning approach, *Jabberwocky* is protected by the First Amendment not because its words represent concepts but because it is recognizable as a poem. By contrast, those acts and utterances that violate the rules of our language games simply do not count as meaningful speech, even if they represent facts or concepts and would therefore be meaningful under the representational approach.

The chapter thus concludes by endorsing the First Amendment's linguistic turn and its effort to find meaning in *use*, rather than in the relationship of language to concepts. Making the most of such an approach, however, is no simple task.[35] As Jack Balkin and Sandy Levinson have put it, language games "refuse clear-cut boundaries, they borrow and steal from other sources, they overlap with other language games, and their governing rules are always in a state of flux and disputation. Lived language games are unruly and unkempt, untamed and untidy, much as life itself is."[36] But if the First Amendment's boundaries depend on them, then such games *must* be tamed. Doctrine must provide guidance; it must be able to identify the First Amendment language games that create the kind of meaning the Constitution requires. The use-meaning approach does not provide easy answers to these problems, but it does provide a better set of questions with which to address them.

In using this approach to address the constitutional value of nonsense, the analysis here shares much with the approaches to instrumental music and nonrepresentational art taken in chapters 1 and 2. As Chen and Tushnet demonstrate, those forms of expression perfectly exemplify the shortcomings of a reliance on representation as the sine qua non of meaning. Art and music can be, and often are, deeply "meaningful," but not because they represent anything *else*. Color, form, rhyme, and structure do not have to represent anything to be worthy of First Amendment coverage—their use just *is* the meaning they convey.

I. Stuff and Nonsense

Making sense of nonsense for First Amendment purposes involves at least two tasks: establishing what nonsense is and determining whether it has constitutional value. This part attempts to accomplish both, first sketching the landscape of meaningless speech and then showing how nonsense relates to the basic values traditionally associated with the First Amendment. The discussion therefore not only describes the scope and value of nonsense but also delivers a preliminary case for its constitutional protection and opens the door for part 2's exploration of the concept of meaning itself.

This part begins in section A by describing nonsense's broad domain. Traditionally, it has been thought that boundary disputes between meaning and nonsense are primarily relevant to the First Amendment in the context of artistic expression and that a capacious view of art can more or less solve the problem. But nonsense contains multitudes, and not all of its forms are easily recognizable as such. The very breadth of nonsense demonstrates the importance of explaining it and also suggests that, unless the First Amendment has been radically misunderstood, the Constitution covers at least some of this meaningless speech.

As a matter of doctrine, however, it is not particularly satisfying to say that nonsense must be protected by the Constitution because there is so much of it. To merit coverage, nonsense must presumably further the values traditionally associated with the First Amendment, such as the marketplace of ideas, autonomy, and democracy. Section B argues that nonsense does exactly that, advancing the autonomous search for unsayable truths, contributing to cognitive advancement despite lacking "meaning" of its own, and even providing valuable outlets for political dissent. It follows that the First Amendment must make room for nonsense, as part 2 argues in more detail.

A. The Definition and Scope of Nonsense

Whatever else Wittgenstein's admonition to "pay attention to your nonsense" suggests, it was a call to recognize nonsense when it arises. That is a difficult but rewarding task, for nonsense takes many forms.[37] Because the goal of this discussion is to have constitutional reasoning drive conceptual analysis rather than the other way around, this section evaluates the scope and constitutional value of nonsense in general terms before elaborating a more rigorous definition of meaning in part 2. The downside of this approach is that it is, as an initial matter, overexpansive: Pollock's paintings, for example, are usually seen as nonrepresentational and therefore qualify as a certain kind of nonsense, despite their undoubted value and First Amendment protection. Indeed, the *point* of the following discussion is to develop an appropriate definition of meaning based on an understanding of what it would exclude. And at least as an initial matter, it is not enough simply to posit that meaning is different from propositional content, for much First Amendment scholarship and doctrine makes precisely that connection.

In an effort to impose some order, the following discussion divides nonsense—"[w]ords or language having no meaning or intelligible ideas"[38]—into two major categories: overt and covert.[39]

1. OVERT NONSENSE

At almost the same time that Russell and Wittgenstein were busy in Cambridge trying to pin down nonsense, Lewis Carroll was busy in Oxford generating more of it. *Jabberwocky*, perhaps his most famous piece of nonsense verse (and a cameo performer in First Amendment doctrine),[40] begins, "'Twas brillig, and the slithy toves / Did gyre and gimble in the wade; / All mimsy were the borogoves, / And the mome raths outgrabe."[41] As far as the average reader can tell,[42] these are symbols with no references; "sound and fury, [s]ignifying nothing."[43] As such, they are *overt* nonsense.[44]

Neither the speaker nor the hearer of overt nonsense believes it to have meaning. Its lack of meaning is thus both intentional and apparent.[45] Some overt nonsense is fanciful, in that it does not purport to convey meaning but rather is designed to create a sense of amusement or delight in the listener. People seem to enjoy such nonsense for the same reasons that babies gurgle at a novel stimulus—it provides a sense of wonder, possibility, and absurdity. But overt nonsense need not have some instrumental reason for existence; it can simply be nonsense for nonsense's sake.[46]

As chapters 1 and 2 have demonstrated, much artistic expression is overtly and sometimes avowedly nonsensical according to this definition. Charles Rosen makes a similar point in the context of literary style: "We should recall here the extraordinary sixteenth-century controversy about style between the admirers of Cicero and of Erasmus, the former, led by Étienne Dolet, believing that style had a beauty independent of the matter of the literary work, and the latter insisting that the beauty of style was wholly dependent on its consonance with meaning."[47]

Of course, one need not look that far to find examples of art that overtly lacks representational meaning. Consider the lyrics of popular songs, from "I Am the Walrus"[48] to "Who Put the Bomp"[49] to "Louie Louie"[50] to those consisting entirely of gibberish.[51]

The relationship between overt nonsense and art is not monogamous, however. Philosophers and linguists frequently rely on overt nonsense as an analytic instrument.[52] The *Tractatus*, for example, openly proclaims itself to lack meaning.[53] The philosophers A. W. Moore and Peter Sullivan explain that Wittgenstein had no choice but to use nonsense to demonstrate the boundaries of meaning itself: "The *Tractatus* consists mostly of nonsense because what Wittgenstein is trying to convey, about language and its limits, is, by its own lights, ineffable. The only way in which he can convey it—the only way in which he can get the reader to 'see the world aright'—is by dint of a special kind of nonsense: what we might call 'illuminating' nonsense."[54]

Unsurprisingly, many linguists have taken a similar approach. For example, Noam Chomsky set out in his dissertation to demonstrate among other things that a sentence can be grammatically correct and yet lack semantic meaning. His famous example was the sentence "Colorless green ideas sleep furiously."[55]

2. COVERT NONSENSE

Whereas the meaninglessness of overt nonsense is self-conscious and apparent to speaker and hearer alike, *covert* nonsense is potentially more insidious. It arises when speakers or hearers (or both) incorrectly believe that they are successfully exchanging meaningful ideas.

Perhaps the most common type of covert nonsense is the straightforward misunderstanding, in which speaker and hearer disagree about the specific meaning of a particular speech act or even about whether the purported speech act has meaning at all. This subsection does not attempt to fully address the relationship between misunderstandings and the freedom of speech—an interesting issue in its own right—but rather tries to identify the particular problems that misunderstandings pose for meaning-dependent approaches to the First Amendment.

Simple misunderstandings occur when the speaker intends one meaning and the listener hears another. Such situations are, of course, extremely common, but some approaches to the definition of speech—taken at face value—might exclude them.[56] Carroll's poetry and Pollock's paintings are "unquestionably shielded" by the First Amendment, but one might reasonably ask whether many people "understand" them. For that matter, one could ask the same of James Joyce's *Finnegans Wake*, Matthew Barney's movies, or any number of other impenetrable artistic works. So, too, are few listeners able to understand the specific meanings of most scientific, scholarly, or even legal speech. And it would be troubling, to say the least, if discussions of the rule against perpetuities or the Higgs boson—or professors' efforts to teach them—lack First Amendment protection simply because so few people comprehend them.

But misunderstandings can be more complicated. In addition to disagreeing about what meaning is conveyed by a purported speech act, people sometimes disagree about whether the act is meaningful at all. Such *deep* misunderstandings arise in at least two ways, which can with some oversimplification be called *lost meaning* and *found meaning*. The former occurs when a speaker intends to convey meaning and the listener fails to recognize not only the specific meaning but also the nature of the act as meaningful. In other words, the listener does not even perceive the purported speech act as an effort to communicate meaning. Consider a computer programmer who expresses herself in code. A nonprogrammer might not only fail to understand the code's specific meaning but also fail to understand that it contains meaning at all.[57]

Found meaning, by contrast, arises when a listener imputes meaning to an act when the putative speaker never meant to convey any. First Amendment theory and doctrine have not focused extensively on the possibility of found meaning, but interesting hypotheticals easily come to mind. Imagine, for example, that a person sees a famous pianist sitting on a bench at her piano. The performer is simply taking a break, thinking about a recent vacation. The starstruck and credulous viewer, however, imagines that she is trying out a new performance of John

Cage's 4′33″, which consists of four and a half minutes of not playing.[58] The viewer has discovered meaning and imputed it to the daydreaming pianist, but no volitional speech has occurred. One could even stipulate that the person on the bench is not a pianist at all but a janitor resting after her shift. Or imagine a traveler strolling in a foreign country, singing the supposedly nonsensical words of his favorite Beatles song. Little does he know that in the country he is visiting, "semolina pilchards"[59] is a grievous and actionable insult. Is the janitor or the tourist "speaking" for First Amendment purposes, notwithstanding the fact that neither intends to communicate any meaning?

First Amendment theory and doctrine do not provide satisfying answers as to whether such unintentional speech is constitutionally covered.[60] Denying constitutional coverage to unintended speech could leave out a wide range of speakers who cannot control their speech acts—those who are coerced or asleep, for example. A person with Tourette syndrome may have involuntary verbal tics that can include a wide variety of "vocalizations," from "grunting, throat clearing, shouting and barking" to "socially inappropriate words and phrases."[61] If such a person were to involuntarily utter an actionable threat or libel, shouldn't she be able to raise the First Amendment as a defense? On the one hand, Tushnet persuasively suggests that a "'reasonable' imputation of meaning to otherwise meaningless words—or symbols?—is sufficient to trigger First Amendment coverage."[62] On the other hand, treating involuntary acts as meaningful speech implies that the people who "spoke" them can be held responsible for meaning they never intended to convey. Transforming their nonsense into speech will not always work to their advantage, as the student in *Morse v. Frederick* learned.

Finally, covert nonsense can arise when both speaker and hearer incorrectly believe that they have communicated meaningful ideas. Even though the parties think they are engaged in communication, their words actually lack meaning. This sounds far-fetched, but according to some accounts of meaning, it happens more often than we might like to think. To a representationalist, for example, language is meaningful only when it refers to some extralinguistic fact, and a great deal of everyday speech fails this test. Wittgenstein himself believed, at least in his early writing, that aesthetics, ethics, and theology "cannot be expressed"[63] and are therefore nonsensical. But of course they are also (as Wittgenstein also believed) enormously significant—many people regard such matters as the very lifeblood of public discourse.

The idea of covert nonsense is somewhat unsettling; its apparent scope is downright disturbing. If much of what we say is nonsensical without our even realizing it, then the boundaries of the First Amendment are not only narrow but unknown. Any time we fail to give meaning to our propositions, despite our best efforts and despite believing that we have done so, we are operating outside of constitutional coverage.

B. The Constitutional Value of Nonsense

Simply describing the broad scope of nonsense demonstrates that the representational-meaning approach provides a poor map of the First Amendment's actual boundaries. That is, the Constitution undoubtedly *does* cover much of the nonsensical speech discussed in the previous section, notwithstanding its lack of representational content. And there must be some reason for this; it is unsatisfying to say that nonsense should be protected by the First Amendment simply because it is plentiful. Appealing as that conclusion might be, it is normatively defensible only if nonsense serves relevant *constitutional* values such as the marketplace of ideas, individual autonomy, and democracy. Earlier chapters have explained these First Amendment values in more detail; the following discussion simply attempts to show that nonsense can further them.

1. THE MARKETPLACE OF IDEAS

The model of the marketplace of ideas—the first and perhaps still most prominent First Amendment theory[64]—rests on the notion that, if left unregulated, good ideas will eventually win out over bad ones. In U.S. law, the theory is traced to Justice Oliver Wendell Holmes's argument that "the best test of truth is the power of the thought to get itself accepted in the competition of the market."[65] Importantly, the truths that the marketplace can supposedly uncover are not narrowly defined and can include political and ethical insights as well as empirical facts.[66] As Justice Louis Brandeis put it in his own statement of the marketplace rationale, "freedom to think as you will and to speak as you think are means indispensable to the discovery and spread of political truth."[67]

Inasmuch as nonsense represents a disconnect between words and ideas, it seems out of place in a marketplace devoted exclusively to the latter—especially when ideas are valuable only as handmaidens to truth.[68] This is particularly apparent under some conceptions of "truth" itself. Just as some analytic approaches find meaning in the relationship between language and extralinguistic facts, so too does the correspondence theory of truth hold that statements are true when they represent "actual" extralinguistic facts. As Russell explained, "a belief is true when there is a corresponding fact, and is false when there is no corresponding fact."[69] A statement that does not correspond to a fact therefore seems meaningless under a formal approach to meaning and false under a correspondence theory of truth. If meaningless statements do not even refer to extralinguistic facts, how can they possibly promote the intellectual search for those facts?

But such an argument unfairly oversimplifies both the normative vision of the marketplace model and the potential cognitive value of nonsense. As to the former, even the harshest critics of the marketplace model do not envision it being animated *solely* by a correspondence theory of truth. Under the marketplace approach, the value of free speech extends beyond the accurate identification of facts. Instead, the vision seems to be of what is called a "coherence" theory of truth, one that identifies as true that which people, through open discussion, come to regard as such.[70] The First Amendment generally shies away from legally enforceable determinations about what is "really" true, at least with regard to speech in public discourse.[71]

Even if one thinks that the First Amendment is concerned only with the conveyance of true facts, it is apparent that doctrine embodies a kind of "epistemological humility" on the part of government.[72] The reasons for this are easy enough to perceive, and they suggest that nonsense may be entitled to protection under a marketplace theory. One such reason is a general distrust of government officials determining the meaning of private speech.[73] That is, if the marketplace model requires judges to be agnostic as to truthfulness, it seems that they should also be agnostic as to meaningfulness.

Some version of this concern has arisen in the context of art and music—as chapters 1 and 2 note, there are good reasons to suspect that judges are not well suited to determine art's meaning, value, or even existence. As Justice Holmes once put it, judging the value of art is a "dangerous undertaking for persons trained only to the law."[74] If we do not trust judges to identify which of many possible meanings a work of art conveys, why would we trust them to identify whether it conveys meaning at all? Imbuing meaning where none is intended can distort speech just as much as other forms of misunderstanding. Consider again Carroll's verse. Some people believe *Jabberwocky* to be overtly nonsensical.[75] Others suggest, to the contrary, that the poem represents not nonsense but a purposeful and illustrative distortion of sense.[76] Who are judges to determine which of these is the better interpretation of Carroll?

Nonsense—overt and otherwise—can also be a useful, perhaps even essential, tool in illuminating certain kinds of truth. Consider again (and again and again) the *Tractatus*. What is the truth value of a book that proclaims itself to be nonsensical? That question has bedeviled and divided philosophers for the better part of a century,[77] and although no clear victor has emerged, their efforts demonstrate that nonsense can play a unique and important role in the intellectual marketplace.

The battle lines of the Tractarian debate are currently drawn between what have been called the "ineffable" and the "resolute" readings. The former, represented prominently by Russell and Peter Hacker, holds that "there are, according to the author of the *Tractatus*, ineffable truths that can be apprehended."[78] As Russell put it in his introduction to the *Tractatus*, "after all, Mr Wittgenstein manages to say a good deal about what cannot be said, thus suggesting to the skeptical reader that possibly there may be some loophole through a hierarchy of languages, or by some other exit."[79] And as Hacker points out, "That there are things that cannot be put into words, but which make themselves manifest is a leitmotif running through the whole of the *Tractatus*."[80] According to the ineffable reading, Wittgenstein's goal was to help us see these things "aright" and then to discard the apparatus that helped us to do so.[81] The book itself is overt nonsense (or at least aims to be, for those who understand it) but still manages to convey meaning.

The "resolute," or "austere," reading, most closely associated with James Conant and Cora Diamond,[82] rejects the notion that there are unsayable truths or different kinds of nonsense.[83] According to this reading, "it is a mistake to think that there is anything informative about nonsense. Nonsense is nonsense and to think of the *Tractatus* as showing some 'essential feature of reality, which reality has all right, but which we cannot say or think it has,' is to make Wittgenstein 'chicken out.'"[84] The purpose of the *Tractatus* is therefore therapeutic, rather than demonstrative—it seeks to cure us of the pointless and potentially harmful effort of trying to find meaning in nonsense.[85] On this reading, "the whole talk of the limits of language is confused; there is nothing that language cannot say. Language can represent every possible fact in the world and there are no other-worldly facts."[86] After all, Wittgenstein himself said, "The limits of my language mean the limits of my world."[87] And although Russell's introduction to the book seems to support the ineffability reading, Wittgenstein thought that Russell had not "got hold of [his] main contention."[88]

This brief description of the ineffable and resolute readings inevitably simplifies and flattens them, in an effort to avoid joining a debate it wishes merely to describe. Subtleties abound; variations are common. The goal here is simply to suggest that on either view nonsense can be cognitively illuminating—meaningless speech, in other words, can have value *as a means to truth*. For adherents of the ineffable view, nonsense can demonstrate the existence of important but perhaps unsayable truths. A great deal of art might do just that.[89] And for adherents of the resolute view, nonsense can be a tool to save us from useless and potentially misleading efforts to establish meaning when none can be found. It is therapeutic—intellectually and not just emotionally so.

But high-level epistemological debates are not the only contexts in which nonsense can contribute to the marketplace of ideas. Much as falsehood can demonstrate truth,[90] nonsense can illuminate meaning by demonstrating its boundaries. The *Tractatus* is not unique in that regard. It has been said that Carroll created his nonsense verse "not to put anything in doubt or to entertain any new conceptual possibilities, but . . . to remind us where sense is to be found."[91] So, too, can engaging with nonsense enable individuals to better comprehend truth and meaning. This is certainly the case with regard to art, which as discussed earlier is often overtly nonsensical. Art can, as the Supreme Court has recognized, "affect public attitudes and behavior in a variety of ways, ranging from direct espousal of a political or social doctrine to the subtle shaping of thought which characterizes all artistic expression,"[92] even when it lacks meaning. As William Charlton puts it, "whereas we outgrow play with spoons and handkerchiefs, our intellectual faculties will always benefit from the quickening effect of good nonsense."[93]

2. AUTONOMY

The most potentially expansive theory of the First Amendment is that speech deserves constitutional protection because and to the degree that it furthers individual autonomy. Martin Redish, perhaps the most prominent defender of this view, has argued that "all forms of expression that further the self-realization value, which justifies the democratic system as well as free speech's role in it, are deserving of full constitutional protection."[94] Ed Baker has similarly argued that speech "should receive constitutional protection . . . because and to the extent that it is a manifestation of individual autonomy."[95] The expansiveness of the autonomy conception leaves its defenders with a vast territory to patrol, because nearly any act can be described as a manifestation of individual autonomy. Indeed, as Tushnet suggests in chapter 2, the very overbreadth of the principle (which could be interpreted to reach such activities as ticket scalping) may be good reason to question its utility as a First Amendment theory.

The breadth of the autonomy view comfortably encompasses many forms of meaningless speech, for nonsense can surely manifest autonomy whether or not it "develop[s] the rational faculties."[96] After all, much of what we think and feel is impossible to express in words. This may be a result of deficiencies in our shared language, our limited individual vocabularies, or "practical, social, or psychological impediments to our using even the linguistic resources available to us."[97] Whatever the reason for these limits, or whether we recognize when they are transgressed, our efforts to express what lies beyond them create a kind of nonsense—statements that are unverifiable, fail to describe any possible state of affairs, or attempt to say what can only be shown.

And yet from the perspective of individual autonomy and self-fulfillment, we may have very good reason not to pass over such things in silence. Though arguably nonsensical, beyond those limits may lie our chaotic, contradictory, and even "ineffable" selves. Efforts to represent them may lack meaning according to some definitions, but they are also a very important part of individual and social human development.[98] Even Wittgenstein seemed to recognize that there is a kind of mystical value in some kinds of nonsense.[99]

As a First Amendment matter, these issues—and the autonomy value of nonsense—are most salient with regard to art and music, the constitutional status of which has been a perennial problem for the First Amendment. Chapters 1 and 2 have already demonstrated the degree to which courts and scholars simply take it for granted that the Amendment *must* cover such artistic speech and yet fail to explain why. Chen and Tushnet note that many have tried to deal with the problem by imputing "ideas" or some other cognitive content to art and music. But this is unsatisfying, precisely because art and music may not intend to express any particular idea. Indeed, to try to put their meaning into words would be impossible—as Isadora Duncan put it, "If I could say it, I wouldn't have to dance it."[100] Rather than trying to impute meaning to such expression, we could instead ask whether nonsense for nonsense's sake—like art for art's sake[101]—serves important First Amendment values.

Among those values, autonomy is the most natural candidate. Surely one of the fundamental goals of artistic expression, after all, is to try to say or represent the inexpressible. To do so is to speak nonsense, and yet no one could doubt the importance of such nonsense to the autonomy and self-development of people speaking it.[102] It can serve the autonomy interests of viewers as well. Aesthetic judgments are part of the "pleasure of freedom itself" and are in that way "disinterested and ruleless, unconstrained by . . . appetite" or "a master concept to which they must conform."[103] Art is therefore sometimes important for individual autonomy precisely *because* its lack of meaning removes it from the realm of knowledge.[104]

This is not to say that the autonomy principle provides an unmitigated case for protecting nonsense. Misleading covert nonsense, for example, can further the autonomy of the person speaking it while simultaneously interfering with the autonomy of those who are tricked by it. Moreover, if autonomy is intertwined with rational cognition, covert nonsense might be a threat to autonomy instead of a means to advance it. Many leading proponents of the autonomy approach seem to hold this view. Redish, for example, refers to "the instrumental value in developing individuals' mental faculties so that they may reach their full *intellectual* potential."[105] Fred Schauer has similarly described the self-realization view of the First Amendment as being based on the human potential for "personal growth, self-fulfillment, and development of the rational faculties."[106] If these views are correct, then autonomy is limited by rationality, and nonsense might lack constitutional salience precisely because it is not subject to analysis on the basis of its rationality.

3. DEMOCRACY

The final major First Amendment value is democracy. As with the autonomy and marketplace approaches, democratic theories of the First Amendment come in many forms. Perhaps most famously, Alexander Meiklejohn argued that the Amendment categorically protects political speech (and only political speech) against government interference.[107] Robert Bork took a similar, albeit narrower, view.[108] More recently, Post has argued that the primary value animating the First Amendment is that of "democratic legitimation": the notion that "First Amendment coverage should extend to all efforts deemed normatively necessary for influencing public opinion."[109]

Because democratic approaches to the First Amendment seem to be based on the content of speech acts,[110] it might not be immediately apparent how nonsense—which lacks cognitive content of any kind—can be entitled to protection. After all, nonsense does not directly convey information about voting. Indeed, Chen argues in chapter 1 that democracy-based visions of the First Amendment cannot be made to cover instrumental music. And yet totalitarian states have banned nonrepresentational and nonsensical art.[111] Sheldon Nahmod points to the Soviet Union, whose leaders believed that "art should serve only to reinforce socialist ideals and thereby inculcate appropriate behavior; nonrepresentational art [was] considered decadent, bourgeois and dangerous."[112]

But as Tushnet points out in chapter 2, these odd outliers are surely just that, and their pathologies are not necessarily the ones with which First Amendment doctrine need be concerned. Moreover, the fact that some oppressive states might seek to suppress nonsense does not explain why democracies should protect it. What positive democratic value does overt nonsense serve? Perhaps, like art, nonsense can help cultivate the kind of citizen on whom a well-functioning democracy depends. Meiklejohn, for example, argued that "[l]iterature and the arts must be protected by the First Amendment. They lead the way toward sensitive and informed appreciation and response to the values out of which the riches of the general welfare are created."[113] This may be a bit of a stretch even on its own terms, but it does suggest a possible connection between nonsense and democracy. Just as engaging with nonsense can help people perceive cognitive truths in the marketplace for ideas, perhaps it can also inform their understanding and appreciation of what Brandeis referred to as "political truth."

A second possibility is that overt nonsense serves as a kind of "safety valve"—a way to release what might otherwise become dangerous dissent.[114] On this reading, speech "is an essential mechanism for maintaining the balance between stability and change."[115] The Merry Pranksters, whose escapades in their brightly decorated bus were catalogued in *The Electric Kool-Aid Acid Test*,[116] often "tootl[ed] the multitudes," which referred "to the way a Prankster would stand with a flute on the bus's roof and play sounds to imitate people's various reactions to the bus."[117] Such activity probably did not convey any particularized message or "idea." But without that outlet, perhaps the Pranksters' basically nonsensical hijinks would have devolved into something more destructive.

A related argument for extending constitutional protection to nonsense draws on institutional considerations that are especially salient for, but not unique to, democracy-based conceptions of the First Amendment: that the Amendment must protect nonsense to fully insulate valuable and meaningful speech. The Supreme Court has long recognized that "First Amendment freedoms need breathing space to survive."[118] This proposition is based on the belief that speech is "delicate and vulnerable, as well as supremely precious in our society. The threat of sanctions may deter [its] exercise almost as potently as the actual application of sanctions."[119] Doctrine has been significantly shaped by that belief, perhaps most prominently in the context of First Amendment standing doctrine, which permits people to attack on free speech grounds a law that would concededly be constitutional as applied to them, so long as the law reaches a substantial amount of protected speech.[120]

The nothingness of nonsense might be exactly the kind of breathing space that sense needs to thrive. After all, the Court has recognized that, if only truthful speech were protected, people would "tend to make only statements which 'steer far wider of the unlawful zone.'"[121] Perhaps if only meaningful speech were protected, people would shy away from pushing the boundaries of logic and language for fear of speaking unprotected nonsense. As the Court reasoned in *Cohen v. California*, "forbid[ding] particular words . . . also run[s] a substantial risk of suppressing ideas in the process."[122] Nonsense might merit protection precisely because of its instrumental value in protecting meaningful speech.

II. The Meaning of Meaning for the First Amendment

The discussion up until this point has described an important but underexplored category of speech—nonsense—and made a preliminary case for its constitutional protection. In the process, it has flanked another target: the very concept of meaning itself. This is dangerous quarry, particularly when wounded by the apparent threat to its claim on the First Amendment's territory. With due concern for the hazards, though, it is difficult to imagine a better way to consider meaning than by, as the preceding discussion has, exploring its absence. The goal of this part is to use that analysis to confront the meaning of "meaning" for First Amendment purposes.

It would be easier, perhaps, to avoid the issue by simply saying that meaning does not matter for the First Amendment. But a wide range of doctrine and scholarship suggests that the easy road is foreclosed and that meaning—generally equated with ideas, viewpoints, or content—is a necessary ingredient of constitutionally salient speech. As John Greenman notes, "Frequently, behavior is said to be covered by the First Amendment if it conveys 'ideas' or 'information.'"[123] This meaning-dependent approach is embedded in constitutional doctrine in various ways and has been buttressed by thoughtful scholarship. Peter Tiersma, for example, proposes that "the first requirement for communication by conduct is that the conduct be meaningful, most often as a matter of convention. This is simply an extension of a basic principle of language: a speaker normally cannot use sounds to communicate unless the sounds have some meaning attached to them."[124] Likewise, Melville Nimmer's influential account of symbolic speech holds that "symbolic speech requires not merely that given conduct results in a meaning effect, but that the actor causing such conduct must intend such a meaning effect by his conduct."[125]

But the meaning-dependent approach also raises difficult problems, for the reasons suggested in part 1: nonsense is pervasive, and much of it has a strong relationship to the First Amendment's core values. Moreover, despite courts' and scholars' apparent insistence on the importance of meaning, few have done much to establish what meaning means. That imprecision, in turn, provides space to craft a doctrinal and theoretical apparatus that allows meaning to play a central role in First Amendment discourse without completely denying constitutional coverage to nonsense. This is no easy task, however, for the necessary tools are scarce and scattered throughout the First Amendment's messy workshop.

Fortunately, craftsmen in adjacent workshops can provide useful guidance. The relationship between meaning and language has been the central obsession of analytic philosophy for the better part of a century. Of course, analytic philosophers are primarily concerned with determining what can meaningfully be said, not what kinds of speech are or should be protected from government sanction. But with regard to the specific issue of meaning, their hard-won advances are directly relevant to the questions that constitutional law has set for itself. Moreover, as the following discussion shows, echoes of their efforts can already be heard in First Amendment discourse.

Two major schools of thought have emerged, which, with regrettably necessary simplification, can be called the *representational* and *use* approaches to meaning. The former, associated with Wittgenstein in his early writings, Bertrand Russell, and logical positivism, finds meaning in the connection between language and extralinguistic concepts.[126] Language that fails to represent such concepts is nonsensical. Much First Amendment discourse implicitly utilizes such an approach. Many legal scholars, including those cited earlier, generally employ a more or less representational approach to meaning by searching for "ideas"[127] or "content."[128] The frequent scholarly explorations of nonrepresentational art also seem motivated by a representational approach, for nonrepresentation is only relevant to the degree that representationalism itself is constitutionally salient.

The lessons of analytic philosophy suggest that these are the wrong questions to ask. As Paul Chevigny explains, "Having abandoned the view of language as a 'copy' of the 'real world,' a set of names for objects, and assertions that have meaning only to the extent that they faithfully represent reality, philosophers increasingly think of language as a system of discourse in which assertions can have 'meaning' and be 'true' not as representations of 'reality' but as ideas for which good reasons can be found in other parts of the system of discourse."[129]

That is, if meaning is relevant for First Amendment purposes, it must be found in the way language is *used*, not in what it represents. The following discussion attempts to show what that entails as a constitutional matter and why it represents an improvement over the representational approach. And yet bringing use meaning to the forefront of First Amendment doctrine drags with it a new set of problems, including the inherent difficulty of identifying the language games that imbue speech with meaning.

The goal of this part is to suggest how First Amendment discourse and doctrine can fruitfully utilize the concept of meaning, not to fully define speech, say anything new about analytic philosophy, or—perish the thought—provide an original or comprehensive reading of Wittgenstein.[130] The following accounts of analytic philosophy will be familiar, if simplified, to philosophers; the First Amendment theory and doctrine will be familiar to legal scholars. Indeed, this is far from the first effort to suggest connections between them. But its angle of approach—through the region of nonsense—is novel for First Amendment scholarship, and it aims to provide a fresh and useful, if complicated and imperfect, way to think about meaning for First Amendment purposes.

A. Representational Meaning

In 1899, Oliver Wendell Holmes, Jr., wrote, "We must think things not words, or at least we must constantly translate our words into the facts for which they stand, if we are to keep to the real and the true."[131] For a man whose contribution to American jurisprudence can largely be measured by his mastery of language,[132] this might come as something of a surprise. The remark suggests that the meaning of words lies in "the facts for which they stand." In that way, it is emblematic of the representational approach to meaning—one that locates meaning in the relationship between language and extralinguistic concepts.[133] Words that do not denote such concepts are nonsensical and, if the doctrinal descriptions set out earlier are accurate, fall outside the boundaries of the First Amendment. But as the remainder of this section shows, such a representational approach has serious defects as a guide for constitutional law.

Holmes is often classified as a pragmatist,[134] and though his circle of scientifically and philosophically inclined friends was broad and deep,[135] it apparently did not include those in Vienna and Cambridge who were concurrently exploring the relationship between "things" and "words." Even as Holmes was penning his monumentally influential free speech opinions and essentially giving the First Amendment its first normative theory, those thinkers—Russell and Wittgenstein prominent but not alone among them—were probing the meaning of meaning itself.[136]

In the early 1900s, Russell was perhaps the world's preeminent logician and mathematician. His *Principia Mathematica* was published in the 1910s, just as Holmes was laying the normative foundations of the First Amendment. As part of his wide-ranging intellectual explorations, Russell contemplated what it means for a statement to have meaning. He eventually came to believe that statements are meaningful, even if not verifiable, so long as they express a possible state of affairs: "a sentence 'p' is significant if 'I believe that p' or 'I doubt that p' or etc., can describe a perceived fact."[137] Thus, a statement like "The king of France is bald" can be meaningful because it denotes a concept, even though the thing it denotes (the king of France) does not exist.[138] Statements that fail to denote are nonsensical. Russell's famous example of such nonsense was the statement "quadruplicity drinks procrastination."[139]

At around the same time as Russell was developing this approach to meaning, he took on a new pupil, whom he at first referred to as "[m]y ferocious German, . . . armour-plated against all assaults of reasoning."[140] Within one academic term, Russell learned that his German was Austrian and quite capable of his own assaultive reasoning. Russell was intellectually smitten: "I love him & feel he will solve the problems I am too old to solve."[141] The ferocious Austrian was, of course, Wittgenstein. For him, as Dennis Patterson says, "all philosophical problems [were] ultimately problems of language."[142] Although the focus on problems of language was consistent throughout Wittgenstein's career, his approach to them can be divided into two basically distinct phases, only the first of which fits the representational mold described here. For the "early" Wittgenstein, author of the spectacularly impenetrable *Tractatus Logico-Philosophicus*, sense consisted in "a determinate relation between a proposition and an independent state of affairs."[143] To explore their "relation," Wittgenstein focused on the relationship between thought and expression. As the preface or "frame" of the *Tractatus* explained,

> The book will, therefore, draw a limit to thinking, or rather—not to thinking, but to the expression of thoughts; for, in order to draw a limit to thinking we should have to be able to think both sides of this limit (we should therefore have to be able to think what cannot be thought).
>
> The limit can, therefore, only be drawn in language and what lies on the other side of the limit will be simply nonsense.[144]

That limit represents the boundary of both meaning and of reality. As Wittgenstein explained in the koan-like propositions of the book itself, "The proposition is a picture of reality. The proposition is a model of the reality as we think it is."[145] Anything that is not a proposition is, strictly speaking, nonsense, for anything that is not a proposition fails to present a picture of reality: "Only the proposition has sense; only in the context of a proposition has a name meaning."[146] It follows that there is no way to comprehend or create reality *but* through language, and thus "[t]he limits of my language mean the limits of my world."[147]

This does not necessarily mean, however, that all concepts are reducible to language. Wittgenstein was obsessed with the notion that some things "can not be expressed by prop[osition]s, but only shown . . . ; which, I believe, is the cardinal problem of philosophy."[148] As Elizabeth Anscombe, a distinguished philosopher and former student of Wittgenstein's, later explained, "[A]n important part is played in the *Tractatus* by the things which, though they cannot be 'said,' are yet 'shewn' or 'displayed.' That is to say: it would be right to call them 'true' if, *per impossible*, they could be said; in fact they cannot be called true, since they cannot be said, but 'can be shewn,' or 'are exhibited,' in the propositions saying the various things that can be said."[149] Whatever the importance of these things, attempts to *say* them inevitably result in nonsense. Holmes seemed to have something similar in mind when he suggested the difference between thinking things and thinking words.

Though Wittgenstein himself apparently later abandoned the effort to find meaning in the relationship between words and things, the search certainly did not end with the *Tractatus*. The influence of the representational approach is palpable in the work of A. J. Ayer, the great English logical positivist, whose *Language, Truth, and Logic* defends among other things the "verification principle." That principle holds that statements are nonsensical when they are not analytically or empirically verifiable.[150] A similar focus on verifiability seems to underlie popular intuitions about the relationship between meaning and truth. For example, Wikipedia's rules provide that "[a]ll material in Wikipedia mainspace, including everything in articles, lists and captions, must be verifiable."[151]

The influence of the representational approach extends, albeit uncredited, to First Amendment doctrine itself. This is perhaps most apparent in what John Greenman calls the Supreme Court's "ideaism"— the principle that "behavior is . . . covered by the First Amendment if it conveys 'ideas' or 'information.'"[152] The notion that ideas—cognitive meanings—are the focus of the First Amendment is so often repeated that it might sometimes pass unnoticed. In *New York Times Co. v. Sullivan*, the Supreme Court explained that the Amendment's "constitutional safeguard . . . 'was fashioned to assure unfettered interchange of ideas for the bringing about of political and social changes desired by the people.'"[153] Since then, the Court has often invoked the principle that "[t]he First Amendment . . . embodies '[o]ur profound national commitment to the free exchange of ideas.'"[154] In *Miller v. California*, for example, the Court seemed to suggest that ideas are so important that the existence of one is sufficient for constitutional coverage: "All ideas having even the slightest redeeming social importance—unorthodox ideas, controversial ideas, even ideas hateful to the prevailing climate of opinion—have the full protection of the [First Amendment's] guaranties."[155] By the same logic, the Court has also indicated that putative speech acts such as fighting words and obscenity fall outside the boundaries of the First Amendment in part because they "are no essential part of any exposition of ideas."[156]

A representational approach to meaning similarly seems to animate some of the Court's efforts to define what kinds of nonverbal conduct qualify for First Amendment coverage. By now, "[i]t is well settled that the First Amendment's protections extend to nonverbal 'expressive conduct' or 'symbolic speech.'"[157] And meaning seems to be the ingredient that makes that extension possible. In *West Virginia State Board of Education v. Barnette*, for example, the Court indicated that expressive conduct (in that case, saluting a flag) is "speech" for constitutional purposes because it conveys "ideas."[158] A similar premise appears in *Spence v. Washington*,[159] the Court's most direct effort to define the essential elements that transform conduct into speech. In that case, the Court set out to evaluate whether conduct is "sufficiently imbued with elements of communication to fall within the scope" of the First Amendment.[160] The test it created asks whether "[a]n intent to convey a particularized message was present, and whether the likelihood was great that the message would be understood by those who viewed it."[161] Conduct that satisfies both prongs of this test is considered to be expressive. *Spence* therefore effectively doubles down on the importance of representational meaning, requiring both that the speaker intend to convey it (in "particularized" form, no less) and also that there be a "great" likelihood that the audience understand it.

Despite the frequent appearances of the representational approach to meaning in First Amendment doctrine, it is a poor guide to what speech the First Amendment actually does or should protect. Indeed, the representational approach to meaning, combined with the meaning-dependent approach to the First Amendment discussed earlier, leads to the problems of underinclusion suggested by part 1. As Greenman points out, ideaism "fails to predict what the First Amendment actually covers."[162] In *United States v. O'Brien*, the Court clarified that the mere intent to convey meaning is not sufficient for First Amendment coverage: "We cannot accept the view that an apparently limitless variety of conduct can be labeled 'speech' whenever the person engaging in the conduct intends thereby to express an idea."[163]

Nor is a connection between language and concept necessary for First Amendment coverage. As Chen demonstrates in chapter 1, music is clearly covered by the First Amendment,[164] even though a great deal of it does not convey meaning in any standard sense. As Richard Posner writes, "even if 'thought,' 'concept,' 'idea,' and 'opinion' are broadly defined, these are not what most music conveys; and even if music is regarded as a language, it is not a language for encoding ideas and opinions."[165] In other ways, too, the Constitution protects efforts to say the unsayable. Justice John Harlan explained in *Cohen v. California* that "much linguistic expression serves a dual communicative function: it conveys not only ideas capable of relatively precise, detached explication, but otherwise *inexpressible* emotions as well."[166]

Under the representational approach to meaning, expression of the "inexpressible" is by definition nonsensical. But as Justice Harlan suggests, and as part 1 argues, it is also properly covered by the First Amendment. It follows that the representational approach, whatever its intuitive appeal, is a poor guide to the boundaries of the First Amendment. If "meaning" is to matter, it must lie elsewhere than in the relationship between speech and concepts.

B. Use Meaning

The best place to find an alternative to the representational approach associated with Russell and Wittgenstein is in the work of Wittgenstein himself. His later thought—especially the enormously influential concept of language games—reshaped the whole of analytic philosophy, putting it on the "linguistic turn" that led to speech-act theory, ordinary-language philosophy, and a host of other important developments. From these developments emerges a new way of thinking about language and meaning that is ultimately a better guide for the First Amendment.

After leaving philosophical work behind for nearly a decade, Wittgenstein returned to Cambridge in 1929 and took a new approach to the relationship between language, meaning, and the world. This work culminated in the posthumous publication of *Philosophical Investigations*. It was here that Wittgenstein "reject[ed] the search for a unified account of language's internal logic, which had occupied the bulk of . . . the *Tractatus*."[167] Indeed, he described the *Philosophical Investigations* as a rejoinder to "what logicians have said about the structure of language. (Including the author of the *Tractatus Logico-Philosophicus*.)"[168]

Instead of the picture theory of meaning that animated Wittgenstein's earlier work, he now focused on "language games" as defining the limits of meaning and, therefore, the world: "I shall also call the whole, consisting of language and the actions into which it is woven, the 'language-game.'"[169] The term, he said, was "meant to bring into prominence the fact that the *speaking* of language is part of an activity, or of a form of life."[170] The nature of these games became Wittgenstein's focus for the rest of his life. As Patterson explains, "The central tenet of Wittgenstein's writing after 1929 is that knowledge is not achieved by the individual subject's grasp of a connection between word and object. Rather, knowledge turns out to be the grasp of the topography of a word's uses in activities into which language is woven."[171]

The language-games approach locates meaning in language's *use*, not in its representation of the world. As Wittgenstein put it in the *Philosophical Investigations*, "For a *large* class of cases—though not for all—in which we employ the word 'meaning' it can be defined thus: the meaning of a word is its use in the language."[172] The way to identify meaning, therefore, is not necessarily to ask whether a putative speaker has given content to signs in his or her propositions but rather whether he or she has followed the rules of the relevant language game. Jack Balkin and Sandy Levinson explain, "As a tradition now identified with Wittgenstein and his successors insists, there are only 'practices,' each constituted by inchoate and unformalizable standards that establish one's statements . . . as 'legitimately assertable' by persons within the interpretive community that constitutes the practice in question."[173]

The tradition to which Balkin and Levinson refer has now spread throughout analytic philosophy. The later Wittgenstein is therefore important not only on his own terms but also because he shaped so many other philosophical developments throughout the past century. The branches on that tree are too numerous to count and too complex to describe but include the work of Paul Grice,[174] the speech-act theory associated most closely with J. L. Austin and John R. Searle,[175] and ordinary-language philosophy.[176]

Most importantly for present purposes, the use-meaning approach has gained traction in First Amendment doctrine and scholarship. Post, for example, argues that Marcel Duchamp's *The Fountain*—a urinal turned on its side—is properly recognized as artistic speech precisely because of the shared norms of the artistic community.[177] This is because it is a "form[] of communication that sociologically we recognize as art."[178] Taking a similar approach, Amy Adler points to the example of Annie Sprinkle, a performance artist who also works in the pornography industry: "When asked if anything made Sprinkle's performance

at the Kitchen [Center for the Performing Arts] 'art' and her performance for *Screw* [magazine] 'pornography,' a spokesman for the Kitchen
said, 'Here it was performed in an art context.'"[179] These are arguments
rooted in use, not in representation.

Such examples raise the question of whether the use approach provides any boundaries whatsoever between meaning and nonsense.
Indeed, if not applied rigorously, the fuzziness inherent in evaluating
language games and social practices can be made to shield nearly any
act or utterance. But although use meaning is potentially more capacious with regard to meaning than the representational approach, it is
not all-encompassing. By establishing a new approach to meaning, the
linguistic turn in analytic philosophy simply creates a new and potentially richer approach to nonsense and language.[180] Rather than arising
from a disjunction between language and extralinguistic facts, speech
is nonsensical when it fails to adhere to the rules of the relevant language game. Jonathan Yovel explains that "one plays a language-game
by the act of following its rules; deviation from the rules is 'not playing
the game,' which produces nonsense in relation to the language-game in
question."[181] Identifying and evaluating meaning, then, requires focus
on how language is actually *used*.

In a variety of ways, the Supreme Court has implicitly endorsed this
view, suggesting that the First Amendment has at least partially taken its
own linguistic turn with regard to meaning. This is a welcome development both descriptively and normatively, for the use-meaning approach
better captures both the actual contours of existing First Amendment
coverage and the constitutional value of what would otherwise seem to
be meaningless speech.

The First Amendment's linguistic turn manifests itself in many areas
of doctrine, perhaps most prominently in cases that tinker with *Spence's*
representationalist machinery. In *Hurley v. Irish-American Gay, Lesbian
and Bisexual Group of Boston, Inc.*, for example, the Court assessed the
constitutional salience of a Hibernian pride parade. The justices conceded that it was difficult to locate a "narrow, succinctly articulable message" in the parade[182] but concluded that no such showing was required.
A unanimous Court held that the parade qualified for protection and
that "if confined to expressions conveying a 'particularized message,'
[the First Amendment] would never reach the unquestionably shielded

painting of Jackson Pollock, music of Arnold Schoenberg, or Jabber-wocky verse of Lewis Carroll."[183] This is effectively a rejection of the representational approach and an endorsement of the idea that meaning lies in form and use.

The distinction between the representational and use approaches animates many other cases as well. Recall *Morse v. Frederick*. On a strictly representational approach, the phrase "BONG HiTS 4 JESUS" seems just as nonsensical as Chomsky's "Colorless green ideas sleep furiously"— each idea might represent a concept, but strung together, they convey nothing sensible.[184] (Conversely, if a group of students displayed the latter on a banner, it might also reasonably be viewed as promoting—or perhaps demonstrating—illegal drug use!) Indeed, the student's declaration that the banner was designed to be nonsense, if accepted, should have taken him outside the realm of *Spence v. Washington*, because no "intent to convey a particularized message was present." To the representationalist, then, the act involved only nonsense. If the First Amendment requires the presence of meaning, then there was no constitutional issue to begin with.

Under a use-meaning approach, by contrast, the fact that the banner's words conveyed no semantic content does not preclude them from having meaning, which derives from use, not representation. That use, the majority concluded, imbued them with drug-promoting meaning, not simply television-attracting meaning. In other words, the use-meaning approach can account for the existence of meaning in the banner, therefore bringing the case within the boundaries of the First Amendment and enabling the more substantive and useful debate over whether the majority identified the *correct* meaning and whether the government had sufficient reason to regulate it.[185]

This is the same basic insight reflected in the First Amendment's attention to context as a component of meaning. The representational approach is relatively, if not entirely, acontextual. Whether a word "really" corresponds to an underlying concept is generally not dependent on the context in which that word is deployed. But First Amendment doctrine itself is deeply attuned to the fact that context can create or change meaning.[186] Even *Spence* recognized that "context may give meaning to [a] symbol."[187] The Court there noted that hanging a flag upside down with peace symbols attached to it related to a "contemporaneous issue of intense public concern"[188] and that observers were likely to recognize Spence's point "at the time that he made it,"[189] even though in a different context it "might be interpreted as nothing more than bizarre behavior."[190] A similar principle seems to be on display (so to speak) in the Court's nude-dancing cases, in which the justices have taken pains to distinguish between "bacchanalian revelries" in barrooms and "a performance by a scantily clad ballet troupe in a theater."[191]

Further hints of the use-meaning approach can be found in the Supreme Court's conclusion that First Amendment coverage extends to practices that form a "significant medium for the communication of ideas,"[192] even if the specific communication at issue does not successfully convey a particularized message.[193] Post has provided the strongest normative justification for this approach, arguing that "First Amendment coverage presumptively extends to media for the communication of ideas, like newspapers, magazines, the Internet, or cinema, which are the primary vehicles for the circulation of the texts that define and sustain the public sphere."[194] It follows that, "[i]n the absence of strong countervailing reasons, whatever is said within such media is covered by the First Amendment."[195] On this approach, *Jabberwocky* is covered by the First Amendment not because its words represent concepts but because it is recognizable as a poem.

The same basic intuition might be animating the appealing but problematic effort to draw a line between "pure speech" and expressive conduct. The Supreme Court has suggested that pure speech—apparently conceived as the spoken or written word, with no accompanying nonverbal action[196]—should receive constitutional coverage,[197] apparently without any further inquiry into its meaningfulness. Expressive conduct, by contrast, is covered only when it is sufficiently imbued with "communicative element[s]" as to bring it within the boundaries of the First Amendment.[198] In other words, it must, at least according to some accounts, convey ideas or meaning.[199] The pure speech / expressive conduct dichotomy is deeply difficult, largely inaccurate, and probably unworkable, for all the reasons that Tushnet gives in his discussion of "nominalism" in chapter 2. But the effort itself demonstrates that meaning may lie in form and use, rather than in representation.[200]

C. Making the Most of the First Amendment's Linguistic Turn

Endorsing use meaning as an alternative to representational meaning is relatively easy; implementing it is not. It should by now be apparent that the boundaries of the First Amendment cannot be explained on the basis of the relationship between language and extralinguistic facts, as the representational-meaning approach would suggest. But to say that those boundaries do or should depend instead on language games raises a new, albeit more useful, set of questions. This section explores a few of them.

First, by focusing on language games rather than on the connection between words and ideas, the approach here would exclude from First Amendment coverage acts that, despite being "communicative" in some sense, are not traditionally recognized as "speech." This could explain why many prominent First Amendment scholars have rejected a generalist account of the constitutional value of form,[201] focusing instead on the transmission of ideas.[202]

This objection is difficult and deceptively complex, as is the best answer to it: that such activities, whatever relationships they might have with the First Amendment's values, simply are not *speech*. Consider Jed Rubenfeld's example of a person who speeds to express disapproval of speed limits[203] or Tushnet's example of ticket scalping in chapter 2. These activities arguably further First Amendment values by advancing the autonomy interests of those who are engaged in them and perhaps even communicate ideas. But so do innumerable other activities, from terrorist attacks to rape. Prohibition of those activities is perfectly constitutional under the First Amendment not because the government interest in doing so is sufficiently strong but because they are not thought to implicate the First Amendment at all. To borrow Schauer's terminology, they are uncovered, not merely unprotected.[204]

The question of what constitutes "speech" is, in turn, an old one for First Amendment theory and doctrine, and the difficulty of articulating anything like a precise definition is familiar. This chapter has focused on one possible component of speech—meaning—not the concept of speech as a whole. The two inquiries might be distinct; perhaps meaning must be accompanied by a volitional act or utterance to constitute speech. To the degree that the discussion here provides lessons for the quest to define speech itself, it is that the answers probably lie in social practices rather than in formal logic. In the end, as Schauer explains, "the very idea of free speech is a crude implement, to the core, protecting acts that its background justifications would not protect, and failing to protect acts that its background justifications would protect."[205]

But the crudeness of the implement raises another and perhaps equally foundational challenge for the use-meaning approach: negotiating the tension between the First Amendment's desire for clear boundaries and language games' resistance to them. As to the former, the importance of clarity in First Amendment doctrine is recognized as valuable in its own right.[206] Language games, however, are a poor guide for establishing clear boundaries. Both in their definition and in their behavior, language games "lack purity."[207] Post, whose First Amendment theory depends on identifying those boundaries, concludes that although we do not "have a very clear or hard-edged account" of the boundaries of public discourse, "it is anthropologically apparent that they do exist and are reflected in constitutional doctrine."[208] Ordinary-language philosophers, too, embrace this lack of clarity as not merely a necessary drawback but a positive feature of their approach. As Toril Moi explains, "Often the blurred concept is exactly what we want. . . . In many cases . . . , it is useless to spend time and energy trying to produce a sharp concept."[209]

The problem is not simply that language games have fuzzy boundaries but that it is difficult to know at what level of generality they should be defined. After all, "use" can refer to an individual speech act or to a broader category of speech acts bearing a family resemblance;[210] language games can involve two people, a group, or an entire community. Ordinary-language philosophy typically takes the former route, focusing on the meaning of *particular* speech acts. The inevitable result is a kind of case-by-case analysis that requires careful consideration of individual speech acts.

But whatever the merits of case-by-case analysis as a philosophical approach to language, it does not necessarily make for good free speech law. Case-by-case ex post analysis is ill suited to provide the kind of articulable ex ante rules that law—and especially First Amendment doctrine—is generally thought to require.[211] First Amendment language games must be defined with sufficient breadth that individuals can tailor their conduct accordingly. A use-meaning approach to the Amendment's boundaries must therefore focus to some degree on form and use, rather than act and use.

The cost of that breadth, however, is inaccuracy. The more broadly a First Amendment language game is defined, the less likely it is to capture the values that justify its protection and the more likely it is to be overinclusive with regard to speech. But that is a cost that the First Amendment encourages us to pay. Defining speech at the level of form rather than that of individual speech acts may be imperfect, but it does help check the government's power to regulate speech by defining its boundaries.

The malleability of the language-game approach also suggests ways to account for new social practices and language games—video games, for example.[212] Defining these as "speech" on the basis of the ideas they convey seems unsatisfying, to say the least. The answer seems to lie instead with the fact that over time they have simply become recognized as such. Admittedly, the power to make that determination is itself a form of speech regulation.[213] But such line drawing is inevitably a part of First Amendment doctrine. It is better that the lines be drawn on the basis of such social practices than on the basis of supposed relationships between words and concepts.

There are no straightforward and simple solutions to these problems. First Amendment doctrine and the language games on which it is based are messy and ongoing projects—an experiment, "as all life is an experiment."[214] The Amendment's "linguistic turn" would yield no clearer answers than the linguistic turn in analytic philosophy. But it would, at the very least, better capture what we mean by meaning and why we think it matters for the First Amendment.

* * *

What is the doctrinal or "practical" significance of this inquiry? At a basic level, the argument is simply that the First Amendment should be—and to a large extent already is—interested in use meaning, rather than representational meaning. It follows that some "nonsense" is entitled to constitutional protection. This conclusion neither is dependent on any conclusion about analytic philosophy nor requires judges, lawyers, or scholars to be philosophers. And yet the philosophical inquiries of the past century are so similar in substance to those needed in the First Amendment context that the former provide useful guidance for the latter.

This chapter also indicates a different approach to establishing whether nonrepresentational art—including instrumental music and nonsensical poetry—should be entitled to constitutional protection. The frequency with which scholars focus specifically on nonrepresentational art suggests that they believe representationalism to be an essential part of defining the First Amendment's scope. The argument here suggests that it is not and that a more useful inquiry would focus on social understandings of art in various contexts.

Relatedly, the search for meaning in social usages rather than in representationalism could extend not just to *whether* a speech act is meaningful but also to *which* of many possible meanings it should have. This raises difficult questions when considered in light of the putative speaker's mental state. On the one hand, that seems perfectly straightforward: surely "Fuck the Draft" had a particular meaning precisely because of the broader social context in which it was used.[215] But if speech is fully defined by what a viewer (subjective or objective) would understand, then even "innocent" speakers—including those who intend no offense—might be found liable for meanings they never meant to convey.

Finally, focusing on the social embeddedness of speech has implications for the degree to which speakers can actually control the meaning of their own speech—whether it has any at all and, if so, what meaning it has. The use-meaning approach described here would effectively deny constitutional coverage to putative speech acts that, though perhaps meaningful to the speaker, do not respect the rules of our shared language games. Our old friend Lewis Carroll provides the perfect illustration:

> "And only *one* for birthday presents, you know. There's glory for you!"
>
> "I don't know what you mean by 'glory,'" Alice said.
>
> Humpty Dumpty smiled contemptuously. "Of course you don't—till I tell you. I meant 'there's a nice knock-down argument for you!'"
>
> "But 'glory' doesn't mean 'a nice knock-down argument,'" Alice objected.

"When *I* use a word," Humpty Dumpty said in rather a scornful tone, "it means just what I choose it to mean—neither more nor less."

"The question is," said Alice, "whether you *can* make words mean so many different things."

"The question is," said Humpty Dumpty, "which is to be master—that's all."[216]

Humpty Dumpty is violating the rules of a language game and thus speaking nonsense, but the question he identifies is essentially the same one asked by analytic philosophers. The use-meaning approach denies that the speaker is inevitably master of meaning, which has a variety of potentially troubling implications—consider again the student in *Morse*, who claimed to be speaking nonsense—that deserve further exploration.

Given that Ludwig Wittgenstein has served as a guide and occasional stalking horse throughout this chapter, it seems appropriate to conclude where the *Tractatus* does. The seventh and final section famously reads, in full, "Whereof one cannot speak, thereof one must be silent."[217] If the boundaries of the First Amendment depend on the presence of representational meaning, then Congress could codify Wittgenstein's admonition without violating the Constitution, because saying what cannot be said is, by definition, nonsense. This chapter has argued that this cannot be the case and that the meaning of speech lies not in its connection to extralinguistic facts but in its use. This road is bumpier, but its imperfection offers better footing than the smooth alternatives. "Back to the rough ground!"[218]

4

Going Further

Additional Problems and Concluding Thoughts

Many other forms of expression share the characteristics of music, art, and nonsense—modes of expression that communicate but rarely, if ever, in a manner that conveys a particularized message. The constitutional questions surrounding such expression—some of which have been around for decades and others of which are emerging only because of new technology—will continue to arise in a wide range of contexts. Like music, art, and nonsense, these forms of expression do not convey an identifiable idea or message, making them equally problematic in terms of traditional arguments for First Amendment coverage. What do the collective insights of our approaches to music, art, and nonsense have to offer to thinking about the constitutional status of other forms of nonrepresentational expression? In what ways do these forms of expression resemble music, art, and nonsense, and in what ways are they materially and analytically distinct?

I. Dance

In some contexts, dance implicates many of the same issues regarding form and meaning as music, art, and nonsense do. "Dance" encompasses a fairly broad range of human activity, so its examination must distinguish it from other forms of movement, such as taking a hike, walking to the grocery store, or jumping rope. By one definition, dance is "[a] rhythmical skipping and stepping, with regular turnings and movements of the limbs and body, usually to the accompaniment of music; either as an expression of joy, exultation, and the like, or as an amusement or entertainment."[1] Note that this definition does little to distinguish what most of us might recognize as dance from many other activities that share some of these characteristics. As Judge Frank

Easterbrook observed in his dissent in *Miller v. City of South Bend*, "The court uses a definition of dancing ('moving the body in a rhythmical way, usually to music' . . .) broad enough to cover most physical activity. Swimmers, roller skaters, ice skaters, walkers, skateboarders, matadors, and construction workers using jackhammers move rhythmically, often to music."[2] Similarly, many formalized athletic competitions also involve movement accompanied by music, including figure skating, gymnastics, and synchronized swimming.

Even to the extent the foregoing definition serves as a somewhat useful starting point, it does not distinguish *among* different forms of dance, which, among other things, can be a performing art, an act of spontaneous individual or ritualistic cultural expression, a manner of social interaction, or a species of erotic entertainment and stimulation. We separate dancing into four contexts, each of which involve important expressive components that might be regarded as speech. We do not mean these categories to be as distinctive as the discussion might suggest; there can be significant overlap. Artistic dancing can be erotic; social dancing surely may have cultural significance. Nonetheless, we categorize them to identify distinctly communicative elements of each category.

A. "Artistic" Dancing

First, consider dance as a performing art, such as ballet, tap, and modern dance, which are routinely choreographed and performed for audiences. Artistic dance bears many of the characteristics of the other forms of expression discussed in this book. First, like music, art, and nonsense, artistic forms of dance are likely to be widely accepted throughout society as a form of expression presumptively covered by the First Amendment. Indeed, artistic dance's status as speech is uncontroversial. Dance is frequently conceived of and performed with the intent to express. Like music, it can help construct, preserve, and express cultural values and history and can be an important manner of reflecting and experiencing emotion.

Yet artistic dance shares some of the problems of categorization we found in other areas. Like visual art, it can be either representational or nonrepresentational. While artistic dance is probably always expressive, it is not always done, and perhaps rarely done, to convey an intended, particularized message. Artistic dance may be completely abstract and lacking in any defined or intentional meaning or may purposefully be nonsense. As David Smith's sculpture, discussed in chapter 1, explores the relationship between shape and space, so some forms of artistic dance explore the relationship between movement and space. Like other art forms, dance is also not subject to an objective determinant of meaning. Thus, it is difficult to define as speech under the First Amendment's doctrinal framework.

Similarly, it is difficult to justify constitutional protection for artistic dance from the perspective of First Amendment theory for many of the same reasons that those theories do not map well onto other forms of artistic expression. Because artistic dance does not necessarily appeal to the cognitive, it does not fit well with democracy-promoting or truth-seeking theories. As with music, however, a broader framing of truth that incorporates the emotional, cultural, and aesthetic might support a truth-seeking theory for the inclusion of artistic dance as speech. And an autonomy-based speech theory might provide some limited justification to the extent that artistic dance is a form of emotional expression and experience for choreographers, dancers, and audience members, which helps to distinguish it, though perhaps only slightly, from other types of physical autonomy.

Moreover, as discussed later with respect to cultural dancing, there are certainly dangers associated with government efforts to regulate dancing because of its expressive elements (as opposed, say, to regulate dancing in the streets as a means of facilitating traffic flow). Like art and music, the reasons for any possible state bans or censorship of artistic dance are likely to implicate interests that are antithetical to the values underlying free speech, including the desire to impose cultural conformity or carry out subjective judgments about the aesthetic value of dances. Of course, to the extent a particular artistic dance performance is overtly political, the state's actions to prohibit its performance may elicit conventional First Amendment objections. For example, in the late 1920s, the Soviet Union imposed *narodnost*, "the requirement that artists pay deliberate attention to the nation and its heritage as an ideological subject of their work." This included control over ballet, which the state hoped would help construct a new idealized, national socialist identity that explicitly rejected the classical forms of art associated with its tsarist past. The choreographer Leonid Yakobson was initially fully supportive of these efforts, rejecting classical ballet because of its association with imperial rule. But as Stalin began to more forcefully impose his directives on the artistic community, Yakobson found himself trying to maintain his aesthetic independence while simultaneously using his choreography to subversively push back politically against state control.[3]

B. Cultural Dancing

Dance varies widely among cultures and can be an important way of expressing a particular group's heritage, one that is often passed on from generation to generation. Cultural dance can express, advance, and preserve both religious and secular cultural values of groups such as indigenous peoples. In certain contexts, cultural dances may even have a specific intended and understood message. Or they may have ritualistic, celebratory meaning that is generally understood even if it lacks a specific message that could be translated into words.

Treatment of cultural dance as speech can be justified on multiple First Amendment theories. If we value cultural pluralism, for example, then facilitating cultural dance as expression may to some degree promote the search for cultural truth and maybe even democratic self-governance, in addition to embracing the autonomy of both individuals and the cultures to which they belong.[4] The arguments here closely track those in the discussion of instrumental music, which can also bear cultural significance.

Perhaps most significantly, the government's reasons for regulating cultural dance are quite likely to conflict with important speech values. States may have an interest in social cohesion through the imposition of cultural orthodoxy that is at odds with the cultures of indigenous peoples, which states may wish to erase. For example, in the late nineteenth century, the U.S. government sought to ban Native American cultural dances through a proclamation issued by the secretary of interior. The purported justifications for such bans resemble the government's arguments for suppressing speech in a wide variety of other contexts. Native American dances were thought to be subject to regulation because of their non-Christian religious nature, the free exercise clause notwithstanding. The government argued that some Native American dances perpetuated the "wild" nature of peoples inclined toward military aggression and violence. Foreshadowing later generations' complaints about rock-and-roll music, the state also suggested that these dances, which were sometimes accompanied by drumming and performed by individuals wearing minimal clothing, could have a corrupting influence on women and generate lustful behavior. Finally, officials suggested that because some Native American dances involved distribution of property, such conduct might interfere with government efforts to encourage Native Americans to accumulate private property. Interestingly, enforcement of the dancing bans was inconsistent, and some officials were more tolerant about dances that resembled social, as opposed to ceremonial, dancing.[5]

Because cultural dance is usually performed and experienced in a different context from artistic dance, the family resemblance argument is a little more difficult to make. Or, at least, we might have to disaggregate cultural dances into many different categories, some of which more closely resemble more traditional expressive forms. Cultural dance may not be political in the sense that we most commonly understand that term and may or may not convey a discrete message, yet it may contribute to political culture, broadly understood.

C. Social Dancing

> Even if this was not a law, which it is, I'm afraid I would have a lot of difficulty endorsing an enterprise [dancing] which is as fraught with genuine peril as I believe this one to be.
> —*Footloose* (1984)

Social dancing—that is, dancing alone or with others for the purposes of social interaction rather than artistic performance—can also be both expressive and associational. Government bans on social dancing have spawned some interesting legal controversies. The Supreme Court addressed the implications of restrictions on such dancing in *City of Dallas v. Stanglin*, where it reviewed a constitutional challenge to a local ordinance that restricted certain classes of dancing establishments to people between the ages of fourteen and eighteen. As described by the Court, the city's purpose for the restriction was "to provide a place where teenagers could socialize with each other, but not be subject to the potentially detrimental influences of older teenagers and young adults."[6] The plaintiff, who operated a skating rink and dance club, asserted that the law unconstitutionally infringed the rights of people between the ages of fourteen and eighteen to associate with persons outside their age bracket.

Association is not explicitly protected by the First Amendment, but the Court has interpreted the Constitution to protect association in certain contexts. It has acknowledged that there is a right to engage in certain intimate personal associations as an element of individual liberty and as a way of engaging "in those activities protected by the First Amendment—speech, assembly, petition for the redress of grievances, and the exercise of religion."[7] But in *Stanglin*, the Court rejected the association claim, concluding that the people gathered in a dance hall for the purpose of social dancing were not engaged in any sort of expressive association that would implicate the First Amendment. The Court instead dismissed this conduct as mere "recreational" dancing.[8] However, this analysis is neither satisfying nor complete. The free speech clause protects government restraints on expression not only in organized, formal political settings but also in private, one-on-one communication. If social dancing counts as speech, then it is speech whether done in one's home or in a commercial dance hall. The dancer can be understood to be communicating and associating with those around him or her or with a specific dance partner.

From a doctrinal perspective, treating social dance as speech runs into problems like those associated with artistic and cultural dancing. Like these other forms, social dancing may sometimes be intended as an expressive act, or it may be done for fun or for exercise. It sometimes may be understood by its "audience" as conveying a message, and many times it may not. Even when it is seen as communicative, it is more likely to be viewed as expressing emotion rather than an identifiable cognitive message.

From the standpoint of First Amendment theory, social dancing is rarely a means of advancing democracy, except perhaps in instances when it is done as part of a formal social protest.[9] Does social dancing contribute to the search for truth? Here is where the overlap among

dance categories becomes important. Social dancing can have important cultural components even when not part of a ritual or other more
traditional cultural dance. Such dancing can serve a function of social
cohesion, which state interference can undermine.

Autonomy arguments for treating social dancing as speech may include claims similar to those regarding instrumental music. Dancing is
often associated with emotion and feeling ("dancing for joy"). Individualized, self-created rhythmic movements can be a form of experience
and expression that is part of the fulfillment of an autonomous emotional life.[10]

Another theoretical argument for covering social dancing as speech
is the surprisingly common impulse of governments to regulate it.
Over the course of history, social dance has been the subject of government bans for many of the same reasons as restrictions on music.
The tango and even the turkey trot and the waltz have been targeted
as conduct that promotes licentiousness and inappropriate sexual contact and suggestiveness.[11] In more contemporary times in the United
States, there have been bans on specific dances popular among teens,
from the twist[12] to the Harlem shake,[13] and on social dances among
young people more generally, as memorialized in the popular (though
not critically acclaimed) film *Footloose*. But fictional accounts aside,
that movie is based on real life events that have arisen in small towns
across America. As Ricardo Ainslie recounts in his book *No Dancin'
in Anson: An American Story of Race and Social Change*, the town of
Anson, Texas, once had an ordinance making it unlawful "for any person or persons, firm or association of persons to carry on, foster or
operate any public dance hall where people assemble for the purpose
of dancing."[14]

Moreover, social dancing bans are not limited to small towns; even
New York City has a little-known restriction. Since 1926, New York has
banned dancing in restaurants and bars that do not have cabaret licenses,
which currently are issued to fewer than 120 establishments. A Brooklyn
bar owner has filed a federal lawsuit challenging the law as a violation
of his and his patrons' First Amendment speech and association rights.
According to the suit, New York imposes onerous conditions and zoning
restrictions that make it very difficult for restaurant and bar owners to
obtain a cabaret license and permit social dancing on their premises.[15]

Governments may attempt to disrupt the social discourse that dancing involves in order to maintain racial and cultural boundaries. As Gerald Torres observes about the Anson ban on social dancing, "The anti-dancing ordinance was a proxy for all of the fears that the traditional leaders had that the close proximity of bodies on the dance floor would lead to other intimacies that would fundamentally alter the social relationships between these groups."[16] Similarly, the historical provenance of the New York City dancing ban resonates with a racial subtext theme. That law was enacted during the Harlem Renaissance, and the plaintiffs claim that the law was originally designed to restrict jazz music in clubs patronized by African Americans and as a means of limiting interracial dancing. Indeed, another provision of that law permitted establishments without cabaret licenses to play "incidental" musical entertainment but prohibited the playing of wind, brass, and percussion instruments, which are more commonly used to perform jazz, until a state court declared that provision unconstitutional. The city subsequently repealed that restriction.[17]

In examining social dancing as speech, extensions of other arguments about nonpropositional expression as speech are perhaps less persuasive. Social dancing may less frequently be associated with any form of meaning than other types of expression are. Its function may bear less of a family resemblance to political or other traditionally protected speech than even other forms of dance do. It is also probably the case that aesthetic theory has less to say about social dancing than about artistic dance and other performing arts.

D. Erotic Dancing

As with art and music, the state's impulse to censor dance has often been driven by its concerns about the harms associated with its sexual provocativeness, real or imagined, as well as its desire to regulate morality. It is not surprising, therefore, that the overwhelming focus of government regulation, case law, and scholarship about dancing involves nude or seminude erotic dancing. Indeed, the Supreme Court has examined the First Amendment implications of state regulation of dance as expression almost exclusively in the context of erotic dancing.[18] Erotic dancing raises different issues than other forms of dance do. For example, how important is the question of aesthetic "value" to deciding that something is speech? We have already seen that there are significant dangers in trying to justify the regulation of other forms of artistic expression on the basis of the state's definition of quality or taste.

Starting again with the doctrinal approach, to the extent that erotic dancing is expressive, it is not likely to be intended or understood to convey a particularized message. But that is also true of virtually all other dance forms. Some specific dances might bear more directly propositional content, but that claim also cuts across the different types of dance we are discussing. Assuming we are talking about nude or seminude dancing that is "merely" suggestive, it is easier to conceive of erotic dance as speech. It is routinely performed in public places for an audience. It is accompanied by music. Many people would argue that it shares artistic components of creativity, rhythm, movement, and coordination with other forms of dance.

From a theoretical standpoint, it is difficult to construct an argument about how erotic dancing promotes democratic self-governance. Arguments about the truth-seeking function of erotic dance may, as in other areas, turn on how we define truth. Like other forms of nonpropositional speech, erotic dancing can be a manner of expressing and experiencing emotion. As Justice David Souter observed, "dancing as a performance directed to an actual or hypothetical audience gives expression at least to generalized emotion or feeling, and where the dancer is nude or nearly so the feeling expressed, in the absence of some contrary clue, is eroticism, carrying an endorsement of erotic experience. Such is the expressive content of the dances described in the record."[19] On this understanding, erotic dancing can be considered to be conduct that facilitates feelings of truth about one's sexuality and emotional life, in contrast to the repression of such feelings.

The law has increasingly suggested room under our Constitution for sexual autonomy,[20] and erotic dancing could therefore be covered under a self-realization justification for free speech. However, if erotic dance is an act of sexual independence, then the question becomes, as we have previously discussed, why it is not covered as a liberty under the Fourteenth Amendment rather than as a type of speech under the First Amendment. That is, as we discuss later in the context of pornography, is erotic dancing more like sex or more like speech?

One distinguishing factor is the degree to which erotic dancing can be considered to be an art form. It could be argued that ballet and modern dance (even if they sometimes have an erotic component) are recognized forms of artistic expression and therefore lay a greater claim to protection as speech than erotic dance does. This introduces the problem of whether the aesthetics of an enterprise ought to be a factor in determining whether it is speech. But if this is relevant, then what are the criteria? Are ballet and modern dance expressive because they are considered to be fine arts and taught in conservatories and other professional training venues? There is also the nontrivial concern about the decision maker. Perhaps the government ought not be in the position to judge aesthetic value, which presents dangers of subjective, discriminatory, and uninformed decisions that have enormous impact on a wide variety of activity that might otherwise be recognized as speech.

This brings us to whether erotic dance is speech because the government's reasons for regulating it are likely to be inconsistent with free speech values. However, this approach is likely to be unilluminating. On the one hand, a serious argument can be made that it is dangerous to allow the government to make decisions about what types of dance are morally or artistically acceptable. These types of judgments are not things that we ordinarily consider the state to be particularly well positioned to make, at least outside of the context of discretionary artistic funding.[21] Moreover, aesthetic and moral judgments about dance may change substantially over time. In earlier generations, Richard Strauss's opera *Salome* was censored or completely banned because of its inclusion of the "Dance of the Seven Veils," but now it is routinely performed in the finest opera houses.

On the other hand, governments have routinely made arguments that erotic dance performed in bars and clubs undermines social morality, is degrading to women, and leads to so-called secondary effects because of the impact that establishments that offer such dancing (among other erotic entertainment) and the customers they draw may have on the surrounding neighborhood.[22] It is of course true that the latter arguments may simply be cover for the state's aesthetic and moral judgments, but this underscores the limitations of the "danger of government censorship" approach to defining speech.

Comparing dance to visual art is also useful. Like art and music, artistic dance bears characteristics that make it resemble traditional forms of expression in important ways. Moreover, as discussed in chapter 2, even if we decided that some forms of dance are more speech-like than others, the risks associated with allowing courts to draw distinctions based on open-ended, subjective standards may outweigh any benefit to having a more individualized analysis. Finally, as with music, aesthetic theory might in some ways be a useful reference point for articulating what types of dance qualify as sufficiently artistic that the medium ought to count as speech.

II. Nonobscene Pornography

A natural follow-up to the discussion of erotic dance is the question of whether nonobscene pornography is speech. Obscenity has long been treated as outside the coverage of the First Amendment, but the Supreme Court's definition of such expression leaves ample room for constitutional coverage of expression that is sexually explicit but not legally "obscene."[23] The regulation of nonobscene pornography has been the subject of a great deal of controversy, including rigorous debates over the constitutionality of government efforts to ban it, such as an Indianapolis ordinance that created a civil damages cause of action against persons who trafficked in pornography or forced pornography on another person.[24]

Like many of the other forms of expression we have discussed, much pornography may not necessarily have an intended message or one that would be understood by its audience. In many forms, it is primarily the depiction of sexual acts. This has led some commentators to dismiss pornography as conduct that is not expressive. Indeed, some academic treatments of pornography advocate an understanding of the First Amendment suggesting that speech that appeals to the noncognitive simply ought not to be covered. Frederick Schauer famously argues that pornography is not speech because its primary purpose is to produce purely physical, rather than mental, stimulation. In his view, pornography is more like a sexual aid than a form of expression.[25] Similarly, as Cass Sunstein argues, "any attempt to distinguish among categories of speech must start with an effort to isolate what is uniquely important about speech in the first place. *Speech that is not intended to communicate a substantive message or that is directed solely to noncognitive capacities may be wholly or largely without the properties that give speech its special status."* Like Schauer, Sunstein contends that pornography appeals solely to sexual arousal rather than cognitive reasoning.[26]

This argument suggests that the First Amendment does not cover expression that is designed to appeal purely to noncognitive, emotional functions. But one could extend the same argument to art, instrumental music, and at least some types of dance. As argued in chapter 2, music is a form of communication that is valuable because of its unique capacity to stir emotion. To the extent music has the capacity to appeal to emotional sensibilities, or even to excite or create a "mood" that enhances the libido, it is also directed at and touches our noncognitive capacities and might, under these arguments, fall outside the bounds of the First Amendment. Conversely, if artistic expression *is* speech covered by the First Amendment on the basis of its appeal to the emotional rather than the cognitive, why don't the same arguments for its inclusion mean that pornography is also speech, the regulation of which courts ought to scrutinize under the First Amendment?

A partial response is that there may be other arguments for covering artistic expression under the First Amendment that are not tied exclusively to its emotionally communicative value but are also tied to the notion of protecting cultural values and experience and distrust of government orthodoxy where cultural and other social values are concerned. Pornography cannot be easily understood to advance a particular cultural value, at least not one recognized as culture in the common understanding of the term.

The First Amendment theory arguments for coverage of pornography closely resemble those discussed earlier with respect to erotic dance. Pornography probably cannot be seen as advancing democracy in either direct or indirect ways. It might be viewed as facilitating emotional expression and experience in ways that both promote the search for erotic or sexual truth and advance individual self-realization. It would be more difficult, though not impossible, to understand pornography as resembling an art form—as speech rather than sex. To the extent we do so, this might lead the government to have to make aesthetic judgments about pornography, meaning that there would have to be criteria for judging whether some pornography is artistic enough to merit First Amendment protection. This may simply be another example of the dilemma over aesthetics as a factor in determining what counts as speech. As Justice John Harlan famously wrote in *Cohen v. California*, "it is . . . often true that one man's vulgarity is another's lyric."[27]

III. Sports

As suggested earlier, some forms of dance closely resemble various forms of athletic performance, with the closest comparisons coming from activities such as gymnastics and figure skating. Genevieve Lakier has argued that competitive athletic events are a form of speech covered by the First Amendment. She points out that, like theater, ballet, and symphonic concerts, spectator sports provide a form of audience-oriented entertainment that is expressive. Applying the *Spence* test, Lakier suggests that the Supreme Court has been less rigid about applying the intent to convey a message requirement when the activity is "audience-oriented." That may be true, but as we have discussed, the Court does so primarily because the intent requirement poses doctrinal problems when applied to art, music, and other forms of speech that are presumptively covered. Lakier notes that sports' entertainment value does not distinguish them from other expressive forms, such as movies, which have been recognized as speech. She also rejects an aesthetics-based distinction between art and sports, noting that many sports seek to communicate messages of "grace and beauty" and that they communicate in other ways as well. Lakier also argues that the competitive nature of sports, often used to distinguish it from artistic performances, does not make it any less communicative but simply reflects the different cultural value that we place on these activities.[28]

Lakier's argument is that determining whether activities are speech under the First Amendment turns largely on the social context in which we understand that conduct. She draws on social science literature to demonstrate that competitive athletes participate in sports not solely to win the competition but also to put on a good performance for the audience and to exhibit skill and excellence. Moreover, she argues, the desire to communicate these messages extends to those who fund, promote, and regulate sports competition as well. Sports are often more spontaneous and less scripted than art, but Lakier claims that this actually enhances the authenticity of sports as expression in ways that make it more like speech than other forms of conduct. From the audience's perspective, sports can be a "powerful vehicle of collective identification," akin perhaps to instrumental music's function as constructing cultural cohesion.[29]

Finally, Lakier's argument for covering sports as speech turns to First Amendment theory. While she acknowledges the counterintuitive nature of the idea that competitive sports promote democracy, she argues for a more expansive vision of that theoretical objective that includes coverage of communicative activities that influence "how members of the polity understand and imagine the world around them." Sports, she argues, "help shape ideas of what virtues matter and who possesses them." Competitive sports also advance the search for truth—while art may promote aesthetic and psychological truth, sports advances thinking about what she calls "moral" truth. Autonomy-based arguments for treating sports as speech turn on the claim that the freedom to engage in sports competition is, like the freedom to write, paint, sculpt, compose, or choreograph, critical to one's self-realization. Lakier argues that "it is hard to think of another genre of performance in which the themes of individual autonomy and self-mastery are more pronounced than they are in sport."[30]

Interestingly, historical examples provide support for the argument that sport is a form of expression that advances self-governance. As part of the 1899 Finnish "Press Days" events to protest increasing Russian control, discussed in chapter 1, rally organizers put together a sports demonstration to communicate the Finns' ability and willingness to wage resistance. As one commentator described it, "The affair bristled with meaning. . . . There was the sheer physical prowess, the primal power, the stark courage on display. What better way for Finns to demonstrate their aptitudes or to reveal their willingness to do battle, be it social or military?"[31]

Lakier's arguments raise interesting questions but also face difficult challenges. Much of her argument rests on the proposition that sports is very much like forms of artistic performance, which are presumptively speech. This is a widely accepted but nonetheless shaky foundation. As we have seen, the notion that art forms are protected is itself not undeniably supportable under current First Amendment doctrine or theory. Moreover, relying on audience-based expression is likely over- and underinclusive. It would exclude recreational sports or sports done for exercise from consideration as speech; but if painting and playing the violin are speech, then they are speech even when done in private without an audience. Why would the same not be true for privately con- ducted sporting activities? Moreover, it is not clear where the line would be drawn about performances before audiences. On her account, is a rodeo speech? What about a monster truck rally?

Furthermore, family-resemblance arguments seem a little harder here than they do in the case of art, music, and nonsense. The exten- sion of First Amendment coverage to competitive sports seems to cre- ate boundary problems similar to those generated by artistic expression. The comment "What part of 'martial *arts*' don't you understand?" sug- gests as much.

IV. Culinary Arts

Unlike visual arts, music, and dance, the culinary arts have never been considered a form of constitutionally protected expression. But there is a nontrivial argument that culinary arts, at least at their highest levels, are a form of expression. Fine culinary preparations are intended by their creators to communicate through appeal not only to taste but to the senses of sight, texture, and smell—the preparation and presentation of food can be as much an aesthetic endeavor as a functional one.[32] While the expressive experience may be somewhat ephemeral, often so is the spoken word or the musical note.

While there is no case law or academic commentary addressing cu- linary artistic expression under the First Amendment, the related field of copyright law has sometimes addressed the question in a somewhat analogous analysis. As one commentator has observed, "a chef may cre- ate art when he designs a dish or a meal that presents patterns of harmo- nious or contrasting flavors, textures, colors, and plating arrangements that are intended to stimulate his patrons' aesthetic sense, and patrons may act as art critics when they contemplate their dishes and appreciate them as visual and flavorful expressions of art."[33] Of course, not all food preparation falls within what we might define as culinary arts. Much cooking is done at the most rudimentary level for the simple purpose of consuming calories to provide basic sustenance. To go back to the sports example, perhaps the difference between cooking and culinary arts is like the difference between playing basketball with one's friends and watching a professional game in a public arena. At the same time, in examining other areas of expression, the Supreme Court has repeatedly warned of the dangers of making aesthetic judgments among different modes of expression as a part of free speech analysis.

Like many of the expressive forms we have discussed, culinary arts do not always provoke a cognitive response in their consumers. However, they communicate in many of the same ways as other nonverbal communication. In this way, culinary arts do bear some family resemblance to other modes of expression that are more widely accepted as speech. For example, culinary arts share many of the features that we have discussed in the context of treating instrumental music as speech. Many people argue that, much like music, culinary artistic expression can be an important manner of conveying emotions and manifesting emotional connections between the cook and his or her "audience," although others dispute that claim.[34] In many cultures, cooking is often viewed as an expression of love, particularly among family members. Cooking and the related communal dining are also critical components of many cultural and religious rituals, such as the Chinese moon festival and the Passover Seder.

First Amendment theory may offer some insights into the expressive nature of food. Even defining democracy quite broadly, it is hard to articulate a specific way in which free culinary expression advances self-governance. As with other art forms, culinary artistic endeavors could be said to promote the search for truth about culture, aesthetics, even emotion. And if we understand the culinary arts to be a project of individualized expression of these same values, we could imagine them as a form of self-realization.

As in other areas, the government's reasons for regulating food may also be of analytical interest. Governments routinely regulate or ban different types of food for a number of ostensibly legitimate reasons, most commonly to promote food safety and prevent animal cruelty. In the face of these restrictions, people have argued that the state has in fact restricted culinary traditions as a means of stamping out a culture.

In California, nonprofit organizations representing the cultural interests of Chinese Americans recently challenged a state law banning the sale of sharks' fins, arguing that the law "was directed at suppressing the practices and traditions of Californians of Chinese national origin."[35] While this is a discrimination claim rather than a speech claim, it demonstrates that some forms of food regulation can be construed as a form of cultural suppression. The suit was ultimately unsuccessful because the law was found to be facially neutral, and the state presented strong reasons that its law advanced interests in preventing extinction of sharks and animal cruelty that were independent of any cultural motivation.[36] For similar reasons, First Amendment claims would likely have failed because the state presented a non-speech-related reason to regulate the underlying conduct.

In other circumstances, culinary bans might have more potentially discriminatory motives. In 2009, Lucca, a walled city situated in the Tuscan region of Italy, adopted an official ban on the opening of new ethnic restaurants in order to preserve the cultural and historical identity of its indigenous cuisine. The ban most affected popular kebab restaurants, suggesting to many people that the ban was motivated not by preserving regional cuisine but by hostility to increasing immigration.[37]

Indeed, the determination of which foods are culturally appropriate is in many instances state driven. For example, the United Nations Educational Scientific and Cultural Organization (UNESCO) has listed some indigenous foods as forms of intangible heritage protected by international law.[38] The United States and several states have banned slaughtering horses for human consumption because they are viewed as recreational and companion animals, even though the agricultural industry routinely kills other mammals for American diets.[39] Americans of Scottish ancestry who wish to celebrate their culture have complained that the traditional dish haggis is effectively prohibited in the United States because of a federal regulation that forbids the use of livestock lungs in human food.[40] In Pittsburgh, there has been mounting controversy over a restaurant called the Conflict Café, which seeks to promote public discourse by serving food indigenous to cultures with which the United States is currently in conflict.[41] In some circles, there were even criticisms of the African American community's embracing of "soul food as a reminder of the cultural genocide perpetrated by slavery."[42]

Finally, another context in which it has been claimed that food has an important expressive component is in the free speech claims of bakery owners who have sought a religious exemption from state laws prohibiting discrimination on the basis of sexual orientation. The bakery owners have suggested in these cases that they do not categorically refuse to provide service to or sell other baked goods to same-sex couples but that there is a special expressive component associated with baking a wedding cake, and therefore they have a First Amendment right to refuse that service. In essence, these suits argue that laws compelling these bakeries to make wedding cakes for same-sex weddings is a form of forced speech, requiring them to engage in expression that endorses a practice they oppose on religious grounds. One of the central points of controversy in such cases is whether baking a cake is speech or conduct. In a recent Colorado decision, the appellate court rejected a bakery's free speech claim on the ground that "the act of designing and selling a wedding cake to all customers free of discrimination does not convey a celebratory message about same-sex weddings likely to be understood by those who view it." Of course, the specific question at issue in the religious bakery owner cases does not control the more general question of whether culinary arts can ever be speech. The Colorado appellate court conceded that "a wedding cake, in some circumstances, may convey a particularized message celebrating same-sex marriage" but concluded that this was not at issue in this case because the bakery owner refused to provide the service without having had any discussions about the cake's design or any written inscriptions.[43]

As a final note, we observe that other forms of nonverbal aesthetic expression could be added to the list of speech that advances both culture and beauty. Fashion, tattoo artistry, and formal garden design, among others, are considered by many people to be expressive in ways that are sufficiently communicative that they should be covered by the First Amendment. If music, art, and nonsense are recognized as speech, why not saggy pants, an abstract tattoo, or "the gardens of Sissinghurst Castle and of Giverny"?[44] As the Seventh Circuit recently observed, "Though plants do not speak, this need not exclude all gardens from the protection of the [free speech] clause, for the clause has been expanded by judicial interpretation to embrace other silent expression, such as paintings."[45]

V. Subliminal Messages in Advertising

Another form of nonpropositional expression is subliminal image advertising. The practice of subliminal advertising involves the inclusion of a hidden message that conveys the seller's true goal ("buy more cigarettes") even though that message does not overtly appear in the body of the advertisement. The few courts that have addressed the issue have concluded that subliminal advertising is not speech.[46]

Subliminal advertising presents a different dilemma for free speech theory than do the issues raised in prior chapters. Unlike the other areas we have discussed, subliminal advertising does purport to convey a message. "Buy more cigarettes" is quite clearly a message, and if subliminal advertising is effective, it is a message that will appeal to the cognitive senses of the viewer. As John Greenman observes, "Subliminal advertising conveys 'I want popcorn'—an idea—through language, and conveying an idea through language is the paradigmatic instance of communication in typical First Amendment discourse."[47] Subliminal advertising therefore meets the first part of the *Spence* test, because it is intended to communicate a message, but not the second, because it is not one that is, at least consciously, understood. One could imagine that the failure of understanding is sufficient to disqualify this practice as speech, but if the listener does indeed buy more cigarettes or popcorn, then the advertising has been effective in communicating its message. Perhaps, then, it is not the case that subliminal advertising is not speech but rather that it is subject to government regulation because it is in some ways like false advertising in that it is deceptive because the message is hidden. But that seems to suggest that it *is* speech and that the government has a compelling reason for regulating it.

Scholars have attempted to distinguish subliminal messages from speech on the basis that they do not, in fact, appeal to cognitive processes. As Sunstein argues, because subliminal advertising is directed solely to noncognitive capacities, it is "entitled to less than full first amendment protection."[48] But if art, music, and nonsense, which also communicate in ways that appeal to the noncognitive, are covered by the First Amendment, the same arguments might apply to this type of advertising, which has not been widely accepted as speech. Commentators suggest that images used to sell tobacco products, such as the "Joe

Camel" logo, can be constitutionally regulated because image advertising does not convey a "particularized message" that appeals to reasoning or cognition but simply communicates a "generalized aesthetic impact producing an emotional response."[49] Indeed, in arguing for the lack of protection, one commentator suggests that image advertising is unprotected precisely *because* it is exactly like instrumental music.[50]

First Amendment theory may be more helpful here than in other categories of nonpropositional expression. Because of the obscured nature of the message, subliminal advertising might be argued to be antithetical to both democracy and the search for truth because rather than facilitating discourse and free thought, it deprives the viewer of the ability to consciously reason through his or her decisions, whether they be political, economic, or otherwise. Similarly, while the freedom to engage in subliminal advertising might advance the speaker's autonomy, it may simultaneously deprive the listener of autonomy by interfering with the process of free decision making. Similar arguments have been made to support the claim that lies should not be protected by the First Amendment.[51]

The government's likely reasons for prohibiting subliminal advertising are also probably more likely to be legitimate rather than contrived as an excuse to distort public discourse (unless such advertising were to be regulated only when carried out by opponents of the government). And it is hard to make a family-resemblance argument here, as subliminal messages do not tend to share many of the characteristics we value in traditional political speech.

VI. New Media

> [W]hatever the challenges of applying the Constitution to ever-advancing technology, "the basic principles of freedom of speech and the press, like the First Amendment's command, do not vary" when a new and different medium for communication appears.
> —*Brown v. Entertainment Merchants Association* (2011)

We close by discussing how the treatment of music, art, and nonsense might inform our judgments about emerging forms of expression available through new media. The courts had to grapple with these questions when movies first became an important medium of artistic expression in the early twentieth century.[52] More contemporary iterations of new media include simulated versions of actions, such as video games and virtual reality, as well as technologically enhanced manners of creating, gathering, and disseminating information, such as data collection, video recording, and digital mapping. State regulation of each of these activities can have substantial implications for free speech values.

A. Video Games and Virtual Reality

Two versions of modern technology that may closely resemble traditional speech are video games and virtual reality. Both involve computer-driven imagery that depicts images, events, sounds, and sometimes dialogue.

In *Brown*, the Supreme Court directly addressed whether video games are speech in a case challenging a 2005 California law that regulated the sale of violent video games to minors. The statute's definition of such video games paralleled in many ways the definition of obscenity under First Amendment law, even though the latter is focused on sexually prurient, rather than violent, material. In reviewing the constitutionality of California's restriction, the Supreme Court held that video games are a form of expression covered by the First Amendment, an argument not even disputed by the state.

Because video games are played by, rather than for, individuals and often do not involve conventional verbal expression, there was at least some question whether their regulation triggered First Amendment considerations. The Court dispensed with this argument in short measure. First, it recognized that it had long since abandoned trying to distinguish between politics and entertainment and reasoned that to do so was a dangerous enterprise. Video games embody components of expression that clearly count as speech when disaggregated; video game characters frequently speak, there are images depicted on the player's computer screen, and instrumental music is often a key component to the games. Thus, the Court noted that "[l]ike the protected books, plays, and movies that preceded them, video games communicate ideas—and even social messages—through many familiar literary devices (such as characters, dialogue, plot, and music) and through features distinctive to the medium (such as the player's interaction with the virtual world)."[53] It is clear, therefore, that the multimedia aspect of video games constitutes their most important expressive component. Consider, in contrast, whether an early version of computerized chess would be properly characterized as speech. The Court did not, however, specify or give examples of the type of messages video games express.

Again, because of rapid technological development, video games and other forms of electronic entertainment not only can reproduce relatively realistic scenarios that can be viewed on screen but also can involve simulations that make viewers feel like they are actually embedded in the experience they are watching. Such technology creates a universe of virtual reality, another form of interactive viewing that makes participants feel sensations that they are actually only observing through an electronic device. Thus, there is substantial, but not complete, overlap between the way that video games and virtual reality programs communicate.

The Supreme Court examined a type of virtual reality in *Ashcroft v. Free Speech Coalition*, in which it struck down parts of the Child Pornography Prevention Act of 1996, which prohibited "virtual child pornography." Such material involves "sexually explicit images that appear to depict minors but were produced without using any real children" but rather were created "using adults who look like minors or by using computer imaging." In some senses, the question of whether virtual reality images are speech is a relatively simple one, perhaps less complex than many of the questions we have addressed in this book. To the extent that virtual imagery is generated by computer technology, it is hard to distinguish it from animation or any other form of moving picture images. Indeed, the *Ashcroft* Court seemed to take it for granted that child pornography created by computer imaging is speech; the only question it addressed was whether that speech should be exempted from First Amendment coverage under *New York v. Ferber*.[54]

Because video games and virtual reality both involve expressive components, they more clearly fall under the umbrella of speech than do other types of technologically enhanced expression. In terms of First Amendment theory, they seem clearly to be an element of expressive and experiential autonomy. The freedom to play video games and experience virtual reality images might also be suggested to advance self-governance. One can imagine video games that contain highly politicized content such that they promote thought about policy issues ranging from gun control to climate change. At first glance, the truth rationale might be a more difficult fit for these modes of expression because they are often by definition fantasy-based and escapist. However, by escaping the real world, participants may be seeking an alternative universe and in that way rejecting the truths of reality. The freedom of speech facilitates freedom of thought, even if that thought is not premised on what the government finds acceptable. Indeed, the *Ashcroft* Court even invoked *Stanley v. Georgia*, noting that "[t]he government 'cannot constitutionally premise legislation on the desirability of controlling a person's private thoughts.'"[55]

There may also be risks that government efforts to regulate video games and virtual reality are motivated by a desire to impose control over thoughts and beliefs that might be facilitated by these technologies. The temptation of the state to focus on the content of such images in imposing regulations may be strong, which suggests that these media should be areas of heightened First Amendment concern. The government, for its part, may argue that the content of these games and images causes harms to both their participants and to third parties should the messages influence the behavior of the participants. In *Brown*, California argued that some video games would promote violent behavior in teenagers. In *Ashcroft*, the federal government claimed that virtual reality child pornography might be used by pedophiles to encourage children to engage in sexual activity or might encourage pedophiles to seek out real child pornography. In both instances, the Court rejected these claims, concluding that in pursuing these legitimate interests, the governments were trying to control thoughts and ideas rather than conduct.

B. Data, Video Recording, and Digital Mapping

In recent years, legal scholars have begun to examine whether the collection and dissemination of data is speech under the First Amendment. The issue has arisen largely because of technological developments that enable massive production, aggregation, and communication of data, activities that can have enormous speech and privacy implications. Moreover, those developments have facilitated the ability of computers to generate information and messages, much of which resemble traditional speech. Data, however, can be collected, recorded, and delivered in many different forms, which raise a variety of dilemmas under free speech law. If data is speech and its collection covered by the First Amendment, many privacy regulations and other government efforts to control data may be at risk. Legal scholars acknowledge such concerns and have examined data as speech on a context-specific basis.

Some scholars have focused on data's function as a form of creating and informing knowledge. For example, Jane Bambauer has observed that much speech is based on data but not all data is speech. Her work explores the tension between concerns about collection of private data and interference with the creation of knowledge, which is sometimes possible only through data gathering. She also acknowledges that while free speech doctrine has typically protected the dissemination of data that already exists or is in the speaker's possession, it has not always been hospitable to the freedom to gather information. Though the act of collecting information is not in and of itself communicative, and therefore does not meet either the intent or understanding elements of *Spence*, Bambauer argues what we have discussed throughout this book—that the *Spence* test does not map well onto inquiries about nonpropositional communication and is better designed to address questions of when the state may regulate conduct that may have both symbolically expressive and nonspeech components.[56]

Bambauer reconceptualizes data gathering not as a simple mechanical task but as the creation of knowledge. Understood as such, she argues, the right to gather and record data is supported by First Amendment theory because it furthers the search for truth, advances deliberative democracy, and fulfills individual self-determination. State laws that regulate data collection interfere with the marketplace of ideas, she argues, because they control the flow of important information that can strongly influence public beliefs and opinions. An important corollary of the free speech right is the right of the speaker's audience to hear what is being said. Bambauer notes that "[a] person's opportunity to receive information and ideas should be protected whether he receives information from another person (a traditional 'speaker') or through his direct observations of the world." With respect to promoting self-governance, she argues that constitutional protection of data collection, even involving information of a personal nature, can be as important in the political realm as in other areas of public discourse and that such information is often a critical component of exposing government wrongdoing and holding officials accountable for their behavior. Finally, Bambauer argues that there is a particularly strong claim that protection of the creation of knowledge through freedom to gather data furthers the interest in autonomy. Access to data can facilitate critical life decision making and promote independent thought.[57]

Others have focused on the problems of understanding data and its transmission as speech, particularly when the information is compiled or communicated by computers rather than humans. For instance, computers employing algorithmic formulas may produce messages that closely resemble human speech, such as when a program aggregates articles about a particular subject and presents the data to readers in a synthesized form, much like a virtual bulletin board. Stuart Benjamin reasons that such expression, though produced from an algorithm, is speech-like and that "[t]he Court has never found a substantive communication that was sendable, receivable, and actually sent to be outside First Amendment coverage unless it fell into one of the Court's articulated exceptions."[58] In contrast, Tim Wu argues that viewing algorithmically created data as speech can lead to absurdly capacious understandings that might include coverage of a car alarm, which collects and communicates a message in a manner that is widely understood but cannot reasonably be characterized as speech. Wu disaggregates computer-generated expression using a functionality model that allows room for state regulation of the functional aspects of the communication process while still providing protection for its expressive component. As he briefly encapsulates his thinking, "Generally, we can distinguish software that serves as a 'speech product' from that which is a 'communication tool.' Communication tools fall into the categories just described: they primarily facilitate the communications of another person, or perform some task for the user. In contrast, speech products are technologies like blog posts, tweets, video games, newspapers, and so on, that are viewed as vessels for the ideas of a speaker, or whose content has been consciously curated."[59]

One pervasive aspect of data gathering is audiovisual recording. Not surprisingly, courts have therefore turned their attention to the question of whether video recording is speech or speech-related conduct.[60] Controversies over restrictions on citizen cell phone recordings of encounters with police, recordings by drones, and surreptitious recordings by undercover investigators have spawned questions about whether such conduct is sufficiently expressive to be entitled to First Amendment protection.

While it would be easy to reflexively dismiss video recording as conduct rather than speech, it is conduct that bears close comparisons to more traditional information gathering that would be unquestionably protected under the First Amendment, such as note taking and journal writing. With the advent of modern technology, recording has become as easy as, perhaps easier than, taking handwritten notes and has the advantage of providing an accurate self-authenticating account of the recorded events, assuming that the video is not altered or edited in ways that undermine its accuracy. Thus, video recording, like other forms of data collection, can be understood as knowledge creation.

In the first comprehensive academic account of image capture, Seth Kreimer carefully lays out the case for the notion that, at least in public, recording images is a form of speech. First, recording may play an important role in holding public officials accountable and in promoting the ability of citizens to meaningfully participate in public dialogue.[61] Recording can also serve a revelatory function with regard to all manner of other types of public knowledge aside from politics, including discovering information necessary for the government to serve the public, revealing private misconduct, and spurring moral and aesthetic debates. It is probably a little harder to find an autonomy-based justification for video recording as a form of speech, though it could certainly be argued that individuals might better achieve self-realization through the autonomous act of video recording as a method of developing their mental and intellectual faculties by informing themselves about the surrounding world.

More recently, it has been argued that even some recordings on private property, and without the consent of the recorded parties, is speech or conduct preparatory to speech under the First Amendment, at least if the recording pertains to a matter of public concern. Such an argument could be used to protect not only those who record police misconduct on their cell phones in public but also undercover journalists or investigators who gain lawful access to private property and secretly record illegal or otherwise newsworthy activities.[62]

A third example of information gathering that is more widely available because of new technology is digital mapping, which shares some of the same characteristics as video recording. Digital mapping is the use of technology to create digital maps of the world, such as Google Earth, in ways that permit users to engage in virtual travel, observing images of locations across the globe from their electronic devices. The speech question is not whether viewing such images is covered by the First Amendment but rather whether the use of technology by individuals or even by automated computers to obtain such data is a type of speech. Like data collection and video recording, digital mapping has the potential to provide vast amounts of information and experience to its viewers but also may generate social problems by interfering with property and privacy interests. There has been much attention paid to the regulation of such mapping to protect those interests but less attention to the constitutional implications of such laws. As Marc Jonathan Blitz has written, there are strong justifications for treating digital mapping as speech. The ability to collect and create virtual maps is a form of information gathering that can result in the advancement of self-governance, generate images that inform the experiences and truths of their viewers, and promote autonomy by ensuring the right to observation. Blitz argues that the First Amendment can be sufficiently expansive to cover digital mapping without sacrificing privacy interests of those who wish not to be observed.[63]

None of the conduct discussed in this section bears much resemblance to traditional speech because while each involves speech-like behavior, the underlying acts frequently do not communicate particular messages. For example, the act of video recording precedes the act of exhibiting that recording, but the latter looks more like the speech we recognize under the First Amendment. Of course, a video can be simultaneously recorded and broadcast, which makes the distinction less clear.[64] In most instances, however, it is not obvious that information and image gathering are sufficiently similar to overt expression of messages such that they should clearly be included as speech.

At the same time, unchecked government regulation of these activities may have profound implications for public discourse. There often may be legitimate interests in regulating data collection, video recording, and digital mapping to protect personal privacy and some tangible property rights, yet the state may also have pernicious motives to suppress access to information critical to the formation of beliefs and ideas. The trick is to sort out which situations truly call for regulation and which generate mistrust of government power such that they require constitutional protection.

* * *

Earlier in this chapter, we wrote of "cultural dance." We have seen a different use of the word *cultural*, as a general account of free speech beyond words. In that account, what counts as an activity covered by the First Amendment is determined not by grand theorizing or granular doctrinal analysis but by what at any specific moment is culturally recognized as "speech." Justice David Souter's canonical statement about Pollock, Schoenberg, and Carroll is then to be understood as an assertion—undoubtedly correct—about contemporary (legal) culture.

Of course, at any specific time, not everything is culturally recognized as speech: the *Stanglin* case, for example, suggests that social dancing is not so recognized (yet?). How some things come to be regarded as covered speech is somewhat mysterious. Advocates for the culturalist view sometimes gesture in the direction of some vaguely identified "social movements," but that seems implausible in at least some contexts: there was a "movement" of abstract expressionism in the mid-twentieth-century United States, but that movement was not something scholars of "social" movements study. And *in media res* claims that some activity heretofore not recognized as covered by the First Amendment *should* be so recognized are, on this culturalist view, arguments for changing our cultural understandings, cast in the form of assertions that "the law" already recognizes them as First Amendment speech.

Our effort throughout this book has been deflationary, at least in one sense: we have argued that reasonably comprehensive approaches to the First Amendment—whether they be doctrinal, predicated on political theory, or resting on aesthetic or linguistic theory—do not provide comprehensive answers to questions about free speech beyond words. Even the most promising approach, which draws on the idea that the topics we have examined bear some sort of family resemblance to speech in words, proves—or at least so we suggest—to provide only sporadic guidance. Perhaps the best that can be done, then, is to assemble bits and pieces from whatever happens to come to hand.

Yet, perhaps, that too says something important not only about free speech beyond words or only about the First Amendment more generally but also about what constitutional law *is*: a legal practice of using what is at hand to address problems as they arise.

ACKNOWLEDGMENTS

Mark V. Tushnet: Chapter 2 has benefited from extended conversations with Rebecca Tushnet. I thank the students in a reading group on art and the First Amendment (Fall term, 2010) for helping me think through the issues addressed here, participants in a seminar at Brown University offered by Corey Breitschneider, and Randall Bezanson, Glenn Cohen, Richard Fallon, Martha Minow, L. Michael Seidman, and Rebecca Zeitlow for their comments on earlier versions.

Alan K. Chen: Chapter 1 is an updated and revised version of an article originally published as "Instrumental Music and the First Amendment," 66 *Hastings Law Journal* 381 (2015). The *Hastings Law Journal* has generously granted permission for its use here. I am most grateful to my coauthors, Mark Tushnet and Joseph Blocher, for the opportunity to collaborate on this fascinating project. Thanks also to Larry Alexander, Rebecca Aviel, the late Randall Bezanson, Ashutosh Bhagwat, Henry Chen, Richard Fallon, Neil Haverstick, John Inazu, Tamara Kuennen, Nancy Leong, William Marshall, Sheldon Nahmod, Helen Norton, Justin Pidot, Tamara Piety, Seana Shiffrin, Michael Siebecker, James Weinstein, R. George Wright, and participants at Jack Balkin's 2013 Yale Freedom of Expression Scholars Conference for their thoughtful comments, insights, and suggestions on earlier versions of this work. My research assistants, Ellen Giarratana, Evan Grimes, Shawn Neal, and Tanya Sevy, and University of Denver Faculty Research Liaison Diane Burkhardt provided indispensable research support. I also thank Dean Marty Katz for his continued support of my work. Finally, thanks to my family for their patience and continued tolerance of the many distractions offered by the First Amendment.

Joseph Blocher: I am immensely grateful to Amy Adler, Mark Bartholomew, Stuart Benjamin, Ashutosh Bhagwat, Josh Chafetz, Alan Chen, Michael Coenen, Kristelia Garcia, Deborah Gerhardt, John Inazu, Adam Kolber, Tamara Piety, Jeff Powell, Jed Purdy, Dana Remus, Seana

Shiffrin, Neil Siegel, Zephyr Teachout, and Mark Tushnet for insightful comments; to participants in the Free Expression Scholars Conference held at Yale Law School in May 2013; and to Kara Duffle, Jordan Fly, Christopher Ford, John Long, and Courtland Tisdale for research assistance.

NOTES

INTRODUCTION

1. Hurley v. Irish-Am. Gay, Lesbian & Bisexual Grp. of Bos., Inc., 515 U.S. 557, 568–69 (1995) (citation omitted).
2. Chaplinsky v. New Hampshire, 315 U.S. 568, 571–72 (1942) (indicating that putative speech acts such as fighting words and obscenity fall outside the boundaries of the First Amendment in part because they "are no essential part of any exposition of ideas").
3. Spence v. Washington, 418 U.S. 405, 410–11 (1974) (articulating test to differentiate expression from unprotected conduct).
4. Frederick Schauer, "The Boundaries of the First Amendment: A Preliminary Exploration of Constitutional Salience," 117 *Harv. L. Rev.* 1765 (2004).
5. Ibid., 1767.
6. Ibid.
7. United States v. Stevens, 559 U.S. 460 (2010).
8. Sorrell v. IMS Health, Inc., 564 U.S. 552 (2011).
9. Brown v. Entm't Merchs. Ass'n, 564 U.S. 786 (2011).
10. Chen notes existing coverage for nonverbal expression (see chapter 1 in this volume); Tushnet argues that words are not necessary and probably not sufficient for First Amendment coverage (see chapter 2 in this volume).
11. United States v. Eichman, 496 U.S. 310, 312 (1990); Texas v. Johnson, 491 U.S. 397, 399 (1989).
12. City of Erie v. Pap's A.M., 539 U.S. 277, 285 (2000).
13. Miller v. California, 413 U.S. 15, 20 (1973) (alteration in original) (quoting Roth v. United States, 354 U.S. 476, 484 (1957)).
14. Chaplinsky v. New Hampshire, 315 U.S. 568, 571–72 (1942).
15. Adam Liptak, "Court's Free-Speech Expansion Has Far-Reaching Consequences," *N.Y. Times*, Aug. 17, 2015 (referring to *Reed v. Town of Gilbert*, a case involving the definition of content neutrality, as "the sleeper case of the last Supreme Court term").
16. Turner Broad. Sys. v FCC, 512 U.S. 622, 642–43 (1994).
17. Ward v. Rock Against Racism, 491 U.S. 781, 791 (1989).
18. Holder v. Humanitarian Law Project, 561 U.S. 1, 28 (2010).
19. The most commonly applicable standard requires a law to be "narrowly tailored to serve a significant governmental interest" and that it leave open "ample alternative channels of communication." *Ward*, 491 U.S. at 791.

20. United States v. Kokinda, 497 U.S. 720, 736 (1990) (treating a solicitation ban as content neutral and upholding it); Heffron v Int'l Soc. for Krishna Consciousness, Inc., 452 U.S. 640, 648 (1981) (same).

21. RAV v City of St Paul, 505 U.S. 377, 385 (1992) ("[B]urning a flag in violation of an ordinance against outdoor fires could be punishable, whereas burning a flag in violation of an ordinance against dishonoring the flag is not.").

22. Hill v. Colorado, 530 U.S. 703, 704 (2000).

23. McCullen v. Coakley, 134 S. Ct. 2518 (2014).

24. Spence v. Washington, 418 U.S. 405, 410–11 (1974).

25. See, e.g., Texas v. Johnson, 491 U.S. 397, 399, 404–6 (1989) (finding flag burning to be speech but without rigorous application of *Spence*); Nat'l Endowment for the Arts v. Finley, 524 U.S. 569 (1998) (assuming artwork to be covered without even discussing *Spence* in detail).

26. Robert H. Bork, "Neutral Principles and Some First Amendment Problems," 47 *Ind. L.J.* 1, 29 (1971) (arguing that the First Amendment protects only "criticisms of public officials and policies, proposals for the adoption or repeal of legislation or constitutional provisions and speech addressed to the conduct of any governmental unit in the country").

27. Robert Post, "Reconciling Theory and Doctrine in First Amendment Jurisprudence," 88 *Calif. L. Rev.* 2353, 2356 (2000).

28. See Alexander Meiklejohn, *Political Freedom* 73 (New York: Harper, 1960) (arguing that establishing truth through a marketplace of ideas "is not merely the 'best' test" but that "[t]here is no other").

29. Abrams v. United States, 250 U.S. 616, 630 (1919) (Holmes, J., dissenting).

30. Whitney v. California, 274 U.S. 357, 375 (1927) (Brandeis, J., concurring).

31. See, e.g., Sheldon H. Nahmod, "Artistic Expression and Aesthetic Theory: The Beautiful, the Sublime, and the First Amendment," 1987 *Wis. L. Rev.* 221, 241.

32. Bleistein v. Donaldson Lithographing Co., 188 U.S. 239, 251 (1903).

33. *Abrams*, 250 U.S. 616.

34. See David Cole, "Agon at Agora: Creative Misreadings in the First Amendment Tradition," 95 *Yale L.J.* 857, 875–78 (1986) (tracing the First Amendment doctrine's "philosophical origins" to John Milton, John Locke, John Stuart Mill, and others). See also John Milton, *Areopagitica: A Speech for the Liberty of Unlicensed Printing* 45 (1644; H. B. Cotterill ed., New York: Macmillan, 1959) ("Let her and falsehood grapple; who ever knew Truth put to the worse in a free and open encounter?").

35. Jacobellis v. Ohio, 378 U.S. 184, 197 (1964) (Stewart, J., concurring).

36. Cf. Joseph C. Hutcheson, Jr., "The Judgment Intuitive: The Function of the 'Hunch' in Judicial Decision," 14 *Cornell L.Q.* 274 (1929).

37. See generally Robert Post, *Democracy, Expertise, and Academic Freedom* (New Haven, CT: Yale University Press, 2012).

38. Hurley v. Irish-Am. Gay, Lesbian & Bisexual Grp. of Bos., Inc., 515 U.S. 557, 568–69 (1995) (citation omitted).

CHAPTER 1. INSTRUMENTAL MUSIC AND THE FIRST AMENDMENT

1. To hear the sound of a C#, see skr33d, "C#/Db 554.37 Hz Tone for Instrument Tuning," YouTube, Feb. 20, 2012, https://www.youtube.com/watch?v=_Ljbw-UpHjw.

2. To hear examples of glissandos as a piano technique, see StockhausenIsMyCat, "Great Pianists' Technique: Glissando," YouTube, Aug. 22, 2011, https://www.youtube.com/watch?v=4iqFvQjdcm8.

3. To hear a demonstration of Tuvan throat singing, see Tonio Delafuente, "Tuvan Throat Singing," YouTube, Sept. 17, 2014, https://www.youtube.com/watch?v=qx8hrhBZJ98.

4. Ludwig Von Beethoven, Symphony No. 5 in C Minor (1808). To hear the beginning of this work, see Classical Archives, "Beethoven—5th Symphony, 1st Movement: Allegro Con Brio," YouTube, Feb. 2, 2008, https://www.youtube.com/watch?v=B7pQytF2nak.

5. The Dave Brubeck Quartet, "Blue Rondo à La Turk," on *Time Out* (Columbia Records, 1959). To hear this recording, see woefulpoe's channel, "The Dave Brubeck Quartet—Blue Rondo à la Turk," Dec. 10, 2009, https://www.youtube.com/watch?v=vKNZqMod-xo.

6. The Jimi Hendrix Experience, "Purple Haze," on *Are You Experienced?* (MCA, 1967). To hear this recording, see The Jimi Hendrix Experience—Topic, "Purple Haze," Aug. 1, 2015, https://www.youtube.com/watch?v=hDy3J_xuGes&index=1&list=PLFLxSw9gDnsthbV_M1jYL1zh5TtptWWzK.

7. For a thoughtful consideration of the coverage question, see Frederick Schauer, "The Boundaries of the First Amendment: A Preliminary Exploration of Constitutional Salience," 117 *Harv. L. Rev.* 1765, 1767 (2004); see also Kent Greenawalt, *Speech, Crime, and the Uses of Language* 54 (New York: Oxford University Press, 1989); John Greenman, "On Communication," 106 *Mich. L. Rev.* 1337 (2008); R. George Wright, "What Counts as 'Speech' in the First Place? Determining the Scope of the Free Speech Clause," 37 *Pepp. L. Rev.* 1217 (2010).

8. First Amendment scholars use various terms to describe this characteristic of speech. In addition to "nonrepresentational," speech that does not convey a particular message has been labeled "nonpropositional" (see, e.g., Randall P. Bezanson, "Art and the Constitution," 93 *Iowa L. Rev.* 1593, 1596 (2008)) and "nonideational" (see, e.g., James Weinstein, "Participatory Democracy as the Central Value of American Free Speech Doctrine," 97 *Va. L. Rev.* 491, 499 n.45 (2011)). This chapter uses the terms interchangeably.

9. First Amendment law is by no means the only area in which music and law uncomfortably coexist. See James Boyle, *The Public Domain: Enclosing the Commons of the Mind* 122 (New Haven, CT: Yale University Press, 2008) ("Music is hard for copyright law to handle."); Michael W. Carroll, "Whose Music Is It Anyway? How We Came to View Musical Expression as a Form of Property," 72 *U. Cin. L. Rev.* 1405, 1407 (2004).

10. Schauer, "Boundaries of the First Amendment," 1773.

11. United States v. Eichman, 496 U.S. 310, 312 (1990); Texas v. Johnson, 491 U.S. 397, 399 (1989).

12. R.A.V. v. City of St. Paul, 505 U.S. 377, 395–96 (1992). But see Virginia v. Black, 538 U.S. 343, 347–48 (2003) (finding that cross burning, while expressive, may be prohibited when accompanied by intent to intimidate).

13. Hurley v. Irish-Am. Gay, Lesbian & Bisexual Grp. of Bos., 515 U.S. 557, 559 (1995).

14. Carey v. Brown, 447 U.S. 455, 460 (1980).

15. City of Erie v. Pap's A.M., 529 U.S. 277, 285 (2000).

16. Tinker v. Des Moines Indep. Cmty. Sch. Dist., 393 U.S. 503, 505–6 (1969).

17. Spence v. Washington, 418 U.S. 405, 406–7, 408, 415 (1974).

18. Ibid., 409.

19. Ibid., 410–11.

20. Another possibility is that the Court intended the *Spence* test to apply only to conduct that is not self-evidently communicative and not to forms of nonverbal artistic expression. See Miller v. Civil City of S. Bend, 904 F.2d 1081, 1125 (7th Cir. 1990) (Easterbrook, J., dissenting) (suggesting that music is not conduct but is closer to pure speech), *rev'd sub nom.* Barnes v. Glen Theatre, Inc., 501 U.S. 560 (1991); see also Seth F. Kreimer, "Pervasive Image Capture and the First Amendment: Memory, Discourse, and the Right to Record," 159 *U. Penn. L. Rev.* 335, 372 (2011) (suggesting that the Court only focuses on whether a message is conveyed when it examines conduct that is not inherently expressive). If this is the case, then the Court's failure to invoke *Spence* in artistic-expression cases is more understandable, though it has been far from clear in drawing this distinction if that was its intent.

21. Texas v. Johnson, 491 U.S. 397, 399, 404–6 (1989).

22. Nat'l Endowment for the Arts v. Finley, 524 U.S. 569, 573 (1998).

23. See Brief for Respondents at 36–37, ibid. (No. 97–371).

24. In chapter 2 in this volume, Mark Tushnet observes that the Court's treatment of the coverage of art in general under the First Amendment has been "remarkably casual."

25. Ward v. Rock Against Racism, 491 U.S. 781, 784–85 (1989). The city argued that the plaintiff's sound technicians might not be as familiar with outdoor sound mixing and with the band shell's acoustics or other surroundings and that musicians would respond to the poor mixing by turning up the volume, thus exacerbating the sound problems the city was trying to address. Ibid., 786; cf. Cooley v. Bd. of Wardens, 53 U.S. 299, 311 (1851) (examining the constitutionality of a statute requiring shipping companies to hire local pilots to navigate their ships into port to enhance safety because of the local pilots' familiarity with the shallow local waters).

26. *Ward*, 491 U.S. at 790 (citations omitted).

27. But see Miller v. Civil City of S. Bend, 904 F.2d 1081, 1096 (7th Cir. 1990) (Posner, J., concurring) (inferring that the *Ward* Court did not mean to limit its holding to music with lyrics), *rev'd sub nom.* Barnes v. Glen Theatre, Inc., 501 U.S. 560 (1991).

28. Southeastern Promotions v. Conrad, 420 U.S. 546, 547–48, 557–58 (1975) (emphasis added). See also Schad v. Borough of Mount Ephraim, 452 U.S. 61, 65 (1981) ("Entertainment, as well as political and ideological speech, is protected; motion pictures, programs broadcast by radio and television, and live entertainment, such as musical and dramatic works, fall within the First Amendment guarantee."").

29. City of Newport v. Fact Concerts, Inc., 453 U.S. 247, 250–51, 271 (1981).

30. Hurley v. Irish-Am. Gay, Lesbian & Bisexual Grp. of Bos., 515 U.S. 557, 561–64, 568–70 (1995) (emphasis added).

31. See Rovi Staff, "Biography of Arnold Schoenberg," AllMusic, accessed Feb. 2, 2015, http://www.allmusic.com/artist/ arnold-schoenberg-mn0000691043/biography.

32. Nurre v. Whitehead, 580 F.3d 1087 (9th Cir. 2009); Stratechuk v. Bd. of Educ., 587 F.3d 597, 610 (3d Cir. 2009). See also Chiasson v. New York City Dep't of Consumer Affairs, 524 N.Y.S.2d 649 (Sup. Ct. N.Y. Cty. 1988) (expressing assumption that live music performance is covered by the First Amendment); Chiasson v. New York City Dep't of Consumer Affairs, 505 N.Y.S.2d 499 (Sup. Ct. N.Y. Cty. 1986) (same).

33. *Nurre*, 580 F.3d at 1093.

34. *Stratechuk*, 587 F.3d at 599, 609–10.

35. Miller v. Civil City of S. Bend, 904 F.2d 1081, 1086, 1089 (7th Cir. 1990) (emphasis added), *rev'd sub nom.* Barnes v. Glen Theatre, Inc., 501 U.S. 560 (1991).

36. *Miller*, 904 F.2d at 1093–94 (Posner, J., concurring). Judge Posner had made a similar observation, also in dicta, in an earlier case. See Reed v. Vill. of Shorewood, 704 F.2d 943, 949–50 (7th Cir. 1983) ("Although the authors of the First Amendment were concerned with protecting political rather than cultural expression . . . and therefore might not have thought it a violation of the First Amendment for Congress to pass a law forbidding the playing of Haydn's string quartets on federal government lands, the modern view is different. If the defendants passed an ordinance forbidding the playing of rock and roll music in the Village of Shorewood, they would be infringing a First Amendment right . . . even if the music had no political message—*even if it had no words*—and the defendants would have to produce a strong justification for thus repressing a form of 'speech'" (emphasis added).).

37. *Miller*, 904 F.2d at 1094. Sergei Prokofiev, *Peter and the Wolf*, op. 67 (1936). To hear a recording of this work, see davidhertzberg, "Prokofiev / Peter Ustinov / Herbert von Karajan, 1960: Peter and the Wolf," YouTube, July 29, 2012, https://www.youtube.com/watch?v=WK_dkBC_Cno.

38. *Miller*, 904 F.2d at 1125 (Easterbrook, J., dissenting). La Monte Young, *The Well-Tuned Piano* (1964, 1973, 1981–present). For a recording of a brief excerpt from *The Well-Tuned Piano*, see https://www.youtube.com/watch?v=9JV-66bGp7Y.

39. The Supreme Court's decision in *Barnes*, reversing *Miller*, does not even discuss music. The word "music" appears only once in the entire decision, in a footnote in Justice Byron White's dissent referring to the definition of dancing. *Barnes*, 501 U.S. at 587 n.1 (White, J., dissenting).

40. A number of scholars have seriously engaged the broader topic of art and freedom of expression. See, e.g., Randall P. Bezanson, *Art and Freedom of Speech* (Urbana: University of Illinois Press, 2009); Amy Adler, "What's Left? Hate Speech, Pornography, and the Problem for Artistic Expression," 84 *Calif. L. Rev.* 1499 (1996); Bezanson, "Art and the Constitution"; Edward J. Eberle, "Art as Speech," 11 *U. Pa. J.L. & Soc. Change* 1 (2007); Marci A. Hamilton, "Art Speech," 49 *Vand. L. Rev.* 73 (1996); Sheldon H. Nahmod, "Artistic Expression and Aesthetic Theory: The Beautiful, the Sublime, and the First Amendment," 1987 *Wis. L. Rev.* 221 (1987).

41. Hamilton, "Art Speech," 121.

42. Ibid., 75.

43. Nahmod, "Artistic Expression and Aesthetic Theory," 226–35.

44. For a variation on this argument suggesting that art can be classified as speech because of the illegitimacy of government motivations for regulating artistic expression, see Frederick Schauer, *Free Speech: A Philosophical Enquiry* 111 (Cambridge: Cambridge University Press, 1982) (suggesting that the proper characterization of artistic expression is a "false problem" because free speech concerns are implicated anytime a regulation is "designed to limit the extent to which people will be *influenced* by a work of art"); Cass R. Sunstein, *Democracy and the Problem of Freedom of Speech* 158 (New York: Free Press, 1993) (claiming that "an effort to regulate music because it stirs up passionate feeling would run afoul of the free speech clause, simply because the justification for regulation is constitutionally off-limits").

45. Another possibility would be a situation when the government claims the work is so disturbing that it might incite an immediate riot or other unlawful action (see Nelson v. Streeter, 16 F.3d 145, 150 (7th Cir. 1994)), though such claims must be viewed with some skepticism. Government regulation of art is more likely to be upheld under a due process challenge but would be subject to a heightened level of scrutiny if art is covered by the First Amendment. In any event, if there is a choice between considering music as speech under the First Amendment or a liberty under the Fourteenth Amendment, there is also a doctrinal reason to focus on speech. The Supreme Court has articulated a preference for analyzing rights under the narrower, more specific provision of the Constitution that might apply rather than under due process. See Graham v. Connor, 490 U.S. 386, 394–95 (1989). For cases addressing musical expression and some form of due process claim, see Pub. Utils. Comm'n v. Pollak, 343 U.S. 451, 454 (1952) (rejecting passengers' free speech and substantive due process claims against the public utilities commission for broadcasting music on streetcars and buses); ibid., 468–69 (Douglas, J., dissenting) (arguing that the government's playing of music was a due process violation because the audience was captive and could not change the station); Jenkins v. Rumsfeld, 412 F. Supp. 1177, 1179 (E.D. Va. 1976) (rejecting a claim by military band members that a law prohibiting them from competing with local musicians for paid music gigs violated their due process rights).

46. Though sometimes the distinction between musical and lyrical content may be difficult to draw, even for censors. In 1968, an El Paso radio station refused to play

Bob Dylan songs because its management found it too difficult to understand the lyrics and was reportedly concerned that the songs might include "politically objectionable or lewd messages." See Meredith E. Rutledge-Borger, "Rock and Roll vs. Censorship," Rock & Roll Hall of Fame, accessed Aug. 23, 2013, https://rockhall.com/blog/post/8840_censorship-in-rock-and-roll-history.

47. See Luke Records, Inc. v. Navarro, 960 F.2d 134, 135, 136 (11th Cir. 1992) (emphasis added).

48. Ibid. Interestingly, however, the lower-court judge in that case specifically suggested the possibility that music without lyrics could be deemed obscene. Skywalker Records, Inc. v. Navarro, 739 F. Supp. 578, 591 (S.D. Fla. 1990) ("[I]t would be difficult, albeit *not impossible*, to find that mere sound without lyrics is obscene" (emphasis added).), *rev'd sub nom. Luke Records*, 960 F.2d 134.

49. The majority of commentary on the 2 Live Crew case appears to come from student notes and comments. See, e.g., Alexis A. Lury, "Time to Surrender: A Call for Understanding and the Re-evaluation of Heavy Metal Music within the Contexts of Legal Liability and Women," 9 *S. Cal. Rev. L. & Women's Stud.* 155, 178–82 (1999); Kirk A. Olson, "Constitutional Law: Can Music Be Considered Obscene? *Skywalker Records, Inc. v. Navarro*—The 2 Live Crew, Obscene or Oppressed?," 44 *Okla. L. Rev.* 513 (1991).

50. See notes 162–90 to this chapter and accompanying text. For observations about the role of race in a different controversy surrounding 2 Live Crew, see Bezanson, *Art and Freedom*, 184–213 (discussing the copyright dispute regarding the band's parody of the Roy Orbison song "Oh, Pretty Woman").

51. See David Munkittrick, "Music as Speech: A First Amendment Category unto Itself," 62 *Fed. Comm. L.J.* 665, 667, 674–85 (2010). Music has been discussed in legal literature as a model for legal interpretation, but that work is not directly relevant to the issues considered in this chapter. See generally Jack M. Balkin, "Verdi's High C," 91 *Tex. L. Rev.* 1687 (2013); Sanford Levinson and J. M. Balkin, "Law, Music, and Other Performing Arts," 139 *U. Pa. L. Rev.* 1597 (1991) (comparing legal interpretation to musicians' interpretation of scores with strict or liberal construction of the composers' intent); Richard A. Posner, "Bork and Beethoven," 42 *Stan. L. Rev.* 1365 (1990) (reviewing Robert H. Bork, *The Tempting of America: The Political Seduction of the Law* (1989)).

52. Munkittrick, "Music as Speech," 668.

53. See 1 Plato, *The Republic* (c. 380 BCE), bk. 4, 424 (3d ed., Benjamin Jowett trans., Oxford: Oxford University Press, 1908).

54. To hear a demonstration of the sound of the tritone, see patdavidmusic, "Ear Training: Practice the Tritone Interval (Aural Training)," YouTube, Sept. 15, 2014, https://www.youtube.com/watch?v=NkJSWsDdQdo.

55. Finlo Rohrer, "The Devil's Music," *BBC News Mag.*, Apr. 28, 2006, http://news.bbc.co.uk/2/hi/4952646.stm.

56. Peter Blecha, *Taboo Tunes: A History of Banned Bands and Censored Songs* 15–16 (San Francisco: Backbeat Books, 2004).

57. To hear a recording of this work, see Scherzo Music, "Stravinsky: The Rite of Spring (Abbado)," YouTube, Oct. 1, 2013, https://www.youtube.com/watch?v=RRyd5zR_3Bc.

58. Blecha, *Taboo Tunes*, 16 (emphasis added). As some people have observed, however, it is not entirely clear whether the audience's reaction was because they were upset about what the music communicated or because they did not understand it at all. See Wright, "What Counts as 'Speech' in the First Place?," 1247 n.169.

59. Michael Haas, *Forbidden Music: The Jewish Composers Banned by the Nazis* 226, 231–35 (New Haven, CT: Yale University Press, 2013); Allan Kozinn, "Mendelssohn, This Is Your Moment," *N.Y. Times*, Feb. 22, 2009; Erik Levi, *Music in the Third Reich* 86, 120 (New York: St. Martin's, 1994).

60. On Soviet censorship of music generally, see Jonathan Green and Nicholas J. Karolides, *Encyclopedia of Censorship* 590 (2d ed., New York: Facts on File, 2005). On censorship of Shostakovich's work in particular, see Janice Ross, *Like a Bomb Going Off: Leonid Yakobson and Ballet as Resistance in Soviet Russia* 95, 130 (New Haven, CT: Yale University Press, 2015); Mansur Mirovalev, "Once-Banned Shostakovich Ballet Triumphs," *Wash. Post*, June 15, 2007, http://www.washingtonpost.com/wp-dyn/content/article/2007/06/15/AR2007061501128_ pf.html.

61. Stephen Moss, "The Hills Are Alive," *Guardian*, Nov. 15, 2001. But see Umar F. Abd-Allah, "Living Islam with Purpose," 7 *UCLA J. Islamic & Near East L.* 17, 24, 30–31 (2008) (observing that the Islamic view on instrumental music is not "immutably fixed" and that some minority viewpoints would permit music to be performed in some contexts); Robert Tait, "Iran's 'Culturally Inappropriate' Rock Hopefuls Struggle to Be Heard," *Guardian*, Aug. 23, 2005.

62. Larry Rohter, "Musical Nomads, Escaping Political Upheaval," *N.Y. Times*, July 30, 2013.

63. Chris Pleasance, "ISIS Police Sentence Musicians to 90 Lashes Because They Were Playing an 'un-Islamic' Electronic Keyboard," *Daily Mail*, Jan. 20, 2015, http://www.dailymail.co.uk/news/article-2918061/ISIS-police-sentence-musicians-lashes-playing-Islamic-electonic-keyboard.html.

64. Munkittrick, "Music as Speech," 673–74.

65. Tom Moon, *1,000 Recordings to Hear before You Die* 76 (New York: Workman, 2008).

66. Franz Biebl, *Ave Maria* (1964). To hear an instrumental version of this work, see DanyellChaos, "Ave Maria by Franz Biebl for Wind/Brass Band," Mar. 8, 2011, https://www.youtube.com/watch?v=Y0ax_22YwtI.

67. Nurre v. Whitehead, 580 F.3d 1087, 1090–91 (9th Cir. 2009). The unsuccessful plaintiffs petitioned the Supreme Court for a writ of certiorari, which was denied. Ibid., *cert. denied*, 559 U.S. 1025 (2010). But see 559 U.S. 1025 (Alito, J., dissenting from denial of certiorari).

68. Stratechuk v. Bd. of Educ., 587 F.3d 597, 610 (3d Cir. 2009). The plaintiffs also challenged the school's policies as violating the First Amendment's Establishment Clause. Ibid., 599.

69. United States v. Davis, 353 F.2d 614 (2d Cir. 1965), *cert. denied*, 384 U.S. 953 (1966) (Stewart, J., dissenting from denial of certiorari). Apparently, Justice Stewart knew it when he heard it (or didn't). Cf. Jacobellis v. Ohio, 378 U.S. 184, 197 (1964) (Stewart, J., concurring) (articulating Justice Stewart's well known struggle to define hard-core pornography by the subjective test, "I know it when I see it").

70. Link Wray & His Waymen, "Rumble," on *Link Wray & the Wraymen* (Epic 1960). To hear a recording of this song, see n3vo5h, "Link Wray—Rumble," Feb. 18, 2012, https://www.youtube.com/watch?v=ucTg6rZJCu4.

71. Adam Bernstein, "Guitarist Link Wray Dies: Influenced Punk, Grunge," *Wash. Post*, Nov. 22, 2005.

72. To hear a recording of this song, see https://www.youtube.com/watch?v=Hvogi73oq6o.

73. Martin Horsfield, "This Record Must Not Be Broadcast," *Guardian*, Sept. 20, 2008.

74. Frank Zappa, *Jazz from Hell* (EMI, 1986). To hear a recording of this album, see Frank Zappa—Topic, "Night School," YouTube, Nov. 8, 2014, https://www.youtube.com/watch?v=bZicPl_b-o8&list=PL8WvZFiJpAr1TmUm9_emg5KOoS-G6xpd2h.

75. Eric Nuzum, *Parental Advisory: Music Censorship in America* 254–55 (New York: Perennial, 2001).

76. These are not the only theories of free speech, but they are the most commonly invoked by both legal scholars and the courts. For a brief discussion of some other speech theories, see Geoffrey R. Stone, Louis Michael Seidman, Cass R. Sunstein, Pamela S. Karlan, and Mark V. Tushnet, *Constitutional Law* 1026–27 (6th ed., New York: Aspen, 2009). Moreover, not all legal theorists agree that utilitarian, "constructivist," or consequentialist approaches are useful to understanding free speech. See, e.g., Larry Alexander, *Is There a Right of Freedom of Expression?* 127–34 (Cambridge: Cambridge University Press, 2005); Andrew Koppelman, "Veil of Ignorance: Tunnel Constructivism in Free Speech Theory," 107 *Nw. U. L. Rev.* 647 (2013).

77. Alexander Meiklejohn, *Free Speech and Its Relation to Self-Government* 888–89 (New York: Harper, 1948).

78. Ibid., 94.

79. Zechariah Chafee, Jr., "Book Review," 62 *Harv. L. Rev.* 891, 900 (1949).

80. See Alexander Meiklejohn, "The First Amendment Is an Absolute," 1961 *Sup. Ct. Rev.* 245, 256 (1961); see also Harry Kalven, "The *New York Times* Case: A Note on 'The Central Meaning of the First Amendment,'" 1964 *Sup. Ct. Rev.* 191, 221 (1964).

81. Meiklejohn, "First Amendment Is an Absolute," 262.

82. Marci Hamilton's work adheres to the notion that art is expression because, in its own way, it promotes democracy, and in this way, she importantly elaborates on Meiklejohn's arguably boundless extension of his democracy-facilitating theory. See generally Hamilton, "Art Speech."

83. Robert H. Bork, "Neutral Principles and Some First Amendment Problems," 47 *Ind. L.J.* 1, 20 (1971).

84. Ibid.
85. Ibid., 24 (citing Whitney v. California, 274 U.S. 357, 375 (1927) (Brandeis, J., concurring)).
86. Ibid., 27.
87. Robert Post, "Participatory Democracy and Free Speech," 97 *Va. L. Rev.* 477, 483 (2011).
88. Ibid. (internal quotation marks omitted).
89. Ibid.
90. Ibid., 486.
91. Robert Post, "Participatory Democracy as a Theory of Free Speech: A Reply," 97 *Va. L. Rev.* 617, 621 (2011).
92. See Koppelman, "Veil of Ignorance," 679 ("Democratic legitimation . . . cannot explain the protection of instrumental music."); see also R. G. Wright, "What Counts as 'Speech' in the First Place," 1222 (observing that not all instrumental music expresses an opinion or has a subject).
93. Weinstein, "Participatory Democracy as the Central Value," 499 n.45.
94. Ibid.
95. Seana Valentine Shiffrin, "A Thinker-Based Approach to Freedom of Speech," 27 *Const. Comment.* 283, 285–86 (2011) (emphasis added; citation omitted); see also C. Edwin Baker, "Autonomy and Free Speech," 27 *Const. Comment.* 251, 271 (2011) ("[C]ompositional music . . . require[s] a stretch to justify as political speech.").
96. Munkittrick, "Music as Speech," 682–83.
97. Ibid., 683–84.
98. But see Baker, "Autonomy and Free Speech," at 278–80 (arguing that the content-discrimination doctrine actually reflects the Court's invocation of an autonomy-based rationale).
99. Greenman, "On Communication," 1348; Munkittrick, "Music as Speech," 676–77.
100. Henry Cowell, "Edgar Varèse," in *American Composers on American Music* 43 (Henry Cowell ed., New York: Frederick Ungar, 1962) ("[Varèse's] music is acrid and telling, with a magnificent hardness of line which used to irritate our naïve listeners greatly, as did also his investigations in the field of emphasis on percussion sounds."); Elaine Barkin, Martin Brody, and Judith Crispin, "Milton Babbitt," in 1 *The Grove Dictionary of American Music* 263, 263–70 (Charles Hiroshi Garrett ed., 2d ed., New York: Oxford University Press, 2013).
101. City of Newport v. Fact Concerts, Inc., 453 U.S. 247, 250–51 (1981).
102. What I mean by "conditionally sufficient" is that expression ought to be protected because it facilitates self-governance but that not all expression is protected because it is political, for example, politically motivated property destruction or violence.
103. John Milton, *Areopagitica: A Speech for the Liberty of Unlicensed Printing* 4 (1644; H. B. Cotterill ed., New York: Macmillan, 1959).
104. John Stuart Mill, *On Liberty* 82–83 (London: John Parker, 1859).
105. Abrams v. United States, 250 U.S. 616, 616–17 (1919).

106. Ibid., 630 (Holmes, J., dissenting).

107. See Eugene Volokh, "In Defense of the Marketplace of Ideas / Search for Truth as a Theory of Free Speech Protection," 97 *Va. L. Rev.* 595, 595 (2011).

108. Greenman, "On Communication," 1348 (emphasis added); see also Weinstein, "Participatory Democracy as the Central Value," 499 n.45 (describing symphonic music as nonideational art).

109. Baker, "Autonomy and Free Speech," 271–72.

110. This is, of course, setting aside the many legitimate concerns about whether the speech marketplace, any more than the economic marketplace, is completely competitive and whether all participants have equal resources and information. See generally Sunstein, *Democracy and the Problem of Free Speech*.

111. Thomas Scanlon, "A Theory of Freedom of Expression," 1 *Phil. & Pub. Aff.* 204, 216 (1972). In later work, Scanlon modified his views about speech and autonomy. See generally T. M. Scanlon, Jr., "Freedom of Expression and Categories of Expression," 40 *U. Pitt. L. Rev.* 519 (1979).

112. Martin H. Redish, "The Value of Free Speech," 130 *U. Pa. L. Rev.* 591, 593 (1982) (internal quotation marks omitted).

113. Baker, "Autonomy and Free Speech," 266. See generally C. Edwin Baker, *Human Liberty and Freedom of Speech* (New York: Oxford University Press, 1992).

114. Baker, "Autonomy and Free Speech," 266–67.

115. Bork, "Neutral Principles," 25; see also chapter 2 in this volume ("Autonomy-related theories are . . . problematic as a way to distinguish artistic expression from essentially all other human activities, which can be ways in which people live autonomously.").

116. Baker, "Autonomy and Free Speech," 256–57; Redish, "Value of Free Speech," 600 ("[T]hat the framers deemed it necessary to create a first amendment at all, rather than merely including speech within the other forms of liberty protected by the fifth amendment, indicates that speech is to receive a constitutional status above and beyond that given to conduct.").

117. There are easier and harder cases that fall within this group, however. Sexual conduct may be a more difficult example to distinguish, since sex can have an important expressive component. See Lawrence v. Texas, 539 U.S. 558, 567 (2003); cf. Stanley v. Georgia, 394 U.S. 557, 568 (1969) (finding, under an autonomy theory, that the private observation of legally obscene material in one's home is protected by the First Amendment).

118. Shiffrin, "Thinker-Based Approach," 289–91.

119. Ibid., 291–92.

120. Ibid., 295.

121. *Stanley*, 394 U.S. at 565, 568.

122. See Miller v. Civil City of S. Bend, 904 F.2d 1081, 1125–26 (7th Cir. 1990) (Easterbrook, J., dissenting) ("All music is rhythmic pressure on the eardrum. Mozart's string quartets, jackhammers, and humpback whales all produce rhythmic compressions."), *rev'd sub nom.* Barnes v. Glen Theatre, Inc., 501 U.S. 560 (1991).

123. Indeed, the freedom *from* sound or noise can also promote important values of autonomy. See generally Tamara R. Piety, *Brandishing the First Amendment: Commercial Expression in America* (Ann Arbor: University of Michigan Press, 2012); George Prochnik, "I'm Thinking. Please. Be Quiet.," *N.Y. Times*, Aug. 25, 2013. Another question about silence is whether the *absence* of sound can ever constitute music, an argument pressed by John Cage's *4'33"*, a piece noteworthy for having absolutely no sound. Although a wide range and variety of sounds may constitute music, consideration of this example of Cage's work falls more properly within the examination of nonsense, discussed in chapter 3.

124. 1 *Shorter Oxford English Dictionary: On Historical Principles* 1866, s.v. "music" (William R. Trumble, Angus Stevenson, and Lesley Brown eds., 5th ed., Oxford: Oxford University Press, 2002).

125. This chapter sets aside, for now, questions about whether there are important differences between popular music and music as a fine art because they are not germane to the main discussion.

126. John Dewey, *Art as Experience* 74 (New York: Minton, Balch, 1934).

127. Greenman, "On Communication," 1348.

128. Gunther Schuller, *Seven Studies on Themes of Paul Klee* (1959). To hear a recording of this work, see Tim Poulus, "Gunther Schuller: Seven Studies on Themes of Paul Klee (BBC SO/Knussen)," YouTube, Aug. 26, 2015, https://www.youtube.com/watch?v=jUmYkbCchWg.

129. See Los Angeles Philharmonic, "Seven Studies on Themes of Paul Klee," accessed December 22, 2015, http://www.laphil.com/philpedia/music/seven-studies-on-themes-of-paul-klee-gunther-schuller.

130. Vivian Perlis and Libby Van Cleve, *Composers' Voices from Ives to Ellington: An Oral History of American Music* 94 (New Haven, CT: Yale University Press, 2005) (quoting Olivia Mattis, "Edgard Varèse and the Visual Arts," Ph.D. diss., Stanford University, 1992).

131. Dmitri Shostakovich, Symphony No. 11 in G Minor (1957). To hear a recording of this work, see Faces of Classical Music, "Dmitri Shostakovich: Symphony No. 11 in G Minor, Op. 103—Mstislav Rostropovich, 2002 (Audio video)," YouTube, Aug. 31, 2014, https://www.youtube.com/watch?v=NzcvPcQYLt4.

132. Laurel E. Fay, *Shostakovich: A Life* 199–202 (New York: Oxford University Press, 1999).

133. Dewey, *Art as Experience*, 245–46.

134. For an interesting account of the multitude of interpretations of one of the most well-known pieces of classical music, see Matthew Guerrieri, *The First Four Notes: Beethoven's Fifth and the Human Imagination* (New York: Knopf, 2012).

135. We consider the expressive elements of dance in greater detail in chapter 4.

136. See Miller v. Civil City of S. Bend, 904 F.2d 1081, 1125 (7th Cir. 1990) (Easterbrook, J., dissenting) ("Ballet rarely approaches absolute music in abstraction."), *rev'd sub nom.* Barnes v. Glen Theatre, Inc., 501 U.S. 560 (1991).

137. Bernstein, "Guitarist Link Wray Dies."

138. Nuzum, *Parental Advisory*, 24–39.

139. Frank Zappa, "G-Spot Tornado," on *Jazz from Hell* (EMI, 1986). To hear a recording of this song, see https://www.youtube.com/watch?v=MfVqYeyxfhw&list=PL8 WvZFiJpAr1TmUm9_emg5KOoSG6xpd2h&index=5.

140. Horsfield, "This Record Must Not Be Broadcast."

141. Ted Gioia, *The History of Jazz* 7 (New York: Oxford University Press, 1997); Robert Palmer, *Deep Blues* 33 (New York: Viking, 1982).

142. Guerrieri, *First Four Notes*, 211–14.

143. On cryptograms or cryptography generally, see Eric Sams, "Cryptography, Musical," in 6 *The New Grove Dictionary of Music and Musicians* 753–58 (Stanley Sadie ed., 2d ed., London: Macmillan, 2001).

144. Marcus du Sautoy, "The Magic Numbers: A Fascination with Figures Runs through the Music of Composers from Mozart to Bach," *Guardian*, Apr. 5, 2013; see also Wright, "What Counts as 'Speech' in the First Place?," 1247 n.170 (suggesting that coded messages, including musical scores, are speech because even though they may not be generally understandable, they have meaning for their intended audience).

145. United States v. O'Brien, 391 U.S. 367, 377 (1968).

146. Claire Wright, "Reconciling Cultural Diversity and Free Trade in the Digital Age: A Cultural Analysis of the International Trade in Content Items," 41 *Akron L. Rev.* 399, 464–65 n.337 (2008) (citing Daniel J. Levitin, *This Is Your Brain on Music: The Science of a Human Obsession* (2006)).

147. Singing has long played a role in protests and social movements as a means for both conveying messages and inspiring participants. From the work of the American folk singers Woody Guthrie and Pete Seeger in the twentieth century to the contemporary protest music of Pussy Riot, musicians have been incorporating social justice messages into their songs in an effort to express dissatisfaction with the status quo. See Bart Barnes, "Folk Singer Wanted Everyone to be Heard," *Wash. Post*, Jan. 29, 2014; Chris Kornelis, "Woody Guthrie Gave Life to Protest Songs He Wrote, Sang," *Wash. Times*, Oct. 11, 2012; Carol Rumens, "Pussy Riot's Punk Prayer Is Pure Protest Poetry," *Guardian*, Aug. 20, 2012, http://www.the-guardian.com/books/2012/aug/20/pussy-riot-punk-prayer-lyrics; see also Buffalo Springfield, "For What It's Worth," on *Buffalo Springfield* (ATCO Records, 1967). The international scope of such expression is widely noted. See Anne Schumann, "The Beat That Beat Apartheid: The Role of Music in the Resistance against Apartheid in South Africa," 14 *Vienna J. Afr. Stud.* 17 (2008); Sebnem Arsu, "The Music Started, and the Protest Paused," *N.Y. Times*, June 15, 2013.

148. Cohen v. California, 403 U.S. 15, 16, 25–26 (1971). For an interesting evaluation of the role of the word *fuck* in American legal culture, see Christopher M. Fairman, "Fuck," 28 *Cardozo L. Rev.* 1711 (2007).

149. Greenman, "On Communication," 1367 n.136.

150. One possibility that is not fully accounted for is that musical expression may be inextricably linked not only to its lyrics and title but also to its social history and

the context in which it is composed, performed, heard, and experienced. If this is the case, then the theoretical attempt to disaggregate music into its component parts may be misguided. If, indeed, music cannot be disentangled from its social history, this would present a strong, alternative claim for why it is covered by the First Amendment. Because this argument is beyond the ambition of this chapter, we set it aside for future discussion.

151. See chapter 2 in this volume; see also Bezanson, *Art and Freedom of Speech*, 280 (describing most art as nonpropositional).

152. Karol Berger, *A Theory of Art* 173–74 (New York: Oxford University Press, 2000) (quoting Kendall L. Walton, *Mimesis as Make-Believe: On the Foundations of the Representational Arts* 56 (Cambridge, MA: Harvard University Press, 1990)).

153. Ibid., 174.

154. See chapter 3. And, of course, a single word's meaning may vary widely depending on its usage, context, and emphasis. See generally Fairman, "Fuck."

155. Berger, *Theory of Art*, 209.

156. Quoted ibid., 210.

157. Quoted in Lawrence Kramer, *Expression and Truth: On the Music of Knowledge* 98 (Berkeley: University of California Press, 2012).

158. Carroll, "Whose Music Is It Anyway?," 1422.

159. See, e.g., Hans Heinrich Eggebrecht, *Understanding Music: The Nature and Limits of Musical Cognition* (Farnham, UK: Ashgate, 2010).

160. Stanley v. Georgia, 394 U.S. 557, 565 (1969).

161. See Munkittrick, "Music as Speech," 670.

162. Douglas Leedy and Charles Corey, "Tuning Systems," in 8 *The Grove Dictionary of American Music* 276, 276–79 (Charles Hiroshi Garrett ed., 2d. ed., New York: Oxford University Press, 2013).

163. Ted Gioia, "Are We All Mistuning Our Instruments, and Can We Blame the Nazis?," *The Daily Beast*, June 6, 2015, http://www.thedailybeast.com/articles/2015/06/06/are-we-all-mistuning-our-instruments-and-can-we-blame-the-nazis.html.

164. Dorothea E. Hast, James R. Cowdery, and Stan Scott, *Exploring the World of Music: An Introduction to Music from a World Music Perspective* 163 (Dubuque, IA: Kendall/Hunt, 1999).

165. Ibid.

166. Palmer, *Deep Blues*, 36–37. For a discussion of the culturally unique polyrhythms of African music, see Gioia, *History of Jazz*, 11.

167. Linda Martin and Kerry Segrave, *Anti-Rock: The Opposition to Rock 'n' Roll* 53 (New York: De Capo, 1993). Of particular interest here is the announcement of a San Antonio city councilman that "[t]he First Amendment should not apply to rock 'n' roll." Ibid., 271.

168. See ibid., 41.

169. Sachal Studios Orchestra, "Take Five," on *Sachal Jazz: Interpretations of Jazz Standards & Bossa Nova* (Sachal Music, 2011). To hear a recording of this work,

see sachalsmusicchannel, "Sachal Studios Orchestra Presents Dave Brubeck's Take Five," YouTube, Mar. 25, 2011, https://www.youtube.com/watch?v=1-lRV7qLD08.

170. See Gioia, *History of Jazz*, 5.
171. Carroll, "Whose Music Is It Anyway?," 1417 ("Music has no intrinsic definition. It is a cultural category consisting of any sounds that those in a society or culture designate as 'music' instead of 'noise,' along with any notation, recording, or other means of capturing or representing such sounds.").
172. Gioia, *History of Jazz*, 200.
173. United Nations Education, Scientific, and Cultural Organization and World Intellectual Property Organization, *Model Provisions for National Laws on the Protection of Expressions of Folklore Against Illicit Exploitation and Other Prejudicial Actions* 9–10 (1985).
174. Nurre v. Whitehead, 580 F.3d 1087, 1091 (9th Cir. 2009).
175. Stratechuk v. Bd. of Educ., 587 F.3d 597, 599 (3d Cir. 2009).
176. Dewey, *Art as Experience*, 223. Because this chapter is concerned only with First Amendment coverage, it does not address the idea that even if instrumental music is covered, it might still be subject to some regulation depending on the context in which it is performed.
177. Church of the Lukumi Babalu Aye, Inc. v. City of Hialeah, 508 U.S. 520, 524 (1993).
178. Kenneth Schweitzer, *The Artistry of Afro-Cuban Batá Drumming* 21–49 (Jackson: University of Mississippi Press, 2013).
179. Moon, *1,000 Recordings*, 52–53; see also Felix Contreras, "How Santería Seeped into Latin Music," NPR.org, Jan. 7, 2015, http://www.npr.org/2015/01/07/375389153/how-santer-a-seeped-into-latin-music?utm_source=npr_email_a_friend&utm_medium=email&utm_content=20150107&utm_campaign=storyshare&utm_term=
180. Abd-Allah, "Living Islam with Purpose," 30–31; Moss, "Hills Are Alive"; Tait, "Iran's 'Culturally Inappropriate' Rock Hopefuls."
181. See Rohrer, "Devil's Music"; Blecha, *Taboo Tunes*, 15–16.
182. Haas, *Forbidden Music*, 231–35.
183. Blair Jackson, Dennis McNally, and Stephen Peters, *Grateful Dead: The Illustrated Trip* 138 (London: Dorling Kindersley, 2003).
184. Scott Mervis, "Insane Clown Posse Is Back in the Dark Carnival," *Pitt. Post-Gazette*, May 20, 2010. These cultures are much more than what might be called "fan clubs" but are, by their nature and self-identification, subcultures of society. In an interesting twist, Insane Clown Posse and some of its fans recently sued the Federal Bureau of Investigation for labeling the Juggalos as a "gang." Dave Itzkoff, "Rap Group Defends Fans, with Lawsuit," *N.Y. Times*, Jan. 9, 2014.
185. Shiffrin, "Thinker-Based Approach," 289–90.
186. Greenman, "On Communication," 1339; Bork, "Neutral Principles," 25.
187. For a general consideration of the nationalistic elements of patriotic symbols, songs, and ceremonies, see Alan K. Chen, "Forced Patriot Acts," 81 *Denv. U. L. Rev.* 703 (2004).

188. Sousa was renowned for infusing his marches with patriotic spirit. Neil Harris, "John Philip Sousa and the Culture of Reassurance," in *Perspectives on John Philip Sousa* 11, 30–31 (Jon Newsom ed., Washington, DC: Library of Congress, 1983). To hear a recording of one of Sousa's most famous marches, "The Stars and Stripes Forever," see United States Marine Band, "Sousa The Stars and Stripes Forever— 'The President's Own' U.S. Marine Band," YouTube, Dec. 8, 2011, https://www.youtube.com/watch?v=a-7XWhyvIpE.

189. Jean Sibelius, *Finlandia*, op. 26 (1899; rev. 1900). *Finlandia* was written in response to the increasing efforts of Russia to impose its own nationalism in Finland. Glenda Dawn Goss, *Sibelius: A Composer's Life and the Awakening of Finland* 239–72 (Chicago: University of Chicago Press, 2009). To hear a recording of this work, see Tarja M, "Jean Sibelius—Finlandia," YouTube, July 23, 2012, https://www.youtube.com/watch?v=F5zg_af9b8c&feature=youtu.be. For an argument that the First Amendment should protect "cultural democracy" as well as democracy in the conventional political sense, see Jack M. Balkin, "Digital Speech and Democratic Culture: A Theory of Freedom of Expression for the Information Society," 79 *N.Y.U. L. Rev.* 1, 3–4 (2004); Jack M. Balkin, "Cultural Democracy and the First Amendment," 110 *Nw. U. L. Rev.* (forthcoming 2016).

190. Ward v. Rock Against Racism, 491 U.S. 781, 790 (1989).

191. Plato, *Republic*, bk. 3, 401.

192. Berger, *Theory of Art*, 120.

193. Donald Jay Grout and Claude V. Palisca, *A History of Western Music* 7–8 (4th ed., New York: Norton, 1988).

194. Isobel Henderson, "Ancient Greek Music," in 1 *The New Oxford History Of Music* 336, 395 (Egon Wellesz ed., 1957).

195. Plato, *Republic*, bk. 4, 424.

196. Grout and Palisca, *History of Western Music*, 8.

197. George Wilhelm Friedrich Hegel, 2 *Aesthetics: Lectures on Fine Art* 934 (T. M. Knox trans., Oxford, UK: Clarendon, 1975). This account follows the lead of Sheldon Nahmod's excellent work on visual arts. See generally Nahmod, "Artistic Expression and Aesthetic Theory."

198. Hegel, 2 *Aesthetics*, 934.

199. Arthur Schopenhauer, 1 *The World as Will and Representation* 261 (E. F. J. Payne trans., Indian Hills, CO: Falcon's Wing, 1958).

200. Dewey, *Art as Experience*, 237.

201. Ibid., 238.

202. Ibid., 239.

203. Ibid.; see Berger, *Theory of Art*, 120 ("Music's historical edge over painting or poetry consists only in this, that, with its inherent tendency toward abstraction, it was able to provide moods without the admixture of anything else earlier than the other arts were.").

204. Andrew Kania, "The Philosophy of Music," in *Stanford Encyclopedia of Philosophy* (Oct. 22, 2007; rev. July 13, 2012), http://plato.stanford.edu/entries/music/3.

205. See, e.g., Meiklejohn, "First Amendment Is an Absolute," 256.

206. See generally Post, "Participatory Democracy and Free Speech."

207. James Weinstein, "Free Speech Values, Hardcore Pornography and the First Amendment: A Reply to Professor Koppelman," 31 *N.Y.U. Rev. L. & Soc. Change* 911, 921 (2007).

208. Martha C. Nussbaum, *Upheavals of Thought: The Intelligence Of Emotions* 1 (Cambridge: Cambridge University Press, 2001); see also Andrew Koppelman, "Free Speech and Pornography: A Response to James Weinstein," 31 *N.Y.U. Rev. L. & Soc. Change* 899, 905 n.42 (2007).

209. See chapter 2 in this volume. Such a declaration is insufficient because in the end, autonomy is promoted by lots of things that are not protected by the First Amendment.

210. Mill, *On Liberty*, 13–14.

211. Scanlon, "Theory of Freedom of Expression," 216.

212. Redish, "Value of Free Speech," 593.

213. Baker, "Autonomy and Free Speech," 253, 271.

214. See Robert J. Zatorre and Valorie N. Salimpoor, "Why Music Makes Our Brain Sing," *N.Y. Times*, June 7, 2013, http://www.nytimes.com/2013/06/09/opinion/sunday/why-music-makes-our-brain-sing.html ("When pleasurable music is heard, dopamine is released in the striatum, . . . which is known to respond to naturally rewarding stimuli like food and sex and which is artificially targeted by drugs like cocaine and amphetamine.").

215. Shiffrin, "Thinker-Based Approach," 289–90.

216. Cf. James Weinstein, "Democracy, Sex and the First Amendment," 31 *N.Y.U. Rev. L. & Soc. Change* 865, 888–92 (2007) (considering the argument that pornography might be protected when the producer's intent is to change attitudes about sexual mores but not when the producer's intent is merely to provide sexual stimulation).

217. To hear a recording of this event, see James Inverne, "Listen to This Chilling Audio as Crowd at Boston Symphony Learns President Kennedy Is Dead," *Time*, Nov. 11, 2013, http://nation.time.com/2013/11/11/boston-symphony-kennedy-assassination/.

218. Ibid.

219. Goss, *Sibelius*, 255, 272.

220. Jed Rubenfeld, "The First Amendment's Purpose," 53 *Stan. L. Rev.* 767, 817–22 (2001).

221. This is not to say that the government has no role in shaping or supporting different cultural values through funding and other types of official support (see Nat'l Endowment for the Arts v. Finley, 524 U.S. 569 (1998)) but that it is important that the state not attempt to interfere with the shaping and natural evolution of various cultures in society.

222. Alexander, *Is There a Right of Freedom of Expression?*, 9.

223. Ibid., 11.

CHAPTER 2. ART AND THE FIRST AMENDMENT

1. Hurley v. Irish-Am. Gay, Lesbian & Bisexual Grp. of Bos., Inc., 515 U.S. 557, 568–69 (1995) (citation omitted).

2. For a discussion of the term *coverage*, see the introduction. Using the phrase "not protected by the First Amendment," the Court has held that recreational dancing is not covered by the First Amendment. Dallas v. Stanglin, 490 U.S. 19, 25 (1989); see also Brown v. Entm't Merchs. Ass'n, 564 U.S. 786, 790 (2011) (using the phrases "qualify for First Amendment protection" and "confer First Amendment protection" to refer to coverage). Justice David Souter, the author of *Hurley*, asserted elsewhere that "dancing as aerobic exercise is likewise outside the First Amendment's concern." Barnes v. Glen Theatre, Inc., 501 U.S. 560, 581 (1991) (Souter, J., concurring in the judgment). One might wonder whether *Stanglin's* treatment of recreational dancing would be the same today, after the commercial success of *Dancing with the Stars*.

3. Much of the secondary literature on art and the First Amendment assumes art's coverage and derives First Amendment rules to deal with specific problems such as the permissible scope of regulation of public art (art owned by public agencies) or of regulation of commercial transactions in art, particularly in public places. For an important discussion of art's coverage under the First Amendment, see Randall P. Bezanson, *Art and Freedom of Speech* (Urbana: University of Illinois Press, 2009). Marci Hamilton, "Art Speech," 49 *Vand. L. Rev.* 73 (1996), argues for giving nonrepresentational art "stringent First Amendment protection" "as a means of protecting vital spheres of personal freedom." Ibid., 78, 77. See also Janet Elizabeth Haws, "Architecture as Art? Not in My Neocolonial Neighborhood: A Case for Providing First Amendment Protections to Expressive Residential Architecture," 2005 *B.Y.U. L. Rev.* 1625 (2005) (arguing that expressive architecture should be covered by the First Amendment by analogy to art's coverage).

4. This chapter attempts to keep close to the doctrinal ground, avoiding controversial accounts of how art "works," although complete abstinence from art theory is almost certainly impossible. For an example of insightful analysis relying on art theory, see Sheldon Nahmod, "Artistic Expression and Aesthetic Theory: The Beautiful, the Sublime, and the First Amendment," 1987 *Wisc. L. Rev.* 221 (1987).

5. "Worry" in the sense "to get or bring into a specified condition by . . . dogged effort." *Oxford English Dictionary Online*, s.v. "worry (v.), 5(c)" (available at www. oed.com).

6. Much constitutional doctrine appears to be animated by a search for this sort of overlapping consensus, with each specific First Amendment principle supported by diverse First Amendment theories, rather than a free-standing doctrine, to use Rawlsian terms. Overlapping consensus, much less free-standing doctrine, may be unavailable here (as elsewhere).

7. Scare quotes are used here because the term *content based* is characteristic of First Amendment discourse, whereas the question to be explored is whether these

regulations deal with materials covered by the First Amendment. One would not ordinarily say that a contractual provision limiting a person's ability to compete with his or her former employer is "content based," although in some sense it is. However we describe such contracts, the underlying question is whether the First Amendment places some special limits on the state's power to regulate them—as of course it does not. So too with artworks: Does the First Amendment place special limits on a government's ability to regulate an artwork because in the government's view it is ugly?

8. Such a regulation is "content based." Whether the city council could justify such a ban by asserting that the sculpture distracts drivers or lowers property values raises separate questions. On the possibility of distraction from viewing "art" works, see Erznoznik v. City of Jacksonville, 422 U.S. 305 (1975) (holding unconstitutional a city ordinance declaring it a public nuisance to present films showing nudity at a drive-in movie theater, where the screen is visible from a public street).

9. Cf. Robert C. Post, "Participatory Democracy and Free Speech," 97 *Va. L. Rev.* 477, 479 (2011) ("the value of autonomy extends not merely to the speech of persons but also to the actions of persons.").

10. Briefly on the justifications for prohibiting ticket scalping: The prohibition prima facie prevents people who value seeing a performance highly from purchasing tickets from ticket holders who value doing so less highly. Ticket scalpers are not exploiting "needs" in any interesting sense. There does not seem to be a strong distributional interest at stake, and to the extent that there is one, banning ticket scalping is ineffective absent price controls on tickets. The public interest in preventing relatively impecunious fans of Lady Gaga from voluntarily exchanging their tickets for large amounts of cash from richer fans is quite unclear and not obviously consistent with underlying values favoring equitable distribution of social goods. And to the extent that performers are concerned about their relatively impecunious fans, they can impose restrictions on access to tickets.

11. See Frederick Schauer, "Categories and the First Amendment: A Play in Three Acts," 34 *Vand. L. Rev.* 265, 270–71 (1981) (describing the distinction). An early Supreme Court decision supporting the coverage/protection distinction is Chaplinsky v. New Hampshire, 315 U.S. 568, 571–72 (1942) (asserting that "[t]here are certain well defined and narrowly limited classes of speech, the prevention and punishment of which have never been thought to raise any Constitutional problem"). For a discussion of the coverage/protection distinction in constitutional law generally, sometimes described as a distinction between "defining" a right and determining whether an infringement on that right is "justified," see David L. Faigman, "Reconciling Individual Rights and Governmental Interests: Madisonian Principles versus Supreme Court Practice," 78 *Va. L. Rev.* 1521, 1522–23 (1993). For a treatment from a jurisprudential perspective, see Robert Alexy, *A Theory of Constitutional Rights* 35–37 (Julian Rivers trans., Oxford: Oxford University Press, 2002).

12. Other constitutional provisions may be relevant. Suppose we conclude, for example, that "dwarf tossing," understood by the participants and observers

as performance art, is not covered by the First Amendment. The participants might mount other constitutional claims against a ban on the activity, such as a libertarian-sounding claim that the ban violates a right protected by the due process clause to engage in consensual and nonharmful activities. (The United Nations Human Rights Committee has issued a report concluding that a ban on dwarf tossing does not violate various human rights, including the right to earn a living and the right to respect for private life. Wackenheim v. France, Communication No. 854/1999, July 15, 2002, CCPR/C/75/D/854/1999.)

13. Except perhaps insofar as the *other* constitutional claims incorporate components associated with First Amendment analysis into their own doctrine.

14. Such a conclusion is not inevitable. The canonical formulation for identifying covered expression that receives a low level of protection against content-based regulation comes from *Chaplinsky*, 315 U.S. 568. Such instances of expression "by [their] very utterance inflict injury . . . [and] are no essential part of any exposition of ideas, and are of such slight social value as a step to truth that any benefit that might be derived from them is clearly outweighed by the social interest in order and morality." Ibid., 572. "Ugly" art might be said by its very appearance to inflict injury, and as discussed in greater detail later, the assertions that art is "part of [an] exposition of ideas" or is "a step to truth" are extremely difficult to defend.

15. Cf. Dallas v. Stanglin, 490 U.S. 19, 25 (1989) ("It is possible to find some kernel of expression in almost every activity a person undertakes—for example, walking down the street or meeting one's friends at a shopping mall—but such a kernel is not sufficient to bring the activity within the protection of the First Amendment.").

16. Or, in the advice given budding writers, "Show, don't tell."

17. To focus on the more substantial questions, the fact that some panhandlers (contingently) sit with signs saying "Homeless and Out of Work" and the like or utter words in asking for money is put aside as a distraction.

18. As the Second Circuit put it when it held unconstitutional New York's ban on begging in Loper v. New York City Police Dep't, 999 F.2d 699, 704 (2d Cir. 1993), "Begging frequently is accompanied by speech indicating the need for food, shelter, clothing, medical care or transportation. Even without particularized speech, however, *the presence of an unkempt and disheveled person holding out his or her hand or a cup to receive a donation itself conveys a message of need for support and assistance*" (emphasis added).

19. Tyson & Brother v. Banton, 273 U.S. 418 (1927), invalidated an anti-ticket-scalping law as a violation of economic due process. The decision lacks precedential value today. Then-professor Robert Bork raised the question of ticket scalping in connection with a discussion of the First Amendment in a law-school class or on an examination nearly thirty years ago. I gave what I describe later as a nominalist response, which I now think inadequate.

20. Distinguishing between panhandling and ticket scalping as "activities" and artworks as "things" for purposes of analyzing their First Amendment coverage can

bear little if any weight. The distinction leads to the odd result—one inconsistent with existing doctrine—that Stravinsky's music for *The Firebird* is covered by the First Amendment but the ballet performed to that music is not.

21. Kleinman v. City of San Marcos, 597 F.3d 323, 324–25 (5th Cir. 2010), *cert. denied*, 562 U.S. 837 (2010). Judge Haynes concurred only in the judgment.

22. *Kleinman*, 597 F.3d at 326–27.

23. Ibid., 328.

24. And yet there is the Visual Artists Rights Act, 17 U.S.C. § 106A(a)(3)(B) (providing a right against destruction of "work[s] of *recognized* stature"; emphasis added).

25. It is similar with the effects on property values, which occur—if they do—because of viewers' adverse reactions to seeing the display. (A look at the Planet K location on Google Maps suggests that the diminution in property values would have to be low. Go to 910 N. Interstate 35, San Marcos, TX 78666.) But cf. Young v. American Mini-Theatres, 427 U.S. 50 (1976) (upholding the regulation of adult entertainment clubs on the basis of their secondary effects on the neighborhood, while acknowledging that those secondary effects occur as a result of the cognitive effects the clubs have on their patrons).

26. The court did not explain why the car/planter was "a utilitarian device." Clearly it was not usable as an automobile, and it seems to me generally agreed that items that have "ordinary" uses can also be works of art. See, e.g., the Saarinen "womb chair" both in its ordinary use and when placed in a museum. A well-designed cactus planter could be both utilitarian and a work of art. Cf. Kieselstein-Cord v. Accessories by Pearl, Inc., 632 F.2d 989 (2d Cir. 1980) (referring to the placement of a category of utilitarian objects in museums as supporting the copyrightability as an artwork of an object with utilitarian uses); discussion of *Hurley* later in this chapter. Finally, the suggestion that the car/planter was "an advertisement" rather than a work of art seems mistaken. (In a footnote, the court observed that it did "not reach the City's contention" that the car/planter was regulable as commercial speech. *Kleinman*, 597 F.3d at 327 n.5.) Print newspapers contain advertisements to increase the newspapers' profitability, and those advertisements are pretty clearly covered by the First Amendment. Cf. N.Y. Times Co. v. Sullivan, 376 U.S. 254 (1964) (providing First Amendment protection to a political advertisement printed in a newspaper).

27. United States v. O'Brien, 391 U.S. 367, 377 (1968).

28. Some people might reasonably think that the claim that a work of art, even *Cadillac Ranch*, lowers local property values is a weak one and that the asserted interests in protecting property values and neighborhood aesthetics are not substantial enough.

29. Here too the label "transgressive" suggests why some people might be motivated to regulate some artworks.

30. Content-neutral laws are sometimes described as laws of general application that in some applications directly affect speech activities. See, e.g., Arcara v. Cloud

Books, Inc., 478 U.S. 697, 705 (1986) ("[N]either the press nor booksellers may claim special protection from governmental regulations of general applicability simply by virtue of their First Amendment protected activities.").

31. The reference here is to "punking" as performance art. See *Urban Dictionary*, s.v. "punked," accessed Nov. 20, 2015, www.urbandictionary.com, especially definitions 1 ("A way to describe someone ripping you off, tricking you, teasing you") and 5 ("What Ashton Kutcher says that makes all the hilarious pranks he pulls on celebrities suddenly okay"). Regarding the criminalization of particular forms, the requirement of impractibility is needed to show that the application of the general criminal law to the artwork has no greater impact on expression than is necessary.

32. The artists have had to navigate the shoals of environmental-protection regulations for permission to install some of their other works. For a brief discussion of some of these difficulties, see Kriston Copps, "Recognizing Jeanne-Claude," *American Prospect*, Nov. 24, 2009, www.prospect.org. One can imagine stringent applications of environmental-protection regulations that would bar the installations in a way that would only modestly protect the environment against permanent damage.

33. Other scholars have used other terms for the same idea. The terms used here bear some resemblance to Bernard Williams's famous "one thought too many" argument against a large number of approaches to practical reasoning about moral questions.

34. Various expressions by Supreme Court justices suggesting that expansive definitions of the First Amendment's coverage ought to be rejected even when the activities are found to be covered but not protected point to some implicit sense that the "too much work" principle should come into play. See, e.g., Clark v. Community for Creative Nonviolence, 462 U.S. 288, 301 (1984) (Burger, C.J., concurring) ("It trivializes the First Amendment to seek to use it as a shield in the manner asserted here," that is, to claim that the activity of sleeping overnight in national parks is covered by the First Amendment); Barnes v. Glen Theatre, Inc., 501 U.S. 560, 566 (1991) (opinion of Rehnquist, C.J.) ("nude dancing of the kind sought to be performed here is expressive conduct within the outer perimeters of the First Amendment, though we view it as only marginally so."). The intuitions behind these expressions may be that using standard First Amendment analysis to reach the conclusion that the activities involved are properly subject to the regulations at issue requires too much work.

35. Indeed, any list of criteria will yield some overinclusive and underinclusive outcomes, and the true question is whether the degree of fit between the criteria (taken cumulatively) and the purposes the classification is designed to serve is "good enough."

36. Archibald MacLeish, "Ars Poetica," in *Collected Poems 1917–1982*, 106, 107 (Boston: Mariner Books, 1985).

37. See James McNeill Whistler, *The Gentle Art of Making Enemies* 127–28 (New York: J. W. Lovell, 1890) ("Art should . . . stand alone, and appeal to the artistic sense

of eye or ear, without confounding this with emotions entirely foreign to it"; and asserting of the work's title, "Now that is what it is. To me it is interesting as a picture of my mother; but what can or ought the public to care about the identity of the portrait?").

38. Cf. Valentine v. Chrestensen, 316 U.S. 52 (1942) (upholding the conviction for distributing a handbill of a person whose handbill advertised on one side a tour of a submarine for which a fee had to be paid and on the other a protest against the city's regulatory system for its wharfs). See also Post, "Participatory Democracy and Free Speech," 487–88 ("The value of autonomy is at stake whenever human beings act or speak, which implies that virtually all government regulation is potentially subject to constitutional review [under the First Amendment]. This is the essential vice of Lochnerism."). The bracketed insertion seems to capture Post's thought more accurately than the sentence as published.

39. For the seemingly applicable standard, see Ward v. Rock Against Racism, 491 U.S. 781, 796 (1989) (content-neutral regulations must be "narrowly tailored to serve a significant governmental interest"). The weakness of the justifications offered to defend ticket-scalping bans against substantive due process attack suggests that the interest at stake might not be "significant," and a complete ban on ticket scalping might not be narrowly tailored in light of the possibility of limiting the ticket scalper's profit to some (small) multiple of the ticket's face value. But see ibid., 798–99 ("[T]he requirement of narrow tailoring is satisfied 'so long as the . . . regulation promotes a substantial government interest that would be achieved less effectively absent the regulation'"; quoting United States v. Albertini, 472 U.S. 641, 689 (1985).)

40. In correspondence, Corey Brettschneider suggested that we could resolve the "too much work" problem by holding that the First Amendment covers artworks but protects them less vigorously than it protects political or other traditional forms of high-value speech. This suggestion raises a number of important questions of First Amendment theory, too many to be explored in detail here. (For example, the high-value/low-value distinction currently tracks the covered/uncovered distinction, but Brettschneider's suggestion would create a third category of covered-but-less-protected material, opening up the possibility that First Amendment doctrine should be structured with numerous layers, each receiving its own level of protection.) For now, my primary observation is that Brettschneider's suggestion would raise questions about the degree of protection to be afforded to works of imaginative literature such as *Ulysses*.

41. The idea of *word equivalents* is developed in more detail later in this chapter, but for present purposes, it is enough to characterize them as works to which a viewer can give propositional content. An example is provided by Chief Justice William Rehnquist's observation that a protestor's burning of an American flag "obviously did convey Johnson's bitter dislike of his country." Texas v. Johnson, 491 U.S. 397, 431 (1989) (Rehnquist, C.J., dissenting). The flag burning is a word equivalent with the propositional content (on Rehnquist's interpretation) "I bitterly dislike this country."

42. In addition, imputing word equivalents to nonrepresentational art is almost certainly a fool's errand. Questions raised by such imputation are discussed in more detail later in this chapter.

43. For a discussion of supplementing a textualist focus on words ("speech") with a textualist focus on mechanical reproduction ("press"), see later in this chapter.

44. *Oxford English Dictionary*, 2d ed., vol. 3, s.v. "commentary," definition 3.b: "Anything that serves for exposition or illustration" (with the following example: "How excellent a Commentary This [Nature] is on the Former [the Scriptures].").

45. One obvious advantage of doing so is that the First Amendment unquestionably covers Joyce's *Ulysses* even if that work has many meanings, few of them political.

46. This interpretation of Holzer's work may be controversial, with other interpretations stressing the importance of the words themselves. The view articulated here is that Holzer's use of words in her works is integral to their force but that the particular words she uses is not.

47. Note, though, that when coupled with *Hurley*'s correct insistence on the multivocality of some covered material—the various interpretations viewers give a group's inclusion in a parade—this argument for First Amendment coverage of nonrepresentational art threatens the trademark law of secondary meaning itself. The person who infringes a secondary-meaning trademark by taking advantage of the image's multivocality has produced material that, on this argument, is covered by the First Amendment. (A descriptive term—and, by inference, an image—may be registered as a trademark only if it has "become descriptive of *the applicant's* goods." 15 U.S.C. § 1052(f) (emphasis added). See Park 'n Fly v. Dollar Park & Fly, 469 U.S. 189 (1985).)

48. As discussed earlier, a finding of coverage is not the same as a finding of protection, and perhaps the infringer can *invoke* the First Amendment because the image is covered by it but is not protected by it because trademark law survives the appropriate level of scrutiny, especially when the protection afforded by trademark law to images with secondary meaning is defined with sufficient narrowness. The structure of the argument is familiar from copyright law. Yet, as before, this analysis seems to me susceptible to the "too much work" critique: we should be able to establish the conclusion with a less elaborate argument.

49. Cohen v. California, 403 U.S. 15, 27 (1971) (Blackmun, J., dissenting). The characterization that Justice Blackmun offered seems to me obviously inapt. Of similar import, but not referring to actual words, is Chief Justice Rehnquist's characterization of flag burning as "the equivalent of an inarticulate grunt or roar." Texas v. Johnson, 491 U.S. 397, 432 (1989) (Rehnquist, C.J., dissenting).

50. Morse v. Frederick, 551 U.S. 393, 401 (2007).

51. Note that in trademark law invented words can become trademarks. Do consumers and competitors have a First Amendment right to use "to xerox" as a synonym for "to use a photocopying machine" or "onesies" as a synonym for "one-piece infant sleepwear" (before the words become generic and lose trademark protection) because they reasonably impute those meanings to the words?

52. An analogy here might be to the visual appearance of an English word transliterated into Greek script (but not translated into Greek). An example: σοκκερ (*soccer* transliterated; the Greek word for soccer is ποδόσφαιρο). The Greek "word" might be meaningless as a Greek word but could be the equivalent of the English word to someone who knows the Greek alphabet but not Greek.

53. The criteria for determining when "enough" viewers converge on a meaning should probably be relatively weak, so that truly idiosyncratic meanings are excluded but odd ones are not.

54. "I was a Flower of the mountain yes when I put the rose in my hair like the Andalusian girls used or shall I wear a red yes and how he kissed me under the Moorish wall and I thought well as well him as another and then I asked him with my eyes to ask again yes and then he asked me would I yes to say yes my mountain flower and first I put my arms around him yes and drew him down to me so he could feel my breasts all perfume yes and his heart was going like mad and yes I said yes I will Yes." James Joyce, *Ulysses* 573 (Paris: Sylvia Beach, 1922). (This quotation is severely truncated.)

55. Central Hudson Gas v. Public Service Comm'n, 447 U.S. 557, 566 (1980).

56. Eldred v. Ashcroft, 537 U.S. 186, 221 (2003).

57. Harper & Row, Publishers v. Nation Enterprises, 471 U.S. 538 (1985).

58. U.S. House of Representatives, *Agreement on Guidelines for Classroom Copying in Not-for-Profit Educational Institutions*, report 94–1476 (1976). The precise status of this agreement is unclear, although some courts have relied on the guidelines to define fair use. See, e.g., Princeton Univ. Press v. Michigan Document Servs., 99 F.3d 1381 (6th Cir. 1996). It seems to have been intended as a safe harbor for uses described as fair by the guidelines; whether the agreement was intended to serve as a delimitation of uses that would not be fair remains controversial.

59. *Harper & Row*, 471 U.S. at 558.

60. The core exemplar here is "confessional poetry," of which Sylvia Plath's "Daddy" is an example. Some confessional poems might identify a person with sufficient specificity to make a claim of reputational damage entirely plausible. The development of online permissions systems might reduce the time needed to obtain permission to the point where no distribution could fairly be called spontaneous. For a more extended discussion of why "copyright's built-in safeguards" might not be sufficient to satisfy non-copyright-based First Amendment requirements, see Rebecca Tushnet, "Copy This Essay: How the Fair Use Doctrine Harms Free Speech and How Copying Serves It," 114 *Yale L.J.* 535 (2004).

61. Buckley v. Valeo, 424 U.S. 1, 48–49 (1976). For a discussion using this observation to challenge *Buckley*'s correctness, see Rebecca Tushnet, "Copyright as a Model for Free Speech Law: What Copyright Has in Common with Campaign Finance Reform, Hate Speech and Pornography Regulation, and Telecommunications Regulation," 42 *B.C. L. Rev.* 1, 44 (2001).

62. For a discussion focusing primarily on art and secondarily on the law, see Anthony Julius, *Transgressions: The Offenses of Art* (Chicago: University of Chicago

Press, 2003). Some recent controversies, such as the withdrawal of city subsidies from the Brooklyn Museum after it exhibited Andres Serrano's *Piss Christ*, demonstrate that some works of transgressive art succeed in that ambition. See Brooklyn Institute of Arts & Sciences v. Giuliani, 64 F. Supp. 2d 184 (F.D.N.Y. 1999), for a discussion of the controversy. Sonya G. Bonneau, "Ex Post Modernism: How the First Amendment Framed Nonrepresentational Art," 39 *Columb. J. L. & Arts* 195 (2015), argues that the canonical reference to Jackson Pollock in discussions of the First Amendment and nonrepresentational art fails to address the issues associated with the forms of art being created today.

63. Busking combines artistic performance (usually musical) with panhandling. SEIU v. City of Houston, 542 F. Supp. 2d 617 (S.D. Tex. 2008), upheld an antibusking ordinance against a First Amendment challenge, finding the ordinance content neutral and adequately justified. Cf. Hobbs v. County of Westchester, 397 F.3d 133 (2d Cir. 2005), upholding against a First Amendment challenge a county's executive order barring a busker, previously convicted of child molestation, from child-oriented performances on public property. The court of appeals found the order content neutral and sufficiently justified. (The busker there made balloon animals.) These cases suggest a pattern in which activities such as panhandling and ticket scalping are held covered by the First Amendment but that regulation of those activities (almost) certainly satisfies the applicable First Amendment standards. For a discussion of whether that pattern can provide the basis for a general approach to nonrepresentational art and the First Amendment, see later in this chapter.

64. Alexander Meiklejohn, "The First Amendment Is an Absolute," 1961 *Sup. Ct. Rev.* 245, 255, 256–57, 262 (1961).

65. The observation that MacLeish "asserted" this in a poem is a commonplace in commentary on it. See, e.g., Michael J. Cummings, "Ars Poetica," Cummings Study Guide, accessed Nov. 23, 2015, www.cummingsstudyguides.net. This citation shows how banal the observation has become.

66. To similar effect, see Lee C. Bollinger, *Uninhibited, Robust, and Wide-Open: A Free Press for a New Century* 46 (Oxford: Oxford University Press, 2010) ("Speech as a means of self-fulfillment and self-realization can be seen as too ill-defined for judges to work with comfortably, *indistinguishable from other meaningful human activities*"; emphasis added.).

67. See especially Jack M. Balkin, "Digital Speech and Democratic Culture: A Theory of Freedom of Expression for the Information Society," 79 *N.Y.U. L. Rev.* 1 (2004).

68. For an exposition of Balkin's historicism, see Jack M. Balkin, *Constitutional Redemption: Political Faith in an Unjust World* (Cambridge, MA: Harvard University Press, 2011).

69. Post, "Participatory Democracy and Free Speech," 486.

70. Robert Post, "Participatory Democracy as a Theory of Free Speech: A Reply," 97 *Va. L. Rev.* 617, 621 (2011).

71. Mutual Film Corp. v. Industrial Comm'n of Ohio, 236 U.S. 230 (1915), *overruled,* Joseph Burstyn, Inc. v. Wilson, 343 U.S. 493 (1952). In *Mutual Film*, the Court addressed the coverage of Ohio's constitutional protection of speech and the press.

72. *Burstyn*, 343 U.S. at 501 ("That books, newspapers, and magazines are published and sold for profit does not prevent them from being a form of expression whose liberty is safeguarded by the First Amendment.")

73. Winters v. New York, 333 U.S. 507, 510 (1948).

74. Ibid., 528 (Frankfurter, J., dissenting). This is true even of poems that seem expressly at least partly didactic. Consider what is lost in saying that the "point" of "Ode on a Grecian Urn" is "'Beauty is truth, truth beauty,—that is all / Ye know on earth, and all ye need to know.'" (Note that Keats has the urn itself "saying" this.) See also Brown v. Entm't Merchs. Ass'n, 131 S. Ct. 2729, 2737 n.4 (2011) ("Reading Dante is unquestionably more cultured and intellectually edifying than playing Mortal Kombat."). The difficulties in distinguishing between didactic imaginative literature—"propaganda through fiction," in Justice Reed's words—and "mere" imaginative literature should not be minimized, and those difficulties might be sufficient to justify a decision not to draw a constitutional distinction between them. But that is a different rationale from the one the Court has offered.

75. See, e.g., Roth v. United States, 354 U.S. 476, 487 (1957) ("The portrayal of sex, e.g., in *art*, literature and scientific works, is not itself sufficient reason to deny material the constitutional protection of freedom of speech and press"; emphasis added.); Miller v. California, 413 U.S. 15, 24 (1973) ("A state offense must also be limited to works which, taken as a whole, appeal to the prurient interest in sex, which portray sexual conduct in a patently offensive way, and which, taken as a whole, do not have *serious* literary, *artistic*, political, or scientific *value*"; emphasis added.).

76. Nat'l Endowment for the Arts v. Finley, 524 U.S. 569 (1998). For a discussion of the case, see Bezanson, *Art and Freedom of Speech*. Bonneau, "Ex Post Modernism," argues that the reference to Pollock is the product of an association of abstract art with free expression, forged in the immediate post-1945 era because of the social and political environment of the times.

77. The possibility that the NEA might deny the subsidy for reasons orthogonal to its interest in art, for example, on the (hypothesized) ground that Pollock was a Communist, is irrelevant here.

78. Hurley v. Irish-Am. Gay, Lesbian & Bisexual Grp. of Bos., Inc., 515 U.S. 557 (1995).

79. Ibid., 574. The resonance between this approach and "reader response" accounts of literature is clear. For an annotated bibliography on reader-response theory, see "Annotated Bibliography," in *Reader-Response Criticism: From Formalism to Post-Structuralism* 233 (Jane P. Tompkins ed., Baltimore: Johns Hopkins University Press, 1980).

80. Rumsfeld v. FAIR, 547 U.S. 47, 66 (2006) (distinguishing between "inherently expressive" conduct and other conduct, only the former of which is protected by the First Amendment, and commenting, "An observer who sees military recruiters

interviewing away from the law school has no way of knowing whether the law school is expressing its disapproval of the military, all the law school's interview rooms are full, or the military recruiters decided for reasons of their own that they would rather interview someplace else."). See also First Vagabonds Church of God v. City of Orlando, 610 F.3d 1274 (11th Cir. 2010) (relying on this passage to hold that a church's activity in providing food to the homeless in a city park, while intended to communicate a message and understood by some viewers to do so, was not "truly communicative"). Consistent with the general pattern identified earlier, on rehearing en banc, the Eleventh Circuit assumed that the activity was expressive but upheld the city's prohibition of the distribution of food as "a reasonable time, place, and manner restriction." First Vagabonds Church of God v. City of Orlando, 638 F.3d 756, 761 (11th Cir. 2011).

81. What counts as "truly idiosyncratic" would have to be quite carefully specified. It is a settled feature in novels dealing with serial killers that the killers can regard what they do as producing works of art, and the very fact that it is a settled feature shows that the imputation of artistry to killings is not idiosyncratic.

82. Cohen v. California, 403 U.S. 15, 26 (1971).

83. Consider here an analysis describing E. E. Cummings's "i sing of Olaf glad and big" as "maintain[ing] that the American ideal of patriotism has been perverted to depraved cruelty as the war machine grinds any opposition to pulp." "i sing of Olaf glad and big—Themes and Meanings," in *Critical Guide to Poetry for Students* (Philip K. Jason ed., eNotes.com, 2002), http://www.enotes.com/topics/sing-olaf-glad-big/themes, https://perma.cc/U76Q-DVQP. The statement is true enough in some sense but obviously lacking a great deal.

84. Two observations here: First, *all* words have noncognitive force, "Abolish the Draft" as much as "Fuck the Draft." The former, perhaps, conveys that the speaker has rationally considered all the relevant policies and has concluded in a dispassionate manner that the draft should be rejected as unsound public policy, the latter that the speaker is passionately committed to the draft's abolition. Second, the presence of words is irrelevant to Justice Harlan's point.

85. Holder v. Humanitarian Law Project, 561 U.S. 1, 27–28 (2010).

86. The classic examples are bans on so-called lifestyle advertising for products, such as tobacco, the consumption of which poses risks to health and life. Lifestyle advertising associates that consumption with lifestyles that the product's producers believe consumers to find attractive.

87. For art, see, e.g., Blanch v. Koons, 467 F.3d 244 (2d Cir. 2006) (magazine photography copied for "high" appropriation art); Leibovitz v. Paramount Pictures Corp., 137 F.3d 109 (2d Cir. 1996) (high-art photography copied for movie poster). For music, see, e.g., Bright Tunes Music v. Harrisongs Music, 420 F. Supp. 177 (S.D.N.Y. 1976) (dealing with the musical similarity between "He's So Fine" and "My Sweet Lord," without regard to lyrics); Bridgeport Music, Inc. v. UMG Recordings, Inc., 585 F.3d 267 (6th Cir. 2009) (holding that any sampling of a sound recording, no matter how de minimis or unrecognizable, is infringing). Only some of these

cases involve arguably "high" art. The classic music-only infringement case not involving any similarity in lyrics, is *Bright Tunes Music*, 420 F. Supp. 177.

88. This suggestion has been made before, though not in precisely these terms. See, e.g., Eugene Volokh and Brett McDonnell, "Freedom of Speech and Independent Judgment Review in Copyright Cases," 107 *Yale L.J.* 2431 (1998); Mark Lemley and Eugene Volokh, "Freedom of Speech and Injunctions in Intellectual Property Cases," 48 *Duke L.J.* 147 (1998).

89. One can tinker with the hypothetical to squeeze it into an existing trademark-dilution cause of action, but perhaps it is better to imagine that the artist could take advantage of some sort of moral-right cause of action. Cf. Visual Artists Rights Act, 17 U.S.C. § 106A(3) (giving a right to creators of works of visual art "to prevent any intentional distortion, mutilation, or other modification of that work which would be prejudicial to his or her honor or reputation"). Under VARA, the question would be whether the alternative frames are a "modification of *that* work," and they probably are not, although again tinkering with the hypothetical could make them so.

90. Perhaps the "family resemblance" approach is sufficiently similar to Balkin's conventionalism as to be vulnerable to the same kinds of criticism leveled against it. So, for example, questions about coverage might be raised in precisely those circumstances where many people do not see even a general family resemblance between the object in question and political speech. An example might be some forms of performance art. The idea of a family resemblance may rely on a certain kind of conventionalism about language, whereas Balkin's approach relies on conventionalism about cultural products themselves. But the notion of family resemblances is notoriously slippery, and the proposition that artworks bear a family resemblance to political speech is not central to the argument here.

91. Winters v. New York, 333 U.S. 507, 510 (1948). The line-drawing exercise is not so difficult as to be beyond judicial capacity. It seems easy to conclude that *Spiral Jetty* and David Smith's sculpture are not propaganda through nonrepresentational art, and it is similar with a great deal of such art (and nonprogrammatic music). Put another way, courts would not inevitably do a bad job were they to try to develop categories smaller than "art" (and, just to be clear, the "rules/standards" literature shows that the possibility that one or a small group of artworks would be misclassified is insufficient in itself to justify seeking larger rather than smaller categories).

CHAPTER 3. NONSENSE AND THE FREEDOM OF SPEECH

1. See Dennis M. Patterson, "Law's Pragmatism: Law as Practice and Narrative," 76 *Va. L. Rev.* 937, 938 (1990) ("It is the thought of Ludwig Wittgenstein which is central to modern philosophy's turn to language. For Wittgenstein, all philosophical problems are ultimately problems of language.").

2. Ludwig Wittgenstein, *Culture and Value* 56e (G. H. von Wright ed., Peter Winch trans., Chicago: University of Chicago Press, 1980); see also Guy Kahane, Edward

Kanterian, and Oskari Kuusela, introduction to *Wittgenstein and His Interpreters* 32 n.23 (Guy Kahane, Edward Kanterian, and Oskari Kuusela eds., Hoboken, NJ: Wiley-Blackwell, 2007) ("Saul Liberman . . . reportedly once introduced a 1940s lecture by the famous Kabbalah scholar Gershom Scholem with the words 'Nonsense is nonsense—but the history of nonsense is scholarship.'").

3. See, e.g., John Greenman, "On Communication," 106 *Mich. L. Rev.* 1337, 1347 (2008) ("Frequently, behavior is said to be covered by the First Amendment if it conveys 'ideas' or 'information.'"); Melville B. Nimmer, "The Meaning of Symbolic Speech under the First Amendment," 21 *UCLA L. Rev.* 29, 61 (1973) ("The crucial question under the first amendment is simply whether meaningful symbols of any type are being employed by one who wishes to communicate to others."); Peter Meijes Tiersma, "Nonverbal Communication and the Freedom of Speech," 1993 *Wis. L. Rev.* 1525, 1559 ("[T]he first requirement for communication by conduct is that the conduct be meaningful, most often as a matter of convention. This is simply an extension of a basic principle of language: a speaker normally cannot use sounds to communicate unless the sounds have some meaning attached to them.").

4. *Merriam-Webster's Collegiate Dictionary* 791 (10th ed. 1996), s.v. "nonsense"; see also William Charlton, "Nonsense," 17 *Brit. J. Aesthetics* 346, 346 (1977) ("The notion of nonsense has been freely used by philosophers of this century, but no full or satisfactory account has been given of it. . . . The English word 'nonsense' seems to apply most appropriately to something which purports to have a sense or meaning, but does not in fact have one.").

5. N.Y. Times Co. v. Sullivan, 376 U.S. 254, 269 (1964) (emphasis added; quoting Roth v. United States, 354 U.S. 476, 484 (1957)); see also Police Dep't of Chi. v. Mosley, 408 U.S. 92, 96 (1972) ("[O]ur people are guaranteed the right to express any thought, free from government censorship.").

6. See Hurley v. Irish-Am. Gay, Lesbian & Bisexual Grp. of Bos., Inc., 515 U.S. 557, 569 (1995) ("As some of these examples show, a narrow, succinctly articulable message is not a condition of constitutional protection, which if confined to expressions conveying a 'particularized message' would never reach the unquestionably shielded painting of Jackson Pollock, music of Arnold Schöenberg, or Jabberwocky verse of Lewis Carroll"; citation omitted; quoting Spence v. Washington, 418 U.S. 405, 411 (1974) (per curiam)).

7. See chapter 2 (providing examples of artists denying the necessity of traditional meaning in their work, including Archibald MacLeish's claim that "[a] poem should not mean but be" (Archibald MacLeish, "Ars Poetica," in *Collected Poems 1917–1982*, 106, 107 (Boston: Mariner Books, 1985)) and William Carlos Williams's refrain, "No ideas but in things" (William Carlos Williams, "A Sort of Song," in 2 *The Collected Poems of William Carlos Williams* 55 (Christopher MacGowan ed., New York: New Directions Books, 2001)); see also Amy M. Adler, "Post-Modern Art and the Death of Obscenity Law," 99 *Yale L.J.* 1359, 1364 (1990) (noting that postmodern art "not only rejected the Modernist demand that art be 'serious,' it

rejected the idea that art must have any traditional 'value' at all"); Adler, "Post-Modern Art," 1367 ("[T]he 80's has been the decade in which art that denies the value of art has become the most valuable art around"; alteration in original; quoting Elizabeth Frank, "Art's Off-the-Wall Critic," *N.Y. Times Mag.*, Nov. 19, 1989, 47, 78)).

8. In chapter 2, Tushnet explores the attractions and perils of "nominalism," which would focus on "words and word equivalents" as the basis of First Amendment analysis. See also Tinker v. Des Moines Indep. Cmty. Sch. Dist., 393 U.S. 503, 505–6 (1969) ("'[P]ure speech' . . . , we have repeatedly held, is entitled to comprehensive protection under the First Amendment."). This chapter focuses primarily on nonsensical language, rather than nonsensical conduct, because it seems to be well accepted that conduct can be nonsensical, whereas the connection between language and nonsense has been largely unexplored. As noted in the conclusion to this chapter, the use-meaning approach would not extend First Amendment coverage to *all* linguistic communication.

9. See Charlton, "Nonsense," 346 ("It would normally be thought fairly damning to say of an utterance or a piece of writing 'That is nonsense.' Yet men of undoubted intelligence, like Edward Lear and Lewis Carroll, have devoted time and pains to writing what they admit is nonsense, and talking nonsense has been regarded as a conversational art."). For a discussion of overt nonsense, see section 1.A.1 in this chapter.

10. Ludwig Wittgenstein, *Tractatus Logico-Philosophicus* § 6.54, 189 (C. K. Ogden ed. and ; trans., New York: Harcourt Brace, 1922). Whether this is really what he intended (and whether he succeeded) is of course another matter. The "meaning" of the *Tractatus*'s avowed lack of sense has been an elusive and perhaps ephemeral grail for analytic philosophers. For a description of the debate over "ineffable" and "resolute" readings, see Leo K. C. Cheung, "The Disenchantment of Nonsense: Understanding Wittgenstein's *Tractatus*, 31 *Phil. Investigations* 197, 201–3 (2008).

11. For a discussion of covert nonsense, see section 1.A.2 in this chapter.

12. Morse v. Frederick, 551 U.S. 393, 396–97 (2007).

13. Ibid., 401.

14. Ibid., 403, 409.

15. See ibid., 401 (quoting Frederick v. Morse, 439 F.3d 1114, 1117–18 (9th Cir. 2006), *rev'd*, 551 U.S. 393 (2007)).

16. Ibid., 444 (Stevens, J., dissenting); see also ibid., 435 (referring to the "nonsense banner").

17. I follow Robert Post's lead by attempting to tell a story in which doctrine and normative commitments are interdependent. See Robert C. Post, *Democracy, Expertise, and Academic Freedom* 5 (New Haven, CT: Yale University Press, 2012) ("To determine the purposes of the First Amendment, therefore, we must consult the actual shape of entrenched First Amendment jurisprudence.").

18. See B. R. Tilghman, "Literature, Philosophy and Nonsense," 30 *Brit. J. Aesthetics* 256, 256 (1990) ("[A] good case can be made that the notion of meaning and all

it implies for the distinction between sense and nonsense has been the primary concern of twentieth-century philosophy, at least Anglo-American philosophy.").

19. See Wittgenstein, *Tractatus*, § 5.6, 149 ("The limits of my language mean the limits of my world.").

20. Borrowing philosophers' tools, with or without acknowledgment, would itself be nothing new for First Amendment doctrine. See David Cole, "Agon at Agora: Creative Misreadings in the First Amendment Tradition," 95 *Yale L.J.* 857, 875–78 (1986) (tracing the First Amendment doctrine's "philosophical origins" to John Milton, John Locke, John Stuart Mill, and others).

21. See section 2.A in this chapter.

22. Herbert Hochberg, preface to *Introducing Analytic Philosophy: Its Sense and Its Nonsense, 1879–2002* (2003) (quoting Russell, "Logical Positivism," in *Logic and Knowledge* 381 (Robert Charles Marsh ed., London: Allen and Unwin, 1956)).

23. Ashcroft v. ACLU, 535 U.S. 564, 573 (2002) (second alteration in original; quoting Harte-Hanks Commc'ns, Inc. v. Connaughton, 491 U.S. 657, 686 (1989)); see also Miller v. California, 413 U.S. 15, 20 (1973) ("All ideas having even the slightest redeeming social importance—unorthodox ideas, controversial ideas, even ideas hateful to the prevailing climate of opinion—have the full protection of the [First Amendment] guaranties"; alteration in original; quoting Roth v. United States, 354 U.S. 476, 484 (1957)).

24. Spence v. Washington, 418 U.S. 405, 410–11 (1974) (per curiam). In *Rumsfeld v. FAIR*, 547 U.S. 47, 66 (2006), the Court suggested that the message must be "created by the conduct itself," not "by the speech that accompanies it."

25. See section 1.B in this chapter.

26. See Wittgenstein, *Tractatus*, § 6.421, 183.

27. Ludwig Wittgenstein, "Ethics, Life and Faith," in *The Wittgenstein Reader* 251, 258 (Anthony Kenny ed., 2d ed., Hoboken, NJ: Wiley-Blackwell, 2006); see also James Boyle, "Anachronism of the Moral Sentiments? Integrity, Postmodernism, and Justice," 51 *Stan. L. Rev.* 493, 519 (1999) (discussing this passage).

28. See Dennis Patterson, "Wittgenstein and Constitutional Theory," 72 *Tex. L. Rev.* 1837, 1854–55 (1994) ("The legacy of philosophy from the middle of this century to the present has been the systematic replacement of foundationalist epistemology with holism, the substitution of referential theories of language with an emphasis on speech as action, and a general movement away from the individual as the foundation of empirical, linguistic, and moral judgment"; footnotes omitted).

29. Dennis Patterson, "Conscience and the Constitution," 93 *Colum. L. Rev.* 270, 303–4 (1993) (book review); see also Owen M. Fiss, "Conventionalism," 58 *S. Cal. L. Rev.* 177, 177 (1985) ("Conventionalism is a viewpoint, most closely associated with the later writings of Wittgenstein, that emphasizes practice and context. It holds, for example, that we understand a concept not when we grasp some fact, but when we can successfully use that concept within a language game or a defined context, and that truth is a function of the agreement of those participating within a practice rather than the other way around"; footnote omitted).

30. Ludwig Wittgenstein, *Philosophical Investigations* § 43 (G. E. M. Anscombe trans., 3d ed., New York: Macmillan, 1969).

31. Ibid., § 7.

32. Joseph Burstyn, Inc. v. Wilson, 343 U.S. 495, 501 (1952).

33. Hurley v. Irish-Am. Gay, Lesbian & Bisexual Grp. of Bos., Inc., 515 U.S. 557, 569 (1995) (quoting Spence v. Washington, 418 U.S. 405, 411 (1974) (per curiam)).

34. Robert Post, "Recuperating First Amendment Doctrine," 47 *Stan. L. Rev.* 1249, 1255 (1995); see also ibid., 1276–77 ("Instead of aspiring to articulate abstract characteristics of speech, doctrine ought to identify discrete forms of social order that are imbued with constitutional value, and it ought to clarify and safeguard the ways in which speech facilitates that constitutional value."). My goal here is, in part, to show that one potential "abstract characteristic[] of speech"—meaning—is in fact derived from "discrete forms of social order." See ibid., 1276–77.

35. See section 2.C in this chapter.

36. Jack M. Balkin and Sanford Levinson, "Constitutional Grammar," 72 *Tex. L. Rev.* 1771, 1802 (1994); see also Wittgenstein, *Tractatus*, § 65 ("Instead of producing something common to all that we call language, I am saying that [language games] have no one thing in common which makes us use the same word for all—but that they are *related* to one another in many different ways.").

37. See Charlton, "Nonsense," 346 ("In general philosophers have gone wrong in supposing that whatever is nonsensical is nonsensical in the same way.").

38. See, e.g., *Oxford Dictionaries*, s.v. "nonsense," accessed Feb. 25, 2014, http://oxforddictionaries.com (defining "nonsense" as "spoken or written words that have no meaning or make no sense").

39. It would be perfectly plausible to slice nonsense in other ways, however—between purposeful and accidental, substantial and mere, illuminating and misleading, and so on. Oskari Kuusela, "Nonsense and Clarification in the *Tractatus*—Resolute and Ineffability Readings and the *Tractatus*' Failure," 80 *Acta Philosophica Fennica* 35, 37 (2006) (distinguishing "between misleading and illuminating nonsense" by noting that "[t]he former is unself-conscious nonsense attempting to say what can only be shown," whereas "[t]he latter is self-conscious nonsense intended to reveal its own nonsensicalness").

The two approaches to meaning discussed in part 2 also suggest their own definitions of nonsense; indeed, the chapter concludes by arguing that "representational" nonsense is constitutionally protected, whereas "use" nonsense is not. Because that argument is dependent in part on the fact that the former would include—and therefore *ex*clude from constitutional coverage—so much everyday nonsense, it is better to start with a more general definition of nonsense.

40. See, e.g., Hurley v. Irish-Am. Gay, Lesbian & Bisexual Grp. of Bos., Inc., 515 U.S. 557, 569 (1995). *Jabberwocky* is perhaps the most famous of Carroll's nonsense, but it is by no means the only example. See, e.g., Lewis Carroll, *Alice's Adventures in Wonderland* 134 (1865; Boston: Lee and Shepard, 1869) ("Never imagine yourself

not to be otherwise than what it might appear to others that what you were or might have been was not otherwise than what you had been would have appeared to them to be otherwise.").

41. Lewis Carroll, *Through the Looking-Glass, and What Alice Found There* 21 (London: Macmillan, 1872).

42. Carroll and Humpty Dumpty—his avatar of nonsense—later provided a glossary of terms.

43. William Shakespeare, *Macbeth*, 5.5.

44. See Kuusela, "Nonsense and Clarification," 37 (describing Peter Hacker's view of overt nonsense); see also P. M. S. Hacker, *Insight and Illusion: Themes in the Philosophy of Wittgenstein* 18–19 (rev. ed., Oxford, UK: Clarendon, 1986) (distinguishing overt and covert nonsense).

45. William Charlton refers to something like this when he discusses "factual" nonsense: "An utterance is factual nonsense if a person uttering it cannot mean what he says without ignoring plain facts, or what are taken to be plain facts." See Charlton, "Nonsense," 352 (distinguishing "factual" from "grammatical" and "logical" nonsense).

46. See ibid., 355 ("A man could not, of course, compose what he knows is nonsense without having a purpose of some sort. But he need have no ulterior purpose, no reason for writing what he writes except that it is nonsense. Lear and Carroll, at least, seem to have written nonsense for its own sake in this way.").

47. Charles Rosen, "Freedom and Art," in *Freedom and the Arts: Essays on Music and Literature* 8–9 (Cambridge, MA: Harvard University Press, 2012).

48. See The Beatles, "I Am the Walrus," *Magical Mystery Tour* (Capitol Records, 1967) ("Semolina pilchards climbing up the Eiffel Tower / Elementary penguin singing Hare Krishna / Man you should have seen them / Kicking Edgar Allan Poe"); see also The Beatles, "Come Together," *Abbey Road* (Capitol Records, 1969) ("He bag production / He got walrus gumboot / He got Ono sideboard / He one spinal cracker").

49. Barry Mann, "Who Put the Bomp," *Who Put the Bomp* (Barry Mann and Gerry Goffin writers; ABC-Paramount, 1961) ("When my baby heard / 'Bomp bah bah bomp' / 'Bah bomp bah bomp bah' / Every word went right into her heart.").

50. The Kingsmen, "Louie, Louie," *The Kingsmen in Person* (Wand Records, 1963); see also Eric Predoehl, "A Short History of the Song 'Louie Louie,'" LouieLouie.net, 1999 (noting that the inscrutable song has "been called everything from a musical joke, pure garbage, the dumbest song ever written, to the quintessential pop single" and that the FBI actually investigated the lyrics to determine whether they are obscene).

51. Adriano Celentano, "Prisencolinensinainciusol," *Nostalrock* (Italdisc, 1973) (consisting of "lyrics" that mimic what American English sounds like to an Italian-speaking listener).

52. Cf. Charlton, "Nonsense," 347 ("Unless they wish to illustrate a philosophic point people seldom compose total nonsense on purpose.").

53. See Wittgenstein, *Tractatus*, § 6.54, 189 ("My propositions are elucidatory in this way: he who understands me finally recognizes them as senseless."). Wittgenstein's use of the word *senseless* rather than *nonsense* is significant, because he posited a difference between the two. For the purposes of the present discussion, however, there is no need to make such a fine distinction: both *senseless* and *nonsense* involve a lack of meaning. See Anat Biletzki and Anat Matar, "Ludwig Wittgenstein," *Stanford Encyclopedia of Philosophy* (Nov. 8, 2002; rev. Mar. 3, 2014), http://plato.stanford.edu ("The characteristic of being senseless applies not only to the propositions of logic but also to other things that cannot be represented, such as mathematics or the pictorial form itself of the pictures that do represent. These are, like tautologies and contradictions, literally sense-less, they have no sense. Beyond, or aside from, senseless propositions Wittgenstein identifies another group of statements which cannot carry sense: the nonsensical ("unsinnig") propositions. Nonsense, as opposed to senselessness, is encountered when a proposition is even more radically devoid of meaning, when it transcends the bounds of sense.").

54. A. W. Moore and Peter Sullivan, "Ineffability and Nonsense," 77 *Proc. Aristotelian Soc'y (Supp.)* 169, 179 (2003). As Wittgenstein explained, the aim of the *Tractatus* was to "draw a limit to thinking," which "can . . . only be drawn in language and what lies on the other side of the limit will be simply nonsense." *Tractatus*, 27.

55. Noam Chomsky, *Syntactic Structures* 15 (The Hague: Mouton, 1957). I am indebted to David Blocher for the example.

56. Cf., e.g., United States v. O'Brien, 391 U.S. 367, 376 (1968) ("[The Court] cannot accept the view that an apparently limitless variety of conduct can be labeled 'speech' whenever the person engaging in the conduct intends thereby to express an idea."); Nimmer, "Meaning of Symbolic Speech," 37 (concluding that "symbolic speech requires not merely that given conduct results in a meaning effect, but that the actor causing such conduct must intend such a meaning effect by his conduct"). To be clear, I do not mean to suggest that these authorities would *actually* exclude misunderstandings from the First Amendment, only that their approaches seem to do so, as stated. Nimmer, for example, posited not only that a "meaning effect" was necessary for symbolic speech but also that the Amendment covered speech lacking "both verbal and cognitive content." Nimmer, "Meaning of Symbolic Speech," 35–36.

57. Cf. Universal City Studios, Inc., v. Corley, 273 F.3d 429, 445 (2d Cir. 2001) ("Communication does not lose constitutional protection as 'speech' simply because it is expressed in the language of computer code. Mathematical formulae and musical scores are written in 'code,' i.e., symbolic notations not comprehensible to the uninitiated, and yet both are covered by the First Amendment.").

58. John Cage, *4'33"* (1952); See Michael Nyman, *Experimental Music: Cage and Beyond* 11 (2d ed., New York: Schirmer Books, 1999) ("[The piece's] first and most famous performance was given by a pianist (David Tudor). . . . Tudor, seated in the normal fashion on a stool in front of the piano, did nothing more nor less

than silently close the keyboard lid at the beginning of, and raise it at the end of each time period.").

59. See The Beatles, "I Am the Walrus," *Magical Mystery Tour* (Capitol Records, 1967).

60. Most likely, neither the pianist, janitor, nor tourist could raise First Amendment claims, given the requirement in *Spence v. Washington* (418 U.S 405, 410–11 (1974)) of "intent to convey a particularized message."

61. National Tourette Syndrome Association, "What Is Tourette Syndrome?," accessed Feb. 25, 2014, www.tourette.org.

62. See chapter 2 in this volume ("Taken together with *Hurley* and *Cohen, Humanitarian Law Project* implies that any activity that enough people regard as having some meaning, noncognitive as well as cognitive, must survive the highest level of scrutiny"; citing Holder v. Humanitarian Law Project, 561 U.S. 1 (2010); Hurley v. Irish-Am. Gay, Lesbian & Bisexual Grp. of Bos., Inc., 515 U.S. 557 (1995); Cohen v. California, 403 U.S. 15 (1971)).

63. See Wittgenstein, *Tractatus*, §§ 6.42–6.421, 183 ("Hence also there can be no ethical propositions. . . . [E]thics cannot be expressed."); see also ibid., § 4.003, 63 ("Most propositions and questions, that have been written about philosophical matters, are not false, but senseless."); Gregory S. Kavka, "Wittgensteinian Political Theory," 26 *Stan. L. Rev.* 1455, 1458 n.7 (1974) (reviewing Hanna Fenichel Pitkin, *Wittgenstein and Justice: On the Significance of Ludwig Wittgenstein for Social and Political Thought* (1972); "Since . . . Wittgenstein holds that propositions of ethics, aesthetics, and religion are not amenable to such analysis, he concludes that such propositions lack cognitive significance. This does not mean that Wittgenstein regards the propositions of aesthetics, ethics, and religion as worthless—such propositions are strictly speaking nonsensical, yet they possess a kind of mystical significance for they try to express that which is important but linguistically inexpressible"; citation omitted).

64. See Alexander Meiklejohn, *Political Freedom* 73 (New York: Harper, 1960) (arguing that establishing truth through a marketplace of ideas "is not merely the 'best' test" but that "[t]here is no other"); see also Joseph Blocher, "Institutions in the Marketplace of Ideas," 57 *Duke L.J.* 821, 823–25 (2008) ("This [marketplace of ideas] theory provided the first justification for a broad freedom of expression commensurate with the sweeping language of the First Amendment itself."); William P. Marshall, "In Defense of the Search for Truth as a First Amendment Justification," 30 *Ga. L. Rev.* 1, 1 (1995) ("In Speech Clause jurisprudence, for example, the oft-repeated metaphor that the First Amendment fosters a marketplace of ideas that allows truth to ultimately prevail over falsity has been virtually canonized.").

65. Abrams v. United States, 250 U.S. 616, 630 (1919) (Holmes, J., dissenting); see also John Milton, *Areopagitica: A Speech for the Liberty of Unlicensed Printing* 45 (1644; H. B. Cotterill ed., New York: Macmillan, 1959) (1644) ("Let her and falsehood grapple; who ever knew Truth put to the worse in a free and open encounter?").

66. See Sorrell v. IMS Health, Inc., 564 U.S. 552, 583 (2011) (Breyer, J., dissenting) ("These test-related distinctions reflect the constitutional importance of maintaining a free marketplace of ideas, a marketplace that provides access to 'social, political, esthetic, moral, and other ideas and experiences'"; quoting Red Lion Broad. Co. v. FCC, 395 U.S. 367, 390 (1969)).

67. Whitney v. California, 274 U.S. 357, 375 (1927) (Brandeis, J., concurring).

68. See chapter 2 in this volume ("What 'idea' does Jackson Pollock's *Blue Poles: No. 11* convey? Even more, what idea does *Ulysses* convey?"); see also Sheldon H. Nahmod, "Artistic Expression and Aesthetic Theory: The Beautiful, the Sublime, and the First Amendment," 1987 *Wis. L. Rev.* 221, 241 ("The [marketplace] theory's emphasis on 'ideas,' however, is troubling, and has the potential for making the first amendment value of art derivative. To the extent that the concept of ideas refers to intellectual and cognitive processes, it does not take account of the noncognitive and emotional aspects of communication which often accompany artistic expression, especially of the nonrepresentational kind.").

69. Bertrand Russell, *The Problems of Philosophy* 84–85 (1912; Rockville, MD: Arc Manor 2008).

70. See Paul G. Chevigny, "Philosophy of Language and Free Expression," 55 *N.Y.U. L. Rev.* 157, 167 (1980) (noting that, under the modern analytic approach, "there is no simple or certain way to know the meanings of words and sentences; even their 'truth' depends on the game in which they are used"). There is of course a danger of tautology here, one that reemerges in efforts to define as "speech" that which people recognize as such.

71. See Hustler Magazine, Inc. v. Falwell, 485 U.S. 46, 51 (1988) ("The First Amendment recognizes no such thing as a 'false' idea"; citing Gertz v. Robert Welch, Inc., 418 U.S. 323, 339 (1974)). As Post notes, the Court has *also* said that "there is no constitutional value in false statements of fact." Post, *Democracy*, 29 (quoting *Gertz*, 418 U.S. at 340); see Post, *Democracy*, 29–31, 43–47 (suggesting that the distinction can be explained based on whether the purportedly false statements are part of public discourse); see also United States v. Alvarez, 132 S. Ct. 2537, 2543 (2012) (striking down the Stolen Valor Act of 2005, Pub. L. No. 109–437, 120 Stat. 3266 (2006), which criminalized lies about certain military medals).

72. Martin H. Redish and Gary Lippman, "Freedom of Expression and the Civic Republican Revival in Constitutional Theory: The Ominous Implications," 79 *Calif. L. Rev.* 267, 271 (1991).

73. See Frederick Schauer, "The Second-Best First Amendment," 31 *Wm. & Mary L. Rev.* 1, 2 (1989) ("Not only the first amendment, but also the very idea of a principle of freedom of speech, is an embodiment of a risk-averse distrust of decisionmakers."); see also Vincent Blasi, "The Pathological Perspective and the First Amendment," 85 *Colum. L. Rev.* 449, 449–50 (1985) (theorizing that in interpreting the First Amendment, courts' "overriding objective at all times should be to equip the first amendment to do maximum service in those historical periods

when intolerance of unorthodox ideas is most prevalent and when governments are most able and most likely to stifle dissent systematically").

74. Bleistein v. Donaldson Lithographing Co., 188 U.S. 239, 251 (1903); see also Miller v. Civil City of S. Bend, 904 F.2d 1081, 1100 (7th Cir. 1990) (en banc) (Posner, J., concurring) ("[A First Amendment claim regarding nude dancing] strikes judges as ridiculous in part because most of us are either middle-aged or elderly men, in part because we tend to be snooty about popular culture, in part because as public officials we have a natural tendency to think political expression more important than artistic expression, in part because we are Americans—which means that we have been raised in a culture in which puritanism, philistinism, and promiscuity are complexly and often incongruously interwoven—and in part because like all lawyers we are formalists who believe deep down that the words in statutes and the Constitution mean what they say, and a striptease is not speech."), *rev'd sub nom.* Barnes v. Glen Theatre, Inc., 501 U.S. 560 (1991).

The question has also proven difficult for persons *not* trained only to the law, as Jeremy Waldron points out: "What [art critics] find is that they cannot agree about the definition of 'art.'" Jeremy Waldron, "Vagueness in Law and Language: Some Philosophical Issues," 82 *Calif. L. Rev.* 509, 530–31 (1994).

75. See Susan Stuart, "Shibboleths and *Ceballos*: Eroding Constitutional Rights through Pseudocommunication," 2008 *B.Y.U. L. Rev.* 1545, 1546 (2008) ("*Jabberwocky* has no meaning, at least that an adult audience could discern."). Indeed, the word *Jabberwocky* has come to be used as a synonym for mere nonsense. See, e.g., Jeanne C. Fromer, "A Psychology of Intellectual Property," 104 *Nw. U. L. Rev.* 1441, 1478 (2010) ("The artistic solution, in effect, is the expression, or vehicle, for the themes, meaning, and emotion essential to the found artistic problem. Without it, artistic expression becomes nothing more than *Jabberwocky*.").

76. See generally, e.g., Peter J. Lucas, "From *Jabberwocky* Back to Old English: Nonsense, Anglo-Saxon and Oxford," in 1 *Language History and Linguistic Modelling* 503 (Raymond Hickey and Stanisław Puppel eds., Boston: De Gruyter Mouton, 1997).

77. See Biletzki and Matar, "Ludwig Wittgenstein" ("'Nonsense' has become the hinge of Wittgensteinian interpretive discussion during the last decade of the 20th century. Beyond the bounds of language lies nonsense—propositions which cannot picture *anything*—and Wittgenstein bans traditional metaphysics to that area. The quandary arises concerning the question of what it is that inhabits that realm of nonsense, since Wittgenstein does seem to be saying that there is something there to be shown (rather than said) and does, indeed, characterize it as the 'mystical.'").

78. P. M. S. Hacker, "Was He Trying To Whistle It?," in *The New Wittgenstein* 353, 368 (Alice Crary and Rupert Read eds., New York: Routledge, 2000). The reference in Hacker's title is to a remark by Wittgenstein's friend, the Cambridge mathematician Frank Ramsey, who wrote that if Wittgenstein was right, "we must then take seriously that [philosophy] is nonsense, and not pretend, as Wittgenstein does,

that it is important nonsense!" Frank Plumpton Ramsey, *The Foundations of Mathematics* 263 (R. B. Braithwaite ed., London: Routledge and Kegan Paul, 1931). Connecting the famous final line of the *Tractatus* to Wittgenstein's well-known habit, Ramsey wrote, "But what we can't say we can't say, and we can't whistle it either." Ibid., 238.

79. See Bertrand Russell, introduction to Wittgenstein, *Tractatus*, 22 (referencing the seventh and final section of the *Tractatus*).

80. Hacker, "Was He Trying to Whistle It?," 353 (emphasis omitted; citation omitted; citing Wittgenstein, *Tractatus*, § 6.522, 187); see also G. E. M. Anscombe, *An Introduction to Wittgenstein's Tractatus* 162 (1971; 4th ed., South Bend, IN: St. Augustine's, 2001) (drawing this same conclusion); Roy Brand, "Making Sense Speaking Nonsense," 35 *Phil. F.* 311, 313 (2004) (same). The ineffable reading appears to be a matter of precedent in the Second Circuit. See Bery v. City of New York, 97 F.3d 689, 695 (2d Cir. 1996) ("The ideas and concepts embodied in visual art have the power to transcend . . . language limitations and reach beyond a particular language group to both the educated and the illiterate.").

81. Cf. Wittgenstein, *Tractatus*, § 6.54, 189 ("My propositions are elucidatory in this way: he who understands me finally recognizes them as senseless, when he has climbed out through them, on them, over them. (He must so to speak throw away the ladder, after he has climbed up on it.)").

82. See generally, e.g., James Conant, "Elucidation and Nonsense in Frege and Early Wittgenstein," in *The New Wittgenstein* 174 (Alice Crary and Rupert Read eds., New York: Routledge, 2000); James Conant, "Must We Show What We Cannot Say?," in *The Senses of Stanley Cavell* 242 (Richard Fleming and Michael Payne eds., Lewisberg, PA: Bucknell University Press, 1989); James Conant, "Two Conceptions of *Die Überwindung der Metaphysik*: Carnap and Early Wittgenstein," in *Wittgenstein in America* 13 (Timothy McCarthy and Sean C. Stidd eds., Oxford, UK: Clarendon, 2001); Cora Diamond, "Throwing Away the Ladder: How to Read the *Tractatus*," in *The Realistic Spirit: Wittgenstein, Philosophy, and the Mind* 179 (Cambridge, MA: MIT Press, 1991); Cora Diamond, "Logical Syntax in Wittgenstein's *Tractatus*," 55 *Phil. Q.* 78 (2005).

83. Edmund Dain, "Contextualism and Nonsense in Wittgenstein's *Tractatus*," 25 *S. Afr. J. Phil.* 91, 92 (2006) ("[T]here are, for austerity, no logically distinct kinds of nonsense; all nonsense, logically speaking, is on a par.").

84. Brand, "Making Sense Speaking Nonsense," 332 (quoting Diamond, "Throwing Away the Ladder," 181). It was Diamond who first wrote that the ineffable interpretation of Wittgenstein read the philosopher as "chickening out." Diamond, "Throwing Away the Ladder," 181.

85. Cheung, "Disenchantment of Nonsense," 200 (concluding that, according to Diamond and Conant, "the *Tractatus* is not trying to help anyone see any unsayable insights" but that "the aim of the *Tractatus* is *merely* to liberate nonsense utterers from nonsense, and that this is to be achieved by the non-frame sentences serving as elucidations"); Marie McGinn, "Between Metaphysics and Nonsense:

Elucidation in Wittgenstein's *Tractatus*," 49 *Phil. Q.* 491, 491–92 (1999); see also Brand, "Making Sense Speaking Nonsense," 326 ("The say/show distinction is meant to liberate us from the mental torture of a mind obsessively occupied with itself, chasing after itself in a movement that is increasingly vacuous, isolated, and cold."); Moore and Sullivan, "Ineffability and Nonsense," 179 ("There is nothing ineffable. There is only the temptation to see sense where it is lacking. Wittgenstein's aim is therapeutic.").

86. Brand, "Making Sense Speaking Nonsense," 330.

87. Wittgenstein, *Tractatus*, § 5.6, 149 (emphasis omitted).

88. As Wittgenstein wrote to Russell, "I'm afraid you haven't really got hold of my main contention, to which the whole business of logical prop[osition]s is only a corollary. The main point is the theory of what can be expressed [*gesagt*] by prop[osition]s—i.e. by language—(and, which comes to the same, what can be *thought*) and what can not be expressed by prop[osition]s, but only shown [*gezeigt*]; which, I believe, is the cardinal problem of philosophy." Ludwig Wittgenstein to Bertrand Russell, Aug. 19, 1919, in *Ludwig Wittgenstein: Letters to Russell, Keynes, and Moore* 71, 71 (G. H. von Wright ed., Oxford, UK: Basil Blackwell, 1974) (alterations in original).

89. Hegel, for one, believed that art was useful—albeit not as much as philosophy—as a guide to truth. See Nahmod, "Artistic Expression," 232 (citing G. W. F. Hegel, 1 *The Philosophy of Fine Art* 15–16 (F. P. B. Osmaston trans., London: G. Bell, 1920)).

90. See N.Y. Times Co. v. Sullivan, 376 U.S. 254, 279 n.19 (1964) ("Even a false statement may be deemed to make a valuable contribution to public debate, since it brings about 'the clearer perception and livelier impression of truth, produced by its collision with error'"; quoting John Stuart Mill, *On Liberty* 33 (London: John Parker, 1859)); Mill, *On Liberty*, 33 (concluding that silencing speech "rob[s] the human race" because even when an opinion is false, its contrast with the truth will more clearly illuminate the latter); Mark Spottswood, "Falsity, Insincerity, and the Freedom of Expression," 16 *Wm. & Mary Bill Rights J.* 1203, 1203 (2008) ("False statements often have value in themselves, and we should protect them even in some situations where we are not concerned with chilling truthful speech. . . . False speech, therefore, is valuable because it is an essential part of a larger system that works to increase society's knowledge.").

91. Tilghman, "Literature, Philosophy and Nonsense," 262.

92. Joseph Burstyn, Inc. v. Wilson, 343 U.S. 495, 501 (1952) (referring to motion pictures); see also Marci A. Hamilton, "Art Speech," 49 *Vand. L. Rev.* 73, 77 (1996) ("Art can carry ideas and information, but it also goes beyond logical, rational and discursive communication. It provides a risk-free opportunity to live in other worlds, enlarging individual perspective and strengthening individual judgment.").

93. Charlton, "Nonsense," 360.

94. Martin H. Redish, "The Value of Free Speech," 130 *U. Pa. L. Rev.* 591, 594 (1982) (footnote omitted). Tim Scanlon once defended a similar viewpoint. See gener-

ally, e.g., Thomas Scanlon, "A Theory of Freedom of Expression," 1 *Phil. & Pub. Aff.* 204 (1972). But he has since done his best to repudiate it. See T. M. Scanlon, "Why Not Base Free Speech on Autonomy or Democracy?," 97 *Va. L. Rev.* 541, 546 (2011) ("As someone who once made a mistaken appeal to autonomy as the centerpiece of a theory of freedom of expression, my position in the Dantean Inferno of free speech debates seems to be repeatedly assailed with misuses of this notion, no matter how I criticize them"; footnote omitted).

95. C. Edwin Baker, "Harm, Liberty, and Free Speech," 70 *S. Cal. L. Rev.* 979, 981 (1997); see also C. Edwin Baker, "Commercial Speech: A Problem in the Theory of Freedom," 62 *Iowa L. Rev.* 1, 6–7 (1976) (arguing that the First Amendment protects a speaker's self-realization).

96. Lawrence Byard Solum, "Freedom of Communicative Action: A Theory of the First Amendment Freedom of Speech," 83 *Nw. U. L. Rev.* 54, 80 (1989) ("[E]xpression may promote human flourishing in ways other than developing the rational faculties. Freedom of speech may allow the expression of powerful emotions and provide an outlet for the creative impulse in a variety of forms, including literature, drama, and the visual arts.").

97. Ibid.

98. See Hamilton, "Art Speech," 79 ("Self-preservation cannot be achieved merely by following principles; it depends on the realization of human potentials, and these can only be brought to light by literature, not by systematic discourse"; quoting Wolfgang Iser, *The Act of Reading: A Theory of Aesthetic Response* 76 (Baltimore: Johns Hopkins University Press, 1978)).

99. See generally James R. Atkinson, *The Mystical in Wittgenstein's Early Writings* (New York: Routledge, 2009).

100. See Hamilton, "Art Speech," 74.

101. See Piarowski v. Ill. Cmty. Coll. Dist. 515, 759 F.2d 625, 628 (7th Cir. 1985) (concluding that the First Amendment protects "purely artistic" expression—"art for art's sake").

102. Leo Tolstoy—whom Wittgenstein "admired and read constantly" (Brand, "Making Sense Speaking Nonsense," 311)—suggested that creating nonsense was perhaps the only thing that humans could do that their own creator could not. See ibid. ("God can do everything, it is true, but there is one thing he cannot do, and that is speak nonsense"; quoting Leo Tolstoy, *The Gospel According to Tolstoy* 11 (David Patterson ed. and trans., Tuscaloosa: University of Alabama Press, 1992)).

103. Anthony T. Kronman, "Is Poetry Undemocratic?," 16 *Ga. St. U. L. Rev.* 311, 324 (1999).

104. See ibid. ("Judgments of beauty are thus free in a twofold sense. They are neither driven by desire nor determined by a rule."); see also Charlton, "Nonsense," 356–59 (evaluating nonsense in terms of Kant's three types of aesthetic effect—the beautiful, the sublime, and the funny—and concluding that the first provides the best "clue"); Harry Kalven, Jr., "The Metaphysics of the Law of Obscenity," 1960 *Sup. Ct. Rev.* 1, 16 (1960) ("[B]eauty has constitutional status too, and . . . the life

of the imagination is as important to the human adult as the life of the intellect."); Nahmod, "Artistic Expression," 231 ("Because art is removed from knowledge and desire, it follows for Kant that art and the beautiful cannot express ideas or take positions.").

105. Martin H. Redish, *Freedom of Expression: A Critical Analysis* 30 (Charlottesville, VA: Michie, 1984) (emphasis added). In Scanlon's original defense of the autonomy position, he argued that, on a Millian approach, "the powers of a state are limited to those that citizens could recognize while still regarding themselves as equal, autonomous, rational agents." Scanlon, "Theory of Freedom of Expression," 215.

106. Frederick Schauer, *Free Speech: A Philosophical Enquiry* 49 (Cambridge: Cambridge University Press, 1982).

107. See Alexander Meiklejohn, *Free Speech and Its Relation to Self-Government* 94 (New York: Harper, 1948) ("The guarantee given by the First Amendment is not, then, assured to all speaking. It is assured only to speech which bears, directly or indirectly, upon issues with which voters have to deal—only, therefore, to the consideration of matters of public interest.").

108. Robert H. Bork, "Neutral Principles and Some First Amendment Problems," 47 *Ind. L.J.* 1, 29 (1971) (arguing that the First Amendment protects only "criticisms of public officials and policies, proposals for the adoption or repeal of legislation or constitutional provisions and speech addressed to the conduct of any governmental unit in the country").

109. Post, *Democracy*, 18; see also James Weinstein, "Participatory Democracy as the Central Value of American Free Speech Doctrine," 97 *Va. L. Rev.* 491, 491 (2011).

110. See, e.g., Meiklejohn, *Free Speech*, 26–27 ("[T]he vital point, as stated negatively, is that no suggestion of policy shall be denied a hearing because it is on one side of the issue rather than another."). Because Post focuses on *media* of communication, this is not necessarily true of his approach, though elsewhere I have questioned whether his theory can really avoid an inquiry into speech's content. See Joseph Blocher, "Public Discourse, Expert Knowledge, and the Press," 87 *U. Wash. L. Rev.* 409, 417–23 (2012).

111. See Hamilton, "Art Speech," 98–100 (discussing examples from post–Cultural Revolution China, communist eastern Europe, Nazi Germany, and elsewhere); cf. Ward v. Rock Against Racism, 491 U.S. 781, 790 (1989) ("Music is one of the oldest forms of human expression. From Plato's discourse in the Republic to the totalitarian state in our own times, rulers have known its capacity to appeal to the intellect and to the emotions, and have censored musical compositions to serve the needs of the state.").

112. Nahmod, "Artistic Expression," 225.

113. See Alexander Meiklejohn, "The First Amendment Is an Absolute," 1961 *Sup. Ct. Rev.* 245, 257 (1961).

114. See, e.g., Stephen G. Gey, "The First Amendment and the Dissemination of Socially Worthless Untruths," 36 *Fla. St. U. L. Rev.* 1, 10–11 (2008) (describing safety-valve theory).

115. Thomas I. Emerson, *The System of Freedom of Expression* 7 (New York: Random House, 1970).

116. Tom Wolfe, *The Electric Kool-Aid Acid Test* (New York: Farrar, Straus and Giroux, 1968).

117. Christopher Lehmann-Haupt, "Ken Kesey, Author of 'Cuckoo's Nest,' Who Defined the Psychedelic Era, Dies at 66," *N.Y. Times*, Nov. 11, 2001; see Wolfe, *Electric Kool-Aid Acid Test*, 100 ("Tootling the Multitudes").

118. NAACP v. Button, 371 U.S. 415, 433 (1963).

119. Ibid.

120. Broadrick v. Oklahoma, 413 U.S. 601, 612, 615 (1973).

121. N.Y. Times Co. v. Sullivan, 376 U.S. 254, 279 (1964) (quoting Speiser v. Randall, 357 U.S. 513, 526 (1958)).

122. Cohen v. California, 403 U.S. 15, 26 (1971).

123. Greenman, "On Communication," 1347; see also Eugene Volokh, "Speech as Conduct: Generally Applicable Laws, Illegal Courses of Conduct, 'Situation-Altering Utterances,' and the Unchartered Zones," 90 *Cornell L. Rev.* 1277, 1304 (2005) ("Under nearly every theory of free speech, the right to free speech is at its core the right to communicate—to persuade and to inform people through the *content* of one's message"; emphasis added).

124. Tiersma, "Nonverbal Communication," 1559. Tiersma creates a two-part test for determining whether nonverbal communication falls within the freedom of speech: "First, action must have meaning, either by way of convention or in some other manner. Second, the actor must intend to communicate by means of the action." Ibid., 1526; see also ibid., 1561 ("An intent to communicate obviously requires an intent to convey information.").

125. Nimmer, "Meaning of Symbolic Speech," 37. Nimmer also explains that "[t]he meaning effect is a signal that registers in the mind of at least one observer. The nonmeaning effect is not dependent upon the reaction of other minds." Ibid., 36. As noted earlier, despite the fact that Nimmer's approach relies on meaning, Nimmer considered it broad enough to reach artistic speech lacking verbal and cognitive content. See ibid., 35.

126. *Representational* is used here as a rough and imperfect label for many related schools of thought, from foundationalism to logical positivism. Paying the inevitable costs of oversimplification nevertheless seems worthwhile, since my purpose here is not to illuminate anything specific to those philosophies but simply to show how, generally speaking, they might inform the First Amendment.

127. See, e.g., Greenman, "On Communication," 1347 (surveying various First Amendment arguments, including one that holds "that communication is the conveyance of 'ideas'").

128. See Volokh, "Speech as Conduct," 1304 ("Under nearly every theory of free speech, the right to free speech is at its core the right to communicate—to persuade and to inform people through the content of one's message.").

129. Chevigny, "Philosophy of Language and Free Expression," 162 (footnote omitted).

130. Wittgenstein's influence is so magnetic that the very act of citing him has become a language game of its own. See Steven L. Winter, "For What It's Worth," 26 *Law & Soc'y Rev.* 789, 796–97 (1992) (noting the signaling value of citations to Wittgenstein "[i]n some legal academic circles"); see also Dennis W. Arrow, "'Rich,' 'Textured,' and 'Nuanced': Constitutional 'Scholarship' and Constitutional Messianism at the Millennium," 78 *Tex. L. Rev.* 149, 149 n.* (1999) (positing the same phenomenon with regard to law review editors).

131. Oliver Wendell Holmes, Jr., "Law in Science and Science in Law," 12 *Harv. L. Rev.* 443, 460 (1899); see also Oliver Wendell Holmes to Harold J. Laski, May 9, 1925, in 1 *Holmes-Laski Letters: The Correspondence of Mr. Justice Holmes and Harold J. Laski, 1916–1935,* 737, 738 (Mark DeWolfe Howe ed., Cambridge, MA: Harvard University Press, 1953) (noting how difficult it is to "think accurately—and think things not words").

132. See Richard A. Posner, introduction to *The Essential Holmes: Selections from the Letters, Speeches, Judicial Opinions, and Other Writings of Oliver Wendell Holmes, Jr.* xvii (Richard A. Posner ed., Chicago: University of Chicago Press, 1992).

133. This does not mean, of course, that each word has only one thing to which it is connected. As Holmes noted elsewhere, "A word is not a crystal, transparent and unchanged, it is the skin of a living thought and may vary greatly in color and content according to the circumstances and the time in which it is used." Towne v. Eisner, 245 U.S. 418, 425 (1918). Conversely, the same "thing" may be connected to multiple words, as in Gottlob Frege's famous example of the "Morning Star" and "Evening Star," both of which refer to Venus. See Gottlob Frege, "Über Sinn und Bedeutung," 100 *Zeitschrift für Philosophie und Philosophische Kritik* 25 (1892), translated in 57 *Phil. Rev.* 209 (1948).

134. See Thomas C. Grey, "Holmes and Legal Pragmatism," 41 *Stan. L. Rev.* 787, 788 (1989) ("Holmes as legal pragmatist is hardly a new idea. His associations with Charles Sanders Peirce and William James, as well as his admiration for John Dewey, have led a number of intellectual historians to count him as an adherent and even a founder of the pragmatist movement.").

135. See generally Louis Menand, *The Metaphysical Club: A Story of Ideas in America* (New York: Farrar, Straus and Giroux, 2001) (describing the social and intellectual "club" that included such luminaries as Holmes, William James, and Charles Saunders Peirce).

136. Starting with Russell and Cambridge means omitting any number of important thinkers, including Gottlob Frege and the Austrian logical positivists, who arguably deserve credit for the very creation of analytic philosophy. However costly, such omissions are necessary for the sake of brevity and clarity. Fuller accounts can be found in Richard M. Rorty, ed., *The Linguistic Turn: Essays in Philosophical Method* (Chicago: University of Chicago Press, 1992).

137. Bertrand Russell, *An Inquiry into Meaning and Truth* 181 (New York: Norton, 1940).

138. See generally Bertrand Russell, "On Denoting," 14 *Mind* 479 (1905) (propounding a "theory of denoting" that holds that "denoting phrases never have any meaning

in themselves, but that every proposition in whose verbal expression they occur has a meaning").

139. Russell, *Inquiry into Meaning and Truth*, 166.

140. Quoted in Ray Monk, *Ludwig Wittgenstein: The Duty of Genius* 40 (New York: Free Press, 1990).

141. Quoted in ibid., 41.

142. Patterson, "Law's Pragmatism," 938.

143. Brand, "Making Sense Speaking Nonsense," 314; see also Kavka, "Wittgensteinian Political Theory," 1457 (concluding that the *Tractatus* is based on the belief that "the function of language is to model or picture the world").

144. Wittgenstein, *Tractatus*, 27.

145. Ibid., § 4.01, 63.

146. Ibid., § 3.3, 51.

147. Ibid., § 5.6, 149 (emphasis omitted); see ibid., § 3.032, 43, 45 ("To present in language anything which 'contradicts logic' is as impossible as in geometry to present by its co-ordinates a figure which contradicts the laws of space; or to give the co-ordinates of a point which does not exist.").

148. See Ludwig Wittgenstein to Bertrand Russell, Aug. 19, 1919, in *Letters to Russell, Keynes, and Moore* 71 (first alteration in original).

149. Anscombe, *Introduction to Wittgenstein's Tractatus*, 162.

150. A. J. Ayer, *Language, Truth and Logic* 41 (1936; New York: Dover, 1952) ("[E]very empirical hypothesis must be relevant to some actual, or possible, experience, so that a statement which is not relevant to any experience is not an empirical hypothesis, and accordingly has no factual content.... [T]his is precisely what the principle of verifiability asserts.").

151. "Wikipedia:Verifiability," Wikipedia, accessed Feb. 25, 2014, http://en.wikipedia. org. Robert Post quotes an earlier version of the rule: "the threshold for inclusion in Wikipedia is verifiability, not truth—that is, whether readers are able to check that material added to Wikipedia has already been published by a reliable source, not whether we think it is true." Post, *Democracy*, 8 (emphasis omitted).

152. Greenman, "On Communication," 1347–48.

153. N.Y. Times Co. v. Sullivan, 376 U.S. 254, 269 (1964) (quoting Roth v. United States, 354 U.S. 476, 484 (1957)); see also Police Dep't of Chi. v. Mosley, 408 U.S. 92, 95–96 (1972) ("[O]ur people are guaranteed the right to express any thought, free from government censorship.").

154. Ashcroft v. ACLU, 535 U.S. 564, 573 (2002) (first alteration in original; quoting Harte-Hanks Commc'ns, Inc. v. Connaughton, 491 U.S. 657, 686 (1989)); see N.Y. State Bd. of Elections v. Lopez Torres, 552 U.S. 196, 208 (2008) ("The First Amendment creates an open marketplace where ideas, most especially political ideas, may compete without government interference."); Virginia v. Black, 538 U.S. 343, 358 (2003) ("The hallmark of the protection of free speech is to allow 'free trade in ideas'"; quoting Abrams v. United States, 250 U.S. 616, 630 (1919) (Holmes, J., dissenting)).

155. Miller v. California, 413 U.S. 15, 20 (1973) (alteration in original; quoting *Roth*, 354 U.S. at 484).
156. Chaplinsky v. New Hampshire, 315 U.S. 568, 571–72 (1942). It also matters that such speech acts "are of such slight social value as a step to truth that any benefit that may be derived from them is clearly outweighed by the social interest in order and morality." Ibid., 572.
157. Amy M. Adler, "Girls! Girls! Girls! The Supreme Court Confronts the G-String," 80 *N.Y.U. L. Rev.* 1108, 1114 n.18 (2005).
158. See W. Va. State Bd. of Educ. v. Barnette, 319 U.S. 624, 632 (1943) ("Symbolism is a primitive but effective way of communicating ideas.").
159. Spence v. Washington, 418 U.S. 405 (1974); see Tiersma, "Nonverbal Communication," 1537 (referring to *Spence* as "the only real test that the Court has articulated to identify 'speech' in the First Amendment sphere"). Tiersma's use of "only" was probably accurate at the time, but it now needs some qualification, given that *Hurley v. Irish-American Gay, Lesbian and Bisexual Group of Boston, Inc.*, 515 U.S. 557 (1995), and other cases seem to have replaced or at the very least altered *Spence*'s test. For example, in *Rumsfeld v. FAIR*, 547 U.S. 47 (2006), rather than applying (or even citing) *Spence*, the Court asked whether the activity at issue was "inherently expressive," such that a viewer could understand its meaning without further explanation. See *FAIR*, 547 U.S. at 66. Excluding military recruiters from campus to express disagreement with the military's policies did not meet this test, the Court found, because such exclusion might well be the result of room scarcity.
160. *Spence*, 418 U.S. at 409; see also Texas v. Johnson, 491 U.S. 397, 406 (1989) ("Johnson's burning of the flag was conduct 'sufficiently imbued with elements of communication' to implicate the First Amendment"; quoting *Spence*, 418 U.S. at 409). But see *Johnson*, 491 U.S. at 432 (Rehnquist, C.J., dissenting) ("[F]lag burning is the equivalent of an inarticulate grunt or roar.").
161. *Spence*, 418 U.S. at 410–11; see R. George Wright, "What Counts as 'Speech' in the First Place? Determining the Scope of the Free Speech Clause," 37 *Pepp. L. Rev.* 1217, 1238 (2010) ("In the absence of the speaker's intent to promote some more or less determinate understanding, we may be skeptical that speech in the constitutional sense is present.").
162. Greenman, "On Communication," 1348; see also Post, "Recuperating First Amendment Doctrine," 1252 (showing that the *Spence* test is overinclusive); Jed Rubenfeld, "The First Amendment's Purpose," 53 *Stan. L. Rev.* 767, 773 (2001) (showing that the *Spence* test is underinclusive).
163. United States v. O'Brien, 391 U.S. 367, 376 (1968).
164. See Ward v. Rock Against Racism, 491 U.S. 781, 790 (1989) ("Music, as a form of expression and communication, is protected under the First Amendment."); see also Reed v. Vill. of Shorewood, 704 F.2d 943, 950 (7th Cir. 1983) ("If the defendants passed an ordinance forbidding the playing of rock and roll music . . . , they would be infringing a First Amendment right, even if the music had no political message—even if it had no words"; citation omitted).

165. Miller v. Civil City of S. Bend, 904 F.2d 1081, 1093 (7th Cir. 1990) (Posner, J., concurring), *rev'd sub nom.* Barnes v. Glen Theatre, Inc., 501 U.S. 560 (1991); see also David Munkittrick, "Music as Speech: A First Amendment Category unto Itself," 62 *Fed. Comm. L.J.* 665, 668 (2010) ("[N]o single First Amendment theory fully explains protection of music as speech."). But see Rosen, "Freedom and Art," 11 ("Felix Mendelssohn found the meaning of music more precise, not less, than language, but that is because music means what it is, not what it says.").

166. Cohen v. California, 403 U.S. 15, 26 (1971) (emphasis added).

167. Ian Bartrum, "Constructing the Constitutional Canon: The Metonymic Evolution of *Federalist 10*," 27 *Const. Comment.* 9, 11 (2010).

168. Wittgenstein, *Philosophical Investigations*, § 23.

169. Ibid., § 7.

170. Ibid., § 23; see also Thomas P. Crocker, "Displacing Dissent: The Role of 'Place' in First Amendment Jurisprudence," 75 *Fordham L. Rev.* 2587, 2613 (2007) ("'Form of life' is a technical term meant to convey the multiplicity of both possible ways of living and possible ways of seeing and responding to the world. The ability to speak a language is the ability to engage in practices within a form of life in which that language has meaning.").

171. Patterson, "Conscience and the Constitution," 303–4; see also Fiss, "Conventionalism," 177 (describing Wittgenstein's view that "we understand a concept not when we grasp some fact, but when we can successfully use that concept within a language game or a defined context").

172. Wittgenstein, *Philosophical Investigations*, § 43; see also Jonathan Yovel, "What Is Contract Law 'About'? Speech Act Theory and a Critique of 'Skeletal Promises,'" 94 *Nw. U. L. Rev.* 937, 939 (2000) (noting that Wittgenstein and the theories of performative language that owe him a debt "all share a basic insight: that language is not primarily about meaning in the traditional, semantic sense associated with representationalism" but rather that "language is primarily about action—speech and texts are 'acts,' and they 'perform' things in the social world and bring about different kinds of effects").

173. Sanford Levinson and J. M. Balkin, "Law, Music, and Other Performing Arts," 139 *U. Pa. L. Rev.* 1597, 1604 (1991) (footnote omitted).

174. Grice's basic argument—vastly oversimplified—was that for A to mean something by X, X must be uttered with an intention of producing some belief or effect in the listener, B, by means of B's recognition of A's intent. See generally H. P. Grice, "Meaning," 66 *Phil. Rev.* 377 (1957). Later, Grice further developed the idea of speaker meaning via analyzing sentences as units of meaning and differentiating between indicative and imperative meaning. See generally H. P. Grice, "Utterer's Meaning, Sentence-Meaning, and Word-Meaning," 4 *Found. Language* 225 (1968).

175. See generally J. L. Austin, *How to Do Things with Words* (Cambridge, MA: Harvard University Press, 1962); John R. Searle, *Expression and Meaning: Studies in the Theory of Speech Acts* (Cambridge: Cambridge University Press,

1979); John R. Searle, *Intentionality: An Essay in the Philosophy of the Mind* (Cambridge: Cambridge University Press, 1983); John R. Searle, *Speech Acts: An Essay in the Philosophy of Language* (Cambridge: Cambridge University Press, 1969).

As suggested by the title of Austin's seminal *How to Do Things with Words*, the central insight of speech-act theory is that speech can *do* things, as for example when a person says, "I am sorry." Uttering those words does not merely report meaning by describing a situation or a state of mind but actually *performs* the act of apologizing. The same can be said of promises (Austin, *How to Do Things with Words*, 10); the words "I do" in the context of a wedding ceremony (ibid., 6); or—as Akhil Amar has suggested, channeling Austin—the phrase "We the People . . . do ordain and establish" in the preamble of the U.S. Constitution (Akhil Reed Amar, *America's Constitution: A Biography* 5 (New York: Random House, 2005)).

176. Toril Moi, "'They Practice Their Trades in Different Worlds': Concepts in Post-structuralism and Ordinary Language Philosophy," 40 *New Literary Hist.* 801, 802 (2009) (defining ordinary-language philosophy as "the philosophical tradition after Wittgenstein and J. L. Austin as established . . . in [Stanley] Cavell's work"). See generally Stanley Cavell, *Must We Mean What We Say? A Book of Essays* (updated ed., Cambridge: Cambridge University Press, 2015).

177. Post, "Recuperating First Amendment Doctrine," 1253–54; cf. Jack M. Balkin, "Digital Speech and Democratic Culture: A Theory of Freedom of Expression for the Information Society," 79 *N.Y.U. L. Rev.* 1, 4 (2004) ("A democratic culture is democratic in the sense that everyone—not just political, economic, or cultural elites—has a fair chance to participate in the production of culture, and in the development of the ideas and meanings that constitute them and the communities and subcommunities to which they belong. . . . Freedom of expression protects the ability of individuals to participate in the culture in which they live.").

178. Robert C. Post, "Participatory Democracy as a Theory of Free Speech: A Reply," 97 *Va. L. Rev.* 617, 621 (2011).

179. Adler, "Post-Modern Art," 1370.

180. See Tilghman, "Literature, Philosophy and Nonsense," 256 ("Wittgenstein went on to provide a still richer exploration of nonsense in the *Philosophical Investigations* where he locates a craving for nonsense in certain deep aspects of our language and our life. It is this craving that he believes is responsible for much of traditional philosophy which, on his view, turns out to be grounded in conceptual confusion and therefore a kind of nonsense.").

181. Yovel, "What Is Contract Law 'About'?," 941; see also Bartrum, "Constructing the Constitutional Canon," 11 ("[A] word's meaning often does not derive from some foundational referent in the world, but, rather, is determined by the use to which it is properly put within a particular language-game.").

182. Hurley v. Irish-Am. Gay, Lesbian & Bisexual Grp. of Bos., Inc., 515 U.S. 557, 569 (1995).

183. Ibid., 568–69 (citation omitted).

184. See Bill Poser, "The Supreme Court Fails Semantics," *Language Log*, July 7, 2007, http://itre.cis.upenn.edu/~myl/languagelog ("[T]he Court has invalidly inferred a particular proposition. The slogan is in fact meaningless in the sense that it expresses no proposition, and Frederick gave a perfectly plausible explanation for the use of a meaningless slogan. The Court was therefore wrong in finding that the banner advocates the use of marijuana.").

185. The meaning (or lack thereof) of the banner would of course be relevant to that inquiry. Indeed, some scholars have suggested that nonsense should be free from government regulation precisely *because* it lacks meaning. See Chevigny, "Philosophy of Language and Free Expression," 164 (arguing that under the early Wittgenstein's view of ethics as nonsense, the "most appropriate argument for freedom of speech would be that people ought to be allowed to say what they please, at least about questions of norms and values, because what they say is meaningless," and that "[t]he government could have no reason to restrain debate that might continue endlessly without hope of a fruitful result"); see also Catherine L. Amspacher and Randel Steven Springer, "Humor, Defamation and Intentional Infliction of Emotional Distress: The Potential Predicament for Private Figure Plaintiffs," 31 *Wm. & Mary L. Rev.* 701, 726 (1990) ("[E]xpressions . . . that courts classify as 'nonsense' or 'fantasy' are protected from defamation suits because, by definition, no one will believe them to be literally true."). This line of reasoning is closely related to the "rationality" challenge that Tushnet describes in chapter 2.

186. See Robert C. Post, "The Constitutional Concept of Public Discourse: Outrageous Opinion, Democratic Deliberation, and *Hustler Magazine v. Falwell*," 103 *Harv. L. Rev.* 601, 676 (1990) ("[T]he judgment that speech is being communicated in a 'public' manner ultimately depends upon the particular context of a specific communicative act.").

187. Spence v. Washington, 418 U.S. 405, 410 (1974).

188. Ibid. That context included "the invasion of Cambodia and the killings at Kent State University, events which occurred a few days prior to [Spence's] arrest." Ibid., 408.

189. Ibid., 410.

190. Ibid.

191. California v. LaRue, 409 U.S. 109, 118 (1972); see Joshua Waldman, "Symbolic Speech and Social Meaning," 97 *Colum. L. Rev.* 1844, 1873 (1997) ("The Supreme Court's nude-dancing cases establish the proposition that constitutional significance may be ascribed to the context in which the dancing takes place.").

192. Joseph Burstyn, Inc. v. Wilson, 343 U.S. 495, 501 (1952).

193. See Hurley v. Irish-Am. Gay, Lesbian & Bisexual Grp. of Bos., Inc., 515 U.S. 557, 569 (1995) (holding that "a narrow, succinctly articulable message is not a condition of constitutional protection").

194. Post, *Democracy*, 20.

195. Ibid.

196. See Susan Jill Rice, "The Search for Valid Governmental Regulations: A Review of the Judicial Response to Municipal Policies Regarding First Amendment Activities," 63 *Notre Dame L. Rev.* 561, 563 (1988) ("Pure speech may be defined as expression in its pristine state, completely isolated from activity."); Carney R. Shegerian, "A Sign of the Times: The United States Supreme Court Effectively Abolishes the Narrowly Tailored Requirement for Time, Place and Manner Restrictions," 25 *Loy. L.A. L. Rev.* 453, 471 (1992) ("Pure speech has been generally defined as communicative expression in a pure state without physical activity.").

197. See, e.g., Tinker v. Des Moines Indep. Cmty. Sch. Dist., 393 U.S. 503, 505–6 (1969) (noting that wearing armbands is "closely akin to 'pure speech' which, we have repeatedly held, is entitled to comprehensive protection under the First Amendment").

198. United States v. O'Brien, 391 U.S. 367, 376 (1968).

199. See, e.g., Nimmer, "Meaning of Symbolic Speech," 37 ("[S]ymbolic speech requires not merely that given conduct results in a meaning effect, but that the actor causing such conduct must intend such a meaning effect by his conduct.").

200. See Post, "Recuperating First Amendment Doctrine," 1257 ("The very concept of a medium presupposes that constitutionally protected expression does not inhere in abstract and disembodied acts of communication of the kind envisioned by *Spence*, but is instead always conveyed through social and material forms of interaction.").

201. See Louis Henkin, "The Supreme Court, 1967 Term—Foreword: On Drawing Lines," 82 *Harv. L. Rev.* 63, 79–80 (1968) ("The meaningful constitutional distinction is not between speech and conduct, but between conduct that speaks, communicates, and other kinds of conduct. If it is intended as expression, if in fact it communicates, especially if it becomes a common comprehensible form of expression, it is 'speech.'"); Melville B. Nimmer, "Does Copyright Abridge the First Amendment Guarantees of Free Speech and Press?," 17 *UCLA L. Rev.* 1180, 1189 (1970) (exploring the argument that the First Amendment protects ideas rather than particular forms of expression).

202. See Nimmer, "Meaning of Symbolic Speech," 34 ("It is the *ideas* expressed, and not just a particular form of expression, that must be protected if the underlying first amendment values are to be realized.").

203. See Rubenfeld, "First Amendment's Purpose," 771–75.

204. See Frederick Schauer, "Categories and the First Amendment: A Play in Three Acts," 34 *Vand. L. Rev.* 265, 267 (1981) (defining the question of "coverage" as "[w]hat marks off the category covered by the first amendment from those other categories of conduct that do not implicate free speech analysis").

205. Schauer, "Second-Best First Amendment," 13.

206. See, e.g., Reno v. ACLU, 521 U.S. 844, 871–72 (1997) (holding a statute void for vagueness under a First Amendment analysis because of its chilling effect on protected speech); Dombrowski v. Pfister, 380 U.S. 479, 497 (1965) (upholding a

federal injunction against state court prosecutions under vague state statutes, on the basis of the prosecutions' "chilling" effect).

207. Balkin and Levinson, "Constitutional Grammar," 1802; see also Chevigny, "Philosophy of Language and Free Expression," 167 ("Wittgenstein's 'language-game' concept has been criticized for a lack of precision."); Biletzki and Matar, "Ludwig Wittgenstein" (noting that Wittgenstein "never explicitly defines" the concept of language game).

208. Post, "Reply," 622–23.

209. Moi, "Concepts in Poststructuralism," 814.

210. See Wittgenstein, *Tractatus*, § 3.311, 51 ("An expression presupposes the forms of all propositions in which it can occur. It is the common characteristic mark of a class of propositions.").

211. See Kolender v. Lawson, 461 U.S. 352, 370 (1983) (White, J., dissenting) ("The Court has held that in such circumstances 'more precision in drafting may be required because of the vagueness doctrine in the case of regulation of expression,' a 'greater degree of specificity' is demanded than in other contexts"; citation omitted; quoting Parker v. Levy, 417 U.S. 733, 756 (1974); Smith v. Goguen, 415 U.S. 566, 573 (1974)); Grayned v. City of Rockford, 408 U.S. 104, 108–9 (1972) ("[B]ecause we assume that man is free to steer between lawful and unlawful conduct, we insist that laws give the person of ordinary intelligence a reasonable opportunity to know what is prohibited, so that he may act accordingly. . . . [W]here a vague statute 'abut[s] upon sensitive areas of basic First Amendment freedoms,' it 'operates to inhibit the exercise of [those] freedoms'"; fourth and fifth alterations in original; footnote omitted; quoting Baggett v. Bullitt, 377 U.S. 360, 372 (1964); Cramp v. Bd. of Pub. Instruction, 368 U.S. 278, 287 (1961)).

212. See Brown v. Entm't Merchs. Ass'n, 131 S. Ct. 2729, 2742 (2011) (striking down, on First Amendment grounds, restrictions on sales of violent video games to minors); see also United States v. Stevens, 559 U.S. 460, 482 (2010) (striking down restrictions on depictions of animal cruelty).

213. See Martin H. Redish and Abby Marie Mollen, "Understanding Post's and Meiklejohn's Mistakes: The Central Role of Adversary Democracy in the Theory of Free Expression," 103 *Nw. U. L. Rev.* 1303, 1343 (2009) ("Whether through its political or its judicial branches, governmental definition of the scope of public discourse is itself a *regulation* of public discourse"; emphasis added).

214. Abrams v. United States, 250 U.S. 616, 630 (1919) (Holmes, J., dissenting).

215. See Cohen v. California, 403 U.S. 15, 16 (1971); see also Spence v. Washington, 418 U.S. 405, 409–10 (1974) (concluding that when the flag was hung from a window with a peace sign taped to it, "the nature of [the] activity, combined with the factual context and environment in which it was undertaken, lead to the conclusion that [Spence] engaged in a form of protected expression").

216. Carroll, *Through the Looking-Glass*, 123–24.

217. Wittgenstein, *Tractatus*, § 7, 189.

218. Wittgenstein, *Philosophical Investigations*, § 107 ("We have got on to slippery ice where there is no friction and so in a certain sense the conditions are ideal, but also, just because of that, we are unable to walk. We want to walk: so we need *friction*. Back to the rough ground!").

CHAPTER 4. GOING FURTHER

1. *Oxford English Dictionary Online*, s.v. "dance," accessed Dec. 11, 2015, www.oed.com.

2. Miller v. Civil City of S. Bend, 904 F.2d 1081, 1126 (7th Cir. 1990) (Easterbrook, J., dissenting), *rev'd sub nom.* Barnes v. Glen Theatre, Inc., 501 U.S. 560 (1991).

3. Janice Ross, *Like a Bomb Going Off: Leonid Yakobson and Ballet as Resistance in Soviet Russia* 11, 90–91, 121, 124, 162 (2015).

4. See Jack M. Balkin, "Digital Speech and Democratic Culture: A Theory of Freedom of Expression for the Information Society," 79 *N.Y.U. L. Rev.* 1, 3–4 (2004) (arguing that freedom of speech should promote a democratic culture not limited to deliberation about public issues); Jack M. Balkin, "Cultural Democracy and the First Amendment," 109 *Nw. U. L. Rev.* (forthcoming 2016).

5. Allison M. Dussias, "Ghost Dance and Holy Ghost: The Echoes of Nineteenth-Century Christianization Policy in Twentieth-Century Native American Free Exercise Cases," 49 *Stan. L. Rev.* 773, 788–94 (1997). There were also claims that Native American dance would detract from missionary efforts to convert Native Americans to Christianity, to educate their children, and to turn them into farmers, though these justifications focus more on the distraction of the dancers from other activities than on the dances' message.

6. City of Dallas v. Stanglin, 490 U.S. 19, 21 (1989).

7. Roberts v. United States Jaycees, 468 U.S. 609, 617–18 (1984).

8. *Stanglin*, 490 U.S. at 21–22, 25.

9. An example of this occurred in Australia in May 2015, when artists and art workers engaged in a dance protest in major cities across the country to protest government cuts to arts funding. See Monica Tan, "Dance Rallies Held across Australia Protest $105m Cut to Arts Funding Body," *Guardian*, May 22, 2015, www.theguardian.com.

10. C. Edwin Baker, "Autonomy and Free Speech," 27 *Const. Comment.* 251, 253, 271 (2011); Seana Valentine Shiffrin, "A Thinker-Based Approach to Freedom of Speech," 27 *Const. Comment.* 283, 289–90 (2011).

11. See Mark Knowles, *The Wicked Waltz and Other Scandalous Dances: Outrage at Couple Dancing in the 19th and Early 20th Centuries* 5, 53–58, 93, 124–28 (Jefferson, NC: McFarland, 2009).

12. In 1962, a Catholic bishop in New York announced a ban on Catholic school students doing the twist. Peter Blecha, *Taboo Tunes: A History of Banned Bands and Censored Songs* 37 (San Francisco: Backbeat Books, 2004). The governments of South Vietnam and Syria banned the twist, and government

officials in Czechoslovakia and Lebanon raided dance clubs to forbid it. Ibid., 37–38.

13. Hayley Tsukayama, "'Harlem Shake' Videos Lead to School Suspensions," *Wash. Post*, Mar. 4, 2013, www.washingtonpost.com (reporting numerous school suspensions of students for producing and posting Harlem shake videos based on their inappropriately suggestive nature). While the Harlem shake is a dance move originating in the 1980s, the version that has been the object of censorship is actually an Internet meme that emerged in 2013 and involves about thirty seconds of video showing an individual dancing among a larger group, followed by the entire group breaking into dance, often wearing unusual costumes. "What's in a Meme? The Harlem Shake," *Economist*, Mar. 9, 2013, www.economist.com. Interestingly, again showing the blurred lines between the social and the political, the Harlem shake became a vehicle of protest in Egypt and Tunisia. Caitlin Dewey, "The 'Harlem Shake' Becomes a Protest in Egypt and Tunisia," *Wash. Post*, Feb. 28, 2013, www.washingtonpost.com.

14. Ricardo Ainslie, *No Dancin' in Anson: An American Story of Race and Social Change* (Lanham, MD: Jason Aronson, 1995). The Anson ordinance stated "[t]hat it shall be unlawful from and after the passage of this ordinance for any person or persons, firm or association of persons to carry on, foster or operate any public dance hall where people assemble for the purpose of dancing in the city of Anson." Quoted in Gerald Torres, "Morenitos, Güeros, y Bolillos," 3 *Tex. Hisp. J.L. & Pol'y* 61, 62–63 (1997) (reviewing Ainslie's book).

15. New York City's cabaret dancing regulations can be found at N.Y.C., N.Y., Code §§ 20–359–370.2 (2014). The lawsuit is Muchmore's Café, LLC v. City of New York, No. 14-cv-05668 RRM-RER (E.D.N.Y. filed Sept. 26, 2014). For an account of the suit, see Sonja West, "A Constitutional Challenge to NYC's Ban on Dancing," *Huffington Post*, June 30, 2015, www.huffingtonpost.com.

16. Torres, "Morenitos, Güeros, y Bolillos," 61.

17. See Chiasson v. New York City Dep't of Consumer Affairs, 524 N.Y.S.2d 649 (Sup. Ct. N.Y. Cty. 1988); Chiasson v. New York City Dep't of Consumer Affairs, 505 N.Y.S.2d 499 (Sup. Ct. N.Y. Cty. 1986).

18. See City of Erie v. Pap's A.M., 529 U.S. 277 (2000); Barnes v. Glen Theatre, Inc., 501 U.S. 560 (1991); Schad v. Borough of Mount Ephraim, 452 U.S. 61 (1981).

19. *Barnes*, 501 U.S. at 581 (Souter, J., concurring in the judgment).

20. Lawrence v. Texas, 539 U.S. 558 (2003); Stanley v. Georgia, 394 U.S. 557 (1969).

21. Nat'l Endowment for the Arts v. Finley, 524 U.S. 569 (1998).

22. City of Renton v. Playtime Theatres, Inc., 475 U.S. 41, 47 (1986).

23. Miller v. California, 413 U.S. 15, 24 (1973). We will set aside pornography in the form of written accounts of sexual acts in books or articles for the purposes of this discussion, which only pertains to nonverbal pornography in the form of drawings, still photographs, and movies.

24. Am. Booksellers Ass'n, Inc. v. Hudnut, 771 F.2d 323 (7th Cir. 1985).

25. Frederick Schauer, "Speech and 'Speech'—Obscenity and 'Obscenity': An Exercise in the Interpretation of Constitutional Language," 67 *Geo. L.J.* 899, 923 (1979).

26. Cass R. Sunstein, "Pornography and the First Amendment," 1986 *Duke L.J.* 589, 606 (1986) (emphasis added). If we accept this to be true, then it is curious how the Supreme Court could exempt sexually explicit material that has "serious . . . artistic . . . value" (*Miller*, 413 U.S. at 24) from the definition of obscenity. Such material might not always appeal to cognitive capacities even if it is classified as art. For a trenchant critique of Sunstein's arguments, see Larry Alexander, "Low Value Speech," 83 *Nw. U. L. Rev.* 547 (1989).

27. Cohen v. California, 403 U.S. 15, 25 (1971).

28. Genevieve Lakier, "Sport as Speech," 16 *U. Pa. J. Const. L.* 1109, 1113–14, 1121–24 (2014).

29. Ibid., 1126–40.

30. Ibid., 1145–50.

31. Glenda Dawn Goss, *Sibelius: A Composer's Life and the Awakening of Finland* 254–55 (Chicago: University of Chicago Press, 2009).

32. Blake Gopnik, "The Big Debate: Can Food Be Serious Art?," *Wash. Post*, Sept. 23, 2009), www.washingtonpost.com.

33. J. Austin Broussard, "An Intellectual Property Food Fight: Why Copyright Law Should Embrace Culinary Innovation," 10 *Vand. J. Ent. & Tech. L.* 691, 718 (2008).

34. Carolyn Korsmeyer, *Making Sense of Taste: Food and Philosophy* 109 (Ithaca, NY: Cornell University Press, 1999).

35. Chinatown Neighborhood Ass'n v. Brown, No. C 12–3759 PJH, 2013 WL 60919, at *3 (N.D. Cal. Jan. 2, 2013), *aff'd*, 539 F. App'x 761 (9th Cir. 2013).

36. Ibid., *6–*7. While not based on cultural discrimination, lawsuits challenging bans on foie gras have been filed by food-industry representatives. Ass'n des Éleveurs de Canards et d'Oies du Québec v. Harris, 729 F.3d 937, 946 (9th Cir. 2013); Illinois Rest. Ass'n v. City of Chicago, No. 06 C 7014, 2008 WL 8915042 (N.D. Ill. Aug. 7, 2008).

37. Rachel Donadio, "A Walled City in Tuscany Clings to its Ancient Menu," *N.Y. Times*, Mar. 12, 2009; Lucy M. Long, "Culinary Tourism," in *The Oxford Handbook of Food History* 389, 402 (Jeffrey M. Pilcher ed., Oxford: Oxford University Press, 2012).

38. Long, "Culinary Tourism," 402.

39. See 16 U.S.C.A. § 1338; Cavel Intern., Inc. v. Madigan, 500 F.3d 551, 552 (7th Cir. 2007) (upholding Illinois ban on slaughterhouses processing horse meat); Empacadora de Carnes de Fresnillo, S.A. de C.V. v. Curry, 476 F.3d 326, 337 (5th Cir. 2007) (upholding similar ban in Texas).

40. Jon Kelly, "The Offal Truth about American Haggis," BBC News, Jan. 24, 2013, www.bbc.com. The federal regulation is 9 C.F.R. § 310.16 (1971).

41. Naureen Khan, "Hummus and Maftoul, with a Side of the Israeli-Palestinian Conflict," Aljazeera America, Nov. 19, 2014, http://america.aljazeera.com.

42. Charles L. Lumpkin, "Soul Food," in 4 *Encyclopedia of African American History, 1986 to the Present* 338, 339 (Paul Finkelman ed., Oxford: Oxford University Press, 2009).

43. See Craig v. Masterpiece Cakeshop, Inc., 370 P.3d 272, 286, 288 (Colo. App. 2015) *petition for cert. filed* (U.S. 2016). See generally Caroline Mala Corbin, "Speech or Conduct? The Free Speech Claims of Wedding Vendors," 65 *Emory L.J.* 241 (2015).

44. See, e.g., Gowri Ramachandran, "Freedom of Dress: State and Private Regulation of Clothing, Hairstyle, Jewelry, Makeup, Tattoos, and Piercing," 66 *Md. L. Rev.* 11, 70 (2006) (arguing that fashion is an important form of First Amendment expression); Anderson v. City of Hermosa Beach, 621 F.3d 1051, 1060–62 (9th Cir. 2010) (holding that tattoos and the tattooing process are speech covered by the First Amendment); Disc. Inn, Inc. v. City of Chicago, 803 F.3d 317, 326 (7th Cir. 2015) (indicating that formal gardens may be expressive in a manner that the First Amendment recognizes).

45. *Disc. Inn*, 803 F.3d at 326.

46. See, e.g., Vance v. Judas Priest, Nos. 86–5844 & 86–3939, 1990 WL 130920, at *4 (Nev. Dist. Ct. Aug. 24, 1990).

47. John Greenman, "On Communication," 106 *Mich. L. Rev.* 1337, 1344 (2008).

48. Sunstein, "Pornography and the First Amendment," 606.

49. O. Lou Reed, "Should the First Amendment Protect Joe Camel? Toward an Understanding of Constitutional 'Expression,'" 32 *Am. Bus. L.J.* 311, 349–50 (1995).

50. Ibid., 341 n.131 ("[A] . . . piece of instrumental music is neither true nor false. It simply *is*. It may be expressive, but it is not speechlike.").

51. See Jonathan D. Varat, "Deception and the First Amendment: A Central, Complex, and Somewhat Curious Relationship," 53 *UCLA L. Rev.* 1107, 1114 (2006). But see Alan K. Chen and Justin Marceau, "High Value Lies, Ugly Truths, and the First Amendment," 68 *Vand. L. Rev.* 1435 (2015).

52. See Joseph Burstyn, Inc. v. Wilson, 343 U.S. 495, 502 (1952) (recognizing motion pictures as a medium of expression and rejecting the argument that modes of entertainment cannot also be speech).

53. Brown v. Entertainment Merchants Association, 131 S. Ct. 2729, 2732–33 (2011).

54. Ashcroft v. Free Speech Coalition, 535 U.S. 234, 239–41, 253 (2002) (citing New York v. Ferber, 458 U.S. 747 (1982)).

55. Ibid., 253 (citing Stanley v. Georgia, 394 U.S. 557, 566 (1969)).

56. Jane Bambauer, "Is Data Speech?," 66 *Stan. L. Rev.* 57, 63–64, 71–77, 82–83 (2014).

57. Ibid., 86–105.

58. Stuart Minor Benjamin, "Algorithms and Speech," 161 *U. Pa. L. Rev.* 1445, 1463–64 (2013).

59. Tim Wu, "Machine Speech," 161 *U. Pa. L. Rev.* 1495, 1496–98 (2013).

60. See, e.g., Glik v. Cunniffe, 655 F.3d 78, 82 (1st Cir. 2011); Animal Legal Def. Fund v. Otter, 118 F. Supp. 3d 1195, 1204–5 (D. Idaho 2015).

61. Seth F. Kreimer, "Pervasive Image Capture and the First Amendment: Memory, Discourse, and the Right to Record," 159 *U. Penn. L. Rev.* 335, 341 (2011).

62. Justin Marceau and Alan K. Chen, "Free Speech and Democracy in the Video Age," 116 *Colum. L. Rev.* 991 (2016).

63. Marc Jonathan Blitz, "The Right to Map (and Avoid Being Mapped): Reconceiving First Amendment Protection for Information-Gathering in the Age of Google Earth," 14 *Colum. Sci. & Tech. L. Rev.* 115, 163–68, 174–81 (2012).

64. Marceau and Chen, "Free Speech and Democracy in the Video Age," 1022–23.

BIBLIOGRAPHY

ARTICLES

Abd-Allah, Umar F. "Living Islam with Purpose." 7 *UCLA Journal of Islamic and Near East Law* 17 (2008).

Adler, Amy M. "Girls! Girls! Girls! The Supreme Court Confronts the G-String." 80 *New York University Law Review* 1108 (2005).

———. "Post-Modern Art and the Death of Obscenity Law." 99 *Yale Law Journal* 1359 (1990).

———. "What's Left? Hate Speech, Pornography, and the Problem for Artistic Expression." 84 *California Law Review* 1499 (1996).

Alexander, Larry. "Low Value Speech." 83 *Northwestern University Law Review* 547 (1989).

Amspacher, Catherine L., and Randel Steven Springer. "Humor, Defamation and Intentional Infliction of Emotional Distress: The Potential Predicament for Private Figure Plaintiffs," 31 *William and Mary Law Review* 701 (1990).

Arrow, Dennis W. "'Rich,' 'Textured,' and 'Nuanced': Constitutional 'Scholarship' and Constitutional Messianism at the Millennium." 78 *Texas Law Review* 149 (1999).

Arsu, Sebnem. "The Music Started, and the Protest Paused." *New York Times*, June 15, 2013.

Baker, C. Edwin. "Autonomy and Free Speech." 27 *Constitutional Commentary* 251 (2011).

———. "Commercial Speech: A Problem in the Theory of Freedom." 62 *Iowa Law Review* 1 (1976).

———. "Harm, Liberty, and Free Speech." 70 *Southern California Law Review* 979 (1997).

Balkin, J. M., and Sanford Levinson. "Constitutional Grammar." 72 *Texas Law Review* 1771 (1994).

Balkin, Jack M. "Cultural Democracy and the First Amendment." 110 *Northwestern University Law Review* (forthcoming 2016).

———. "Digital Speech and Democratic Culture: A Theory of Freedom of Expression for the Information Society." 79 *New York University Law Review* 1 (2004).

———. "Verdi's High C." 91 *Texas Law Review* 1687 (2013).

Bambauer, Jane. "Is Data Speech?" 66 *Stanford Law Review* 57 (2014).

Barkin, Elaine, Martin Brody, and Judith Crispin. "Milton Babbitt." In 1 *The Grove Dictionary of American Music* 263 (Charles Hiroshi Garrett ed., 2d ed.). New York: Oxford University Press, 2013.

Barnes, Bart. "Folk Singer Wanted Everyone to Be Heard." *Washington Post*, January 29, 2012.

Bartrum, Ian. "Constructing the Constitutional Canon: The Metonymic Evolution of *Federalist 10*." 27 *Constitutional Commentary* 9 (2010).

Benjamin, Stuart Minor. "Algorithms and Speech." 161 *University of Pennsylvania Law Review* 1445 (2013).

Bernstein, Adam. "Guitarist Link Wray Dies: Influenced Punk, Grunge." *Washington Post*, November 22, 2005.

Bezanson, Randall P. "Art and the Constitution." 93 *Iowa Law Review* 1593 (2008).

Biletzki, Anat, and Anat Matar. "Ludwig Wittgenstein." *Stanford Encyclopedia of Philosophy*. November 8, 2002; rev. March 3, 2014. http://plato.stanford.edu.

Blasi, Vincent. "The Pathological Perspective and the First Amendment." 85 *Columbia Law Review* 449 (1985).

Blitz, Marc Jonathan. "The Right to Map (and Avoid Being Mapped): Reconceiving First Amendment Protection for Information-Gathering in the Age of Google Earth." 14 *Columbia Science and Technology Law Review* 115 (2012).

Blocher, Joseph. "Institutions in the Marketplace of Ideas." 57 *Duke Law Journal* 821 (2008).

———. "Public Discourse, Expert Knowledge, and the Press." 87 *University of Washington Law Review* 409 (2012).

Bonneau, Sonya G. "Ex Post Modernism: How the First Amendment Framed Nonrepresentational Art." 39 *Columbia Journal of Law and the Arts* 195 (2015).

Bork, Robert H. "Neutral Principles and Some First Amendment Problems." 47 *Indiana Law Journal* 1 (1971).

Boyle, James. "Anachronism of the Moral Sentiments? Integrity, Postmodernism, and Justice." 51 *Stanford Law Review* 493 (1999).

Brand, Roy. "Making Sense Speaking Nonsense." 35 *Philosophical Forum* 311 (2004).

Broussard, J. Austin. "An Intellectual Property Food Fight: Why Copyright Law Should Embrace Culinary Innovation." 10 *Vanderbilt Journal of Entertainment and Technology Law* 691 (2008).

Carroll, Michael W. "Whose Music Is It Anyway? How We Came to View Musical Expression as a Form of Property." 72 *University of Cincinnati Law Review* 1405 (2004).

Chafee, Zechariah, Jr. "Book Review." 62 *Harvard Law Review* 891 (1949).

Charlton, William. "Nonsense." 17 *British Journal of Aesthetics* 346 (1977).

Chen, Alan K. "Forced Patriot Acts." 81 *Denver University Law Review* 703 (2004).

Chen, Alan K., and Justin Marceau. "High Value Lies, Ugly Truths, and the First Amendment." 68 *Vanderbilt Law Review* 1435 (2015).

Cheung, Leo K. C. "The Disenchantment of Nonsense: Understanding Wittgenstein's *Tractatus*." 31 *Philosophical Investigations* 197 (2008).

Chevigny, Paul G. "Philosophy of Language and Free Expression." 55 *New York University Law Review* 157 (1980).

Cole, David. "Agon at Agora: Creative Misreadings in the First Amendment Tradition." 95 *Yale Law Journal* 857 (1986).

Conant, James. "Elucidation and Nonsense in Frege and Early Wittgenstein." In *The New Wittgenstein* 174 (Alice Crary and Rupert Read eds.). New York: Routledge, 2000.

———. "Must We Show What We Cannot Say?" In *The Senses of Stanley Cavell* 242 (Richard Fleming and Michael Payne eds.). Lewisberg, PA: Bucknell University Press, 1989.

———. "Two Conceptions of *Die Überwindung der Metaphysik*: Carnap and Early Wittgenstein." In *Wittgenstein in America* 13 (Timothy McCarthy and Sean C. Stidd eds.). Oxford, UK: Clarendon, 2001.

Contreras, Felix. "How Santería Seeped into Latin Music." NPR.org, January 7, 2015. http://www.npr.org/2015/01/07/375389153/how-santer-a-seeped-into-latin-music?utm_source=npr_email_a_friend&utm_medium=email&utm_content=20150107&utm_campaign=storyshare&utm_term=.

Copps, Kriston. "Recognizing Jeanne-Claude." *American Prospect*, November 24, 2009. www.prospect.org.

Corbin, Caroline Mala. "Speech or Conduct? The Free Speech Claims of Wedding Vendors." 65 *Emory Law Journal* 241 (2015).

Cowell, Henry. "Edgar Varèse." In *American Composers on American Music* 43 (Henry Cowell ed.). New York: Frederick Ungar, 1962.

Crocker, Thomas P. "Displacing Dissent: The Role of 'Place' in First Amendment Jurisprudence." 75 *Fordham Law Review* 2587 (2007).

Cummings, Michael J. "Ars Poetica." Cummings Study Guide. Accessed November 23, 2015, www.cummingsstudyguides.net.

Dain, Edmund. "Contextualism and Nonsense in Wittgenstein's *Tractatus*." 25 *South African Journal of Philosophy* 91 (2006).

Dewey, Caitlin. "The 'Harlem Shake' Becomes a Protest in Egypt and Tunisia." *Washington Post*, February 28, 2013. www.washingtonpost.com.

Diamond, Cora. "Logical Syntax in Wittgenstein's *Tractatus*." 55 *Philosophical Quarterly* 78 (2005).

———. "Throwing Away the Ladder: How to Read the *Tractatus*." In *The Realistic Spirit: Wittgenstein, Philosophy, and the Mind* 179. Cambridge, MA: MIT Press, 1991.

Donadio, Rachel. "A Walled City in Tuscany Clings to Its Ancient Menu." *New York Times*, March 12, 2009.

du Sautoy, Marcus. "The Magic Numbers: A Fascination with Figures Runs through the Music of Composers from Mozart to Bach." *Guardian*, April 5, 2013.

Dussias, Allison M. "Ghost Dance and Holy Ghost: The Echoes of Nineteenth-Century Christianization Policy in Twentieth-Century Native American Free Exercise Cases." 49 *Stanford Law Review* 773 (1997).

Eberle, Edward J. "Art as Speech." 11 *University of Pennsylvania Journal of Law and Social Change* 1 (2007).

Faigman, David L. "Reconciling Individual Rights and Government Interests: Madisonian Principles versus Supreme Court Practice." 78 *Virginia Law Review* 1521 (1993).

Fairman, Christopher M. "Fuck." 28 *Cardozo Law Review* 1711 (2007).

Fiss, Owen M. "Conventionalism." 58 *Southern California Law Review* 177 (1985).

Frege, Gottlob. "Über Sinn und Bedeutung." 100 *Zeitschrift für Philosophie und Philosophische Kritik* 25 (1892). Translated in 57 *Phil. Rev.* 209 (1948).

Fromer, Jeanne C. "A Psychology of Intellectual Property." 104 *Northwestern University Law Review* (2010).

Gey, Stephen G. "The First Amendment and the Dissemination of Socially Worthless Untruths." 36 *Florida State University Law Review* 1 (2008).

Gioia, Ted. "Are We All Mistuning Our Instruments, and Can We Blame the Nazis?" *The Daily Beast*, June 6, 2015. http://www.thedailybeast.com/articles/2015/06/06/are-we-all-mistuning-our-instruments-and-can-we-blame-the-nazis.html.

Gopnik, Blake. "The Big Debate: Can Food Be Serious Art?" *Washington Post*, September 23, 2009. www.washingtonpost.com.

Greenman, John. "On Communication." 106 *Michigan Law Review* 1337 (2008).

Grey, Thomas C. "Holmes and Legal Pragmatism." 41 *Stanford Law Review* 787 (1989).

Grice, H. P. "Meaning." 66 *Philosophical Review* 377 (1957).

———. "Utterer's Meaning, Sentence-Meaning, and Word-Meaning." 4 *Foundations of Language* 225 (1968).

Hacker, P. M. S. "Was He Trying to Whistle It?" In *The New Wittgenstein* 353 (Alice Crary and Rupert Read eds.). New York: Routledge, 2000.

Hamilton, Marci A. "Art Speech." 49 *Vanderbilt Law Review* 73 (1996).

Harris, Neil. "John Philip Sousa and the Culture of Reassurance." In *Perspectives on John Philip Sousa* 11 (Jon Newsom ed.). Washington, DC: Library of Congress, 1983.

Haws, Janet Elizabeth. "Architecture as Art? Not in My Neocolonial Neighborhood: A Case for Providing First Amendment Protections to Expressive Residential Architecture." 2005 *Brigham Young University Law Review* 1625 (2005).

Henderson, Isobel. "Ancient Greek Music." In 1 *The New Oxford History of Music* 336 (Egon Wellesz ed.). Oxford: Oxford University Press, 1957.

Henkin, Louis. "The Supreme Court, 1967 Term—Foreword: On Drawing Lines." 82 *Harvard Law Review* 63 (1968).

Holmes, Oliver Wendell, Jr. "Law in Science and Science in Law." 12 *Harvard Law Review* 443 (1899).

Horsfield, Martin. "This Record Must Not Be Broadcast." *Guardian*, September 20, 2008.

Hutcheson, Joseph C., Jr. "The Judgment Intuitive: The Function of the 'Hunch' in Judicial Decision." 14 *Cornell Law Quarterly* 274 (1929).

Inverne, James. "Listen to This Chilling Audio as Crowd at Boston Symphony Learns President Kennedy Is Dead." *Time*, November 11, 2013. http://nation.time.com/2013/11/11/boston-symphony-kennedy-assassination.

"i sing of Olaf glad and big—Themes and Meanings." In *Critical Guide to Poetry for Students* (Philip K. Jason ed.). eNotes.com, 2002. http://www.enotes.com/topics/sing-olaf-glad-big/themes, https://perma.cc/U76Q-DVQP.

Itzkoff, Dave. "Rap Group Defends Fans, with Lawsuit." *New York Times*, January 9, 2014.

Kalven, Harry, Jr. "The Metaphysics of the Law of Obscenity." 1960 *Supreme Court Review* 1 (1960).

———. "The *New York Times* Case: A Note on 'The Central Meaning of the First Amendment." 1964 *Supreme Court Review* 191 (1964).

Kania, Andrew. "The Philosophy of Music." In *Stanford Encyclopedia of Philosophy*. October 22, 2007; rev. July 13, 2012. http://plato.stanford.edu/entries/music/3.

Kavka Gregory S. "Wittgensteinian Political Theory." 26 *Stanford Law Review* 1455 (1974).

Kelly, Jon. "The Offal Truth about American Haggis." BBC News, January 24, 2013. www.bbc.com.

Khan, Naureen. "Hummus and Maftoul, with a Side of the Israeli-Palestinian Conflict." Aljazeera America, November 19, 2014. http://america.aljazeera.com.

Koppelman, Andrew. "Free Speech and Pornography: A Response to James Weinstein." 31 *New York University Review of Law and Social Change* 899 (2007).

———. "Veil of Ignorance: Tunnel Constructivism in Free Speech Theory." 107 *Northwestern University Law Review* 647 (2013).

Kornelis, Chris. "Woody Guthrie Gave Life to Protest Songs He Wrote, Sang." *Washington Times*, October 11, 2012.

Kozinn, Allan. "Mendelssohn, This Is Your Moment." *New York Times*, February 22, 2009.

Kreimer, Seth F. "Pervasive Image Capture and the First Amendment: Memory, Discourse, and the Right to Record." 159 *University of Pennsylvania Law Review* 335 (2011).

Kronman, Anthony T. "Is Poetry Undemocratic?" 16 *Georgia State University Law Review* 311 (1999).

Kuusela, Oskari. "Nonsense and Clarification in the *Tractatus*—Resolute and Ineffability Readings and the *Tractatus*' Failure." 80 *Acta Philosophica Fennica* 35 (2006).

Lakier, Genevieve. "Sport as Speech." 16 *University of Pennsylvania Journal of Constitutional Law* 1109 (2014).

Leedy, Douglas, and Charles Corey. "Tuning Systems." In 8 *The Grove Dictionary of American Music* 276 (Charles Hiroshi Garrett ed., 2d ed.). New York: Oxford University Press, 2013.

Lehmann-Haupt, Christopher. "Ken Kesey, Author of 'Cuckoo's Nest,' Who Defined the Psychedelic Era, Dies at 66." *New York Times*, November 11, 2001.

Lemley Mark A., and Eugene Volokh. "Freedom of Speech and Injunctions in Intellectual Property Cases." 48 *Duke Law Journal* 147 (1998).

Levinson, Sanford, and J. M. Balkin. "Law, Music, and Other Performing Arts." 139 *University of Pennsylvania Law Review* 1597 (1991).

Liptak, Adam. "Court's Free-Speech Expansion Has Far-Reaching Consequences." *New York Times*, August 15, 2015.

Long, Lucy M. "Culinary Tourism." In *The Oxford Handbook of Food History* 389 (Jeffrey M. Pilcher ed.). Oxford: Oxford University Press, 2012.

Los Angeles Philharmonic. "Seven Studies on Themes of Paul Klee." Accessed December 22, 2015, http://www.laphil.com/philpedia/music/seven-studies-on-themes-of-paul-klee-gunther-schuller.

Lucas, Peter J. "From *Jabberwocky* Back to Old English: Nonsense, Anglo-Saxon and Oxford." In 1 *Language History and Linguistic Modeling* 503 (Raymond Hickey and Stanisław Puppel eds.). Boston: De Gruyter Mouton, 1997.

Lumpkin, Charles L. "Soul Food." In 4 *Encyclopedia of African American History, 1896 to the Present* 338 (Paul Finkelman ed.). Oxford: Oxford University Press, 2009.

Lury, Alexis A. "Time to Surrender: A Call for Understanding and the Re-evaluation of Heavy Metal Music within the Contexts of Legal Liability and Women." 9 *Southern California Review of Law and Women's Studies* 155 (1999).

Marceau, Justin, and Alan K. Chen. "Free Speech and Democracy in the Video Age." 116 *Columbia Law Review* 991 (2016).

Marshall, William P. "In Defense of the Search for Truth as a First Amendment Justification." 30 *Georgia Law Review* 1 (1995).

McGinn, Marie. "Between Metaphysics and Nonsense: Elucidation in Wittgenstein's *Tractatus*." 49 *Philosophical Quarterly* 491 (1999).

Meiklejohn, Alexander. "The First Amendment Is an Absolute." 1961 *Supreme Court Review* 245 (1961).

Mervis, Scott. "Insane Clown Posse Is Back in the Dark Carnival." *Pittsburgh Post-Gazette*, May 20, 2010.

Mirovalev, Mansur. "Once-Banned Shostakovich Ballet Triumphs." *Washington Post*, June 15, 2007, http://www.washingtonpost.com/wp-dyn/content/article/2007/06/15/AR2007061501128_pf.html.

Moi, Toril. "'They Practice Their Trades in Different Worlds': Concepts in Post-structuralism and Ordinary Language Philosophy." 40 *New Literary History* 801 (2009).

Moore, A. W., and Peter Sullivan. "Ineffability and Nonsense." 77 *Proceedings of the Aristotelian Society (Supplementary Volumes)* 169 (2003).

Moss, Stephen. "The Hills Are Alive." *Guardian*, November 15, 2001.

Munkittrick, David. "Music as Speech: A First Amendment Category unto Itself." 62 *Federal Communications Law Journal* 665 (2010).

Nahmod, Sheldon. "Artistic Expression and Aesthetic Theory: The Beautiful, the Sublime, and the First Amendment." 1987 *Wisconsin Law Review* 221 (1987).

National Tourette Syndrome Association. "What Is Tourette Syndrome?" Accessed February 25, 2014, www.tourette.org.

Nimmer, Melville B. "Does Copyright Abridge the First Amendment Guarantees of Free Speech and Press?" 17 *UCLA Law Review* 1180 (1970).

———. "The Meaning of Symbolic Speech under the First Amendment." 21 *UCLA Law Review* 29 (1973).

Olson, Kirk A. "Constitutional Law: Can Music Be Considered Obscene? *Skywalker Records, Inc. v. Navarro*—The 2 Live Crew, Obscene or Oppressed?" 44 *Oklahoma Law Review* 513 (1991).

Patterson, Dennis M. "Conscience and the Constitution." 93 *Columbia Law Review* 270 (1993).

———. "Law's Pragmatism: Law as Practice and Narrative." 76 *Virginia Law Review* 937 (1990).

———. "Wittgenstein and Constitutional Theory." 72 *Texas Law Review* 1837 (1994).

Pleasance, Chris. "ISIS Police Sentence Musicians to 90 Lashes Because They Were Playing an 'Un-Islamic' Electronic Keyboard." *Daily Mail*, January 20, 2015. http://www.dailymail.co.uk/news/article-2918061/ISIS-police-sentence-musicians-lashes-playing-Islamic-electonic-keyboard.html.

Poser, Bill. "The Supreme Court Fails Semantics." *Language Log*, July 7, 2007. http://itre.cis.upenn.edu/myl/languagelog.

Posner, Richard A. "Bork and Beethoven." 42 *Stanford Law Review* 1365 (1990).

———. Introduction to *The Essential Holmes: Selections from the Letters, Speeches, Judicial Opinions, and Other Writings of Oliver Wendell Holmes, Jr.* ix (Richard A. Posner ed.) Chicago: University of Chicago Press, 1992.

Post, Robert C. "The Constitutional Concept of Public Discourse: Outrageous Opinion, Democratic Deliberation, and *Hustler Magazine v. Falwell*." 103 *Harvard Law Review* 601 (1990).

———. "Participatory Democracy and Free Speech." 97 *Virginia Law Review* 477 (2011).

———. "Participatory Democracy as a Theory of Free Speech: A Reply." 97 *Virginia Law Review* 617 (2011).

———. "Reconciling Theory and Doctrine in First Amendment Jurisprudence." 88 *California Law Review* 2353 (2000).

———. "Recuperating First Amendment Doctrine." 47 *Stanford Law Review* 1249 (1995).

Predoehl, Eric. "A Short History of the Song 'Louie Louie.'" LouieLouie.net, 1999.

Prochnik, George. "I'm Thinking. Please. Be Quiet." *New York Times*, August 25, 2013.

Ramachandran, Gowri. "Freedom of Dress: State and Private Regulation of Clothing, Hairstyle, Jewelry, Makeup, Tattoos, and Piercing." 66 *Maryland Law Review* 11 (2006).

Redish, Martin H. "The Value of Free Speech." 130 *University of Pennsylvania Law Review* 591 (1982).

Redish, Martin H., and Gary Lippman. "Freedom of Expression and the Civic Republican Revival in Constitutional Theory: The Ominous Implications." 79 *California Law Review* 267 (1991).

Redish Martin H., and Abby Marie Mollen. "Understanding Post's and Meiklejohn's Mistakes: The Central Role of Adversary Democracy in the Theory of Free Expression." 103 *Northwestern University Law Review* 1303 (2009).

Reed, O. Lou. "Should the First Amendment Protect Joe Camel? Toward an Understanding of Constitutional 'Expression.'" 32 *American Business Law Journal* 311 (1995).

Rice, Susan Jill. "The Search for Valid Governmental Regulations: A Review of the Judicial Response to Municipal Policies Regarding First Amendment Activities." 63 *Notre Dame Law Review* 561 (1988).

Rohrer, Finlo. "The Devil's Music." *BBC News Magazine*, April 28, 2006. http://news.bbc.co.uk/2/hi/4952646.stm.

Rohter, Larry. "Musical Nomads, Escaping Political Upheaval." *New York Times*, July 30, 2013.

Rubenfeld, Jed. "The First Amendment's Purpose." 53 *Stanford Law Review* 767 (2001).

Rumens, Carol. "Pussy Riot's Punk Prayer Is Pure Protest Poetry." *Guardian*, August 20, 2012. http://www.theguardian.com/books/2012/aug/20/pussy-riot-punk-prayer-lyrics.

Russell, Bertrand. "On Denoting." 14 *Mind* 479 (1905).

Rutledge-Borger, Meredith E. "Rock and Roll vs. Censorship." Rock and Roll Hall of Fame and Museum. Accessed August 23, 2013, https://rockhall.com/blog/post/8840_censorship-in-rock-and-roll-history.

Sams, Eric. "Cryptography, Musical." In 6 *The New Grove Dictionary of Music and Musicians* 753 (Stanley Sadie ed., 2d ed.). London: Macmillan, 2001.

Scanlon, T. M. "Why Not Base Free Speech on Autonomy or Democracy?" 97 *Virginia Law Review* 541 (2011).

Scanlon, T. M., Jr. "Freedom of Expression and Categories of Expression." 40 *University of Pittsburgh Law Review* 519 (1979).

Scanlon, Thomas. "A Theory of Freedom of Expression." 1 *Philosophy and Public Affairs* 204 (1972).

Schauer, Frederick. "The Boundaries of the First Amendment: A Preliminary Exploration of Constitutional Salience." 117 *Harvard Law Review* 1765 (2004).

———. "Categories and the First Amendment: A Play in Three Acts." 34 *Vanderbilt Law Review* 265 (1981).

———. "The Second-Best First Amendment." 31 *William and Mary Law Review* 1 (1989).

———. "Speech and 'Speech'—Obscenity and 'Obscenity': An Exercise in the Interpretation of Constitutional Language." 67 *Georgetown Law Journal* 899 (1979).

Schumann, Anne. "The Beat That Beat Apartheid: The Role of Music in the Resistance against Apartheid in South Africa." 14 *Vienna Journal of African Studies* 17 (2008).

Seabrooke, Lily. "Poetry Analysis: E. E. Cummings." Helium.com, 2015. Accessed December 22, 2015, www.helium.com.

Shegerian, Carney R. "A Sign of the Times: The United States Supreme Court Effectively Abolishes the Narrowly Tailored Requirement for Time, Place and Manner Restrictions." 25 *Loyola of Los Angeles Law Review* 453 (1992).

Shiffrin, Seana Valentine. "A Thinker-Based Approach to Freedom of Speech." 27 *Constitutional Commentary* 251 (2011).

Solum, Lawrence Byard. "Freedom of Communicative Action: A Theory of the First Amendment Freedom of Speech." 83 *Northwestern University Law Review* 54 (1998).

Spottswood, Mark. "Falsity, Insincerity, and the Freedom of Expression." 16 *William and Mary Bill of Rights Journal* 1203 (2008).

Staff, Rovi. "Biography of Arnold Schoenberg." AllMusic, 2015. Accessed February 2, 2015, http://www.allmusic.com/artist/arnold-schoenberg-mn0000691043/biography.

Stuart, Susan. "Shibboleths and *Ceballos*: Eroding Constitutional Rights through Pseudocommunication." 2008 *Brigham Young University Law Review* 1545 (2008).

Sunstein, Cass R. "Pornography and the First Amendment." 1986 *Duke Law Journal* 589 (1986).

Tait, Robert. "Iran's 'Culturally Inappropriate' Rock Hopefuls Struggle to Be Heard." *Guardian*, August 23, 2005.

Tan, Monica, "Dance Rallies Held across Australia Protest $105m Cut to Arts Funding Body." *Guardian*, May 22, 2015. www.theguardian.com.

Tiersma, Peter Meijes. "Nonverbal Communication and the Freedom of 'Speech.'" 1993 *Wisconsin Law Review* 1525 (1993).

Tilghman, B. R. "Literature, Philosophy and Nonsense." 30 *British Journal of Aesthetics* 256 (1990).

Torres, Gerald. "Morenitos, Güeros, y Bolillos." 3 *Texas Hispanic Journal of Law and Policy* 61 (1997).

Tsukayama, Hayley. "'Harlem Shake' Videos Lead to School Suspensions." *Washington Post*, March 4, 2013. www.washingtonpost.com.

Tushnet, Rebecca. "Copyright as a Model for Free Speech Law: What Copyright Has in Common with Campaign Finance Reform, Hate Speech and Pornography Regulation, and Telecommunications Regulation." 42 *Boston College Law Review* 1 (2001).

———. "Copy This Essay: How Fair Use Doctrine Harms Free Speech and How Copying Serves It." 114 *Yale Law Journal* 535 (2004).

Varat, Jonathan D. "Deception and the First Amendment: A Central, Complex, and Somewhat Curious Relationship." 53 *UCLA Law Review* 1107 (2006).

Volokh, Eugene. "In Defense of the Marketplace of Ideas / Search for Truth as a Theory of Free Speech Protection." 97 *Virginia Law Review* 595 (2011).

———. "Speech as Conduct: Generally Applicable Laws, Illegal Courses of Conduct, 'Situation-Altering Utterances,' and the Unchartered Zones." 90 *Cornell Law Review* 1277 (2005).

Volokh, Eugene, and Brett McDonnell. "Freedom of Speech and Independent Judgment Review in Copyright Cases." 107 *Yale Law Journal* 2431 (1998).

Waldman, Joshua. "Symbolic Speech and Social Meaning." 97 *Columbia Law Review* 1844 (1997).

Waldron, Jeremy. "Vagueness in Law and Language: Some Philosophical Issues." 82 *California Law Review* 509 (1994).

Weinstein, James. "Democracy, Sex and the First Amendment." 31 *New York University Review of Law and Social Change* 865 (2007).

———. "Free Speech Values, Hardcore Pornography and the First Amendment: A Reply to Professor Koppelman." 31 *New York University Review of Law and Social Change* 911 (2007).

———. "Participatory Democracy as the Central Value of American Free Speech Doctrine." 97 *Virginia Law Review* 491 (2011).

West, Sonja. "NYC's Ban on Dancing." *Huffington Post*, June 30, 2015. www.huffingtonpost.com.

"What's in a Meme? The Harlem Shake." *Economist*, March 9, 2013. www.economist. com.

Winter, Steven L. "For What It's Worth." 26 *Law and Society Review* 789 (1992).

Wright, Claire. "Reconciling Cultural Diversity and Free Trade in the Digital Age: A Cultural Analysis of the International Trade in Content Items." 41 *Akron Law Review* 399 (2008).

Wright, R. George. "What Counts as 'Speech' in the First Place? Determining the Scope of the Free Speech Clause." 37 *Pepperdine Law Review* 1217 (2010).

Wu, Tim. "Machine Speech." 161 *University of Pennsylvania Law Review* 1495 (2013).

Yovel, Jonathan. "What Is Contract Law 'About'? Speech Act Theory and a Critique of 'Skeletal Promises.'" 94 *Northwestern University Law Review* 937 (2000).

Zatorre, Robert J., and Valorie N. Salimpoor. "Why Music Makes Our Brain Sing." *New York Times*, June 7, 2013. http://www.nytimes.com/2013/06/09/opinion/sunday/why-music-makes-our-brain-sing.html.

BOOKS

Ainslie, Ricardo. *No Dancin' in Anson: An American Story of Race and Social Change.* Lanham, MD: Jason Aronson, 1995.

Alexander, Larry. *Is There a Right of Freedom of Expression?* Cambridge: Cambridge University Press, 2005.

Alexy, Robert. *A Theory of Constitutional Rights.* Translated by Julian Rivers. Oxford: Oxford University Press, 2002.

Amar, Akhil Reed. *America's Constitution: A Biography.* New York: Random House, 2005.

Anscombe, G. E. M. *An Introduction to Wittgenstein's Tractatus.* 1971. 4th ed. South Bend, IN: St. Augustine's, 2001.

Atkinson, James R. *The Mystical in Wittgenstein's Early Writings.* New York: Routledge, 2009.

Austin, J. L. *How to Do Things with Words.* Cambridge, MA: Harvard University Press, 1962.

Ayer, A. J. *Language, Truth, and Logic.* 1936. New York: Dover, 1952.

Baker, C. Edwin. *Human Liberty and Freedom of Speech.* New York: Oxford University Press, 1992.

Balkin, Jack M. *Constitutional Redemption: Political Faith in an Unjust World.* Cambridge, MA: Harvard University Press, 2011.

Berger, Karol. *A Theory of Art.* New York: Oxford University Press, 2000.

Bezanson, Randall P. *Art and Freedom of Speech.* Urbana: University of Illinois Press, 2009.

Blecha, Peter. *Taboo Tunes: A History of Banned Bands and Censored Songs.* San Francisco: Backbeat Books, 2004.

Bollinger, Lee C. *Uninhibited, Robust, and Wide-Open.* Oxford: Oxford University Press, 2010.

Boyle, James. *The Public Domain.* New Haven, CT: Yale University Press, 2008.

Carroll, Lewis. *Alice's Adventures in Wonderland.* Boston: Lee and Shepard, 1869.

———. *Through the Looking-Glass, and What Alice Found There*. London: Macmillan, 1872.

Cavell, Stanley. *Must We Mean What We Say? A Book of Essays*. Updated ed. Cambridge: Cambridge University Press, 2015.

Chomsky, Noam. *Syntactic Structures*. The Hague: Mouton, 1957.

Dewey, John. *Art as Experience*. New York: Minton, Balch, 1934.

Diamond, Cora. *The Realistic Spirit*. Cambridge, MA: MIT Press, 1995.

Eggebrecht, Hans Heinrich. *Understanding Music: The Nature and Limits of Musical Cognition*. Farnham, UK: Ashgate, 2010.

Emerson, Thomas I. *The System of Freedom of Expression*. New York: Random House, 1970.

Fay, Laurel E. *Shostakovich: A Life*. New York: Oxford University Press, 1999.

Gioia, Ted. *The History of Jazz*. New York: Oxford University Press, 1997.

Goss, Glenda Dawn. *Sibelius: A Composer's Life and the Awakening of Finland*. Chicago: University of Chicago Press, 2009.

Green, Jonathon, and Nicholas J. Karolides. *Encyclopedia of Censorship*. 2d ed. New York: Facts on File, 2005.

Greenawalt, Kent. *Speech, Crime, and the Uses of Language*. New York: Oxford University Press, 1989.

Grout, Donald Jay, and Claude V. Palisca. *A History of Western Music*. 4th ed. New York: Norton, 1988.

Guerrieri, Matthew. *The First Four Notes: Beethoven's Fifth and the Human Imagination*. New York: Knopf, 2012.

Haas, Michael. *Forbidden Music: The Jewish Composers Banned by the Nazis*. New Haven, CT: Yale University Press, 2013.

Hacker, P. M. S. *Insight and Illusion: Themes in the Philosophy of Wittgenstein*. Rev. ed. Oxford, UK: Clarendon, 1986.

Hast, Dorothea E., James R. Cowdery, and Stan Scott. *Exploring the World of Music: An Introduction to Music from a World Music Perspective*. Dubuque, IA: Kendall/Hunt, 1999.

Hegel, George Wilhelm Friedrich. *Aesthetics: Lectures on Fine Arts*. 2 vols. Translated by T. M. Knox. Oxford, UK: Clarendon, 1975.

Hochberg, Herbert. *Introducing Analytic Philosophy: Its Sense and Nonsense, 1879–2002*. Frankfurt: Ontos Verlag, 2003.

Holmes, Oliver Wendell, Jr., and Harold J. Laski. *Holmes-Laski Letters: The Correspondence of Mr. Justice Holmes and Harold J. Laski, 1916–1935*. Edited by Mark DeWolfe Howe. 2 vols. Cambridge, MA: Harvard University Press, 1953.

Huxley, Aldous. "The Rest Is Silence." In *Music at Night and Other Essays*. London: Chatto and Windus, 1931.

Jackson, Blair, Dennis McNally, and Stephen Peters. *Grateful Dead: The Illustrated Trip*. London: Dorling Kindersley, 2003.

Joyce, James. *Ulysses*. Paris: Sylvia Beach, 1922.

Julius, Anthony. *Transgressions*. Chicago: University of Chicago Press, 2002.

Kahane, Guy, Edward Kanterian, and Oskari Kuusela. *Wittgenstein and His Interpreters*. Hoboken, NJ: Wiley-Blackwell, 2007.

Knowles, Mark. *The Wicked Waltz and Other Scandalous Dances: Outrage at Couple Dancing in the 19th and Early 20th Centuries*. Jefferson, NC: McFarland, 2009.

Korsmeyer, Carolyn. *Making Sense of Taste: Food and Philosophy*. Ithaca, NY: Cornell University Press, 1999.

Kramer, Lawrence. *Expression and Truth: On the Music of Knowledge*. Berkeley: University of California Press, 2012.

Levi, Erik. *Music In the Third Reich*. New York: St. Martin's, 1994.

MacLeish, Archibald. *Collected Poems, 1917–1982*. Boston: Mariner Books, 1985.

Martin, Linda, and Kerry Segrave. *Anti-Rock: The Opposition to Rock 'n' Roll*. New York: De Capo, 1993.

Meiklejohn, Alexander. *Free Speech and Its Relation to Self-Government*. New York: Harper, 1948.

———. *Political Freedom*. New York: Harper, 1960.

Menand, Louis. *The Metaphysical Club: A Story of Ideas in America*. New York: Farrar, Straus and Giroux, 2001.

Mill, John Stuart. *On Liberty*. London: John Parker, 1859.

Milton, John. *Areopagitica: A Speech for the Liberty of Unlicensed Printing*. 1644. Edited by H. B. Cotterill. New York: Macmillan, 1959.

Monk, Ray. *Ludwig Wittgenstein: The Duty of Genius*. New York: Free Press, 1990.

Moon, Tom. *1,000 Recordings to Hear before You Die*. New York: Workman, 2008.

Nussbaum, Martha C. *Upheavals of Thought*. Cambridge: Cambridge University Press, 2001.

Nuzum, Eric. *Parental Advisory: Music Censorship in America*. New York: Perennial, 2001.

Nyman, Michael. *Experimental Music: Cage and Beyond*. 2d ed. New York: Schirmer Books, 1999.

Palmer, Robert. *Deep Blues*. New York: Viking, 1982.

Perlis, Vivian, and Libby Van Cleve. *Composers' Voices from Ives to Ellington*. New Haven, CT: Yale University Press, 2005.

Piety, Tamara R. *Brandishing the First Amendment: Commercial Expression in America*. Ann Arbor: University of Michigan Press, 2012.

Plato. *The Republic*. c. 380 BCE. Translated by Benjamin Jowett. 3d ed. 2 vols. Oxford: Oxford University Press, 1908.

Post, Robert. *Democracy, Expertise, and Academic Freedom*. New Haven, CT: Yale University Press, 2012.

Ramsey, Frank Plumpton. *The Foundations of Mathematics*. Edited by R. B. Braithwaite. London: Routledge and Kegan Paul, 1931.

Redish, Martin H. *Freedom of Expression: A Critical Analysis*. Charlottesville, VA: Michie, 1984.

Rorty, Richard M., ed. *The Linguistic Turn: Essays in Philosophical Method*. Chicago: University of Chicago Press, 1992.

Rosen, Charles. *Freedom and the Arts: Essays on Music and Literature*. Cambridge, MA: Harvard University Press, 2012.

Ross, Janice. *Like a Bomb Going Off: Leonid Yakobson and Ballet as Resistance in Soviet Russia*. New Haven, CT: Yale University Press, 2014.

Russell, Bertrand. *An Inquiry into Meaning and Truth*. New York: Norton, 1940.

———. *The Problems of Philosophy*. Rockville, MD: Arc Manor, 2008.

Schauer, Frederick F. *Free Speech: A Philosophical Enquiry*. Cambridge: Cambridge University Press, 1982.

Schopenhauer, Arthur. *The World as Will and Representation*. 2 vols. Translated by E. F. J. Payne. Indian Hills, CO: Falcon's Wing, 1958.

Schweitzer, Kenneth. *The Artistry of Afro-Cuban Batá Drumming*. Jackson: University of Mississippi Press, 2013.

Searle, John R. *Expression and Meaning: Studies in the Theory of Speech Acts*. Cambridge: Cambridge University Press, 1979.

———. *Intentionality: An Essay in the Philosophy of Mind*. Cambridge: Cambridge University Press, 1983.

———. *Speech Acts: An Essay in the Philosophy of Language*. Cambridge: Cambridge University Press, 1995.

Stone, Geoffrey R., Louis Michael Seidman, Cass R. Sunstein, Pamela S. Karlan, and Mark V. Tushnet. *Constitutional Law* (6th ed.). New York: Aspen, 2009.

Sunstein, Cass R. *Democracy and the Problem of Free Speech*. New York: Free Press, 1993.

Tompkins, Jane P., ed. *Reader-Response Criticism: From Formalism to Post-Structuralism*. Baltimore: Johns Hopkins University Press, 1980.

Whistler, James MacNeill. *The Gentle Art of Making Enemies*. New York: J. W. Lovell, 1890.

Williams, William Carlos. *The Collected Poems of William Carlos Williams*. 2 vols. Edited by Christopher McGowan. New York: New Directions Books, 2001.

Wittgenstein, Ludwig. *Culture and Value*. Edited by G. H. von Wright. Translated by Peter Winch. Chicago: University of Chicago Press, 1980.

———. *Letters to Russell, Keynes, and Moore*. Edited by G. H. von Wright. Oxford, UK: Basil Blackwell, 1974.

———. *Philosophical Investigations*. Translated by G. E. M. Anscombe. 3d ed. New York: Macmillan, 1969.

———. *Tractatus Logico-Philosophicus*. Edited and translated by C. K. Ogden. New York: Harcourt Brace, 1922.

———. *The Wittgenstein Reader*. Edited by Kenny Anthony. 2d ed. Hoboken, NJ: Wiley-Blackwell, 2006.

Wolfe, Tom. *The Electric Kool-Aid Acid Test*. New York: Farrar, Straus and Giroux, 1968.

CASES

Abrams v. United States, 250 U.S. 616 (1919).

American Booksellers Association, Inc. v. Hudnut, 771 F.2d 323 (7th Cir. 1985).

Anderson v. City of Hermosa Beach, 621 F.3d 1051 (9th Cir. 2010).

Animal Legal Defense Fund v. Otter, 118 F. Supp. 3d 1195 (D. Idaho 2015).

Arcara v. Cloud Books, Inc., 478 U.S. 697 (1986).

Ashcroft v. ACLU, 535 U.S. 564 (2002).

Ashcroft v. Free Speech Coalition, 535 U.S. 234 (2002).

Association des Éleveurs de Canards et d'Oies du Québec v. Harris, 729 F.3d 937 (9th Cir. 2013).

Barnes v. Glen Theatre, Inc., 501 U.S. 560 (1991).

Bery v. City of New York, 97 F.3d 689 (2d Cir. 1996).

Blanch v. Koons, 467 F.3d 244 (2d Cir. 2006).

Bleistein v. Donaldson Lithographing Co., 188 U.S. 239 (1903).

Bridgeport Music, Inc. v. UMG Recordings, Inc., 585 F.3d 267 (6th Cir. 2009).

Bright Tunes Music v. Harrisongs Music, 420 F. Supp. 177 (S.D.N.Y. 1976).

Broadrick v. Oklahoma, 413 U.S. 601 (1973).

Brooklyn Institute of Arts & Sciences v. Giuliani, 64 F. Supp. 2d 184 (F.D.N.Y. 1999).

Brown v. Entertainment Merchants Association, 564 U.S. 786 (2011).

Buckley v. Valeo, 424 U.S. 1 (1976).

California v. LaRue, 409 U.S. 109 (1972).

Carey v Brown, 447 U.S. 455 (1980).

Cavel International, Inc. v. Madigan, 500 F.3d 551 (7th Cir. 2007).

Central Hudson Gas v. Public Service Commission, 447 U.S. 557 (1980).

Chaplinsky v. New Hampshire, 315 U.S. 568 (1942).

Chiasson v. New York City Department of Consumer Affairs, 505 N.Y.S.2d 499 (Sup. Ct. N.Y. Cty. 1986).

Chiasson v. New York City Department of Consumer Affairs, 524 N.Y.S.2d 649 (Sup. Ct. N.Y. Cty. 1988).

Chinatown Neighborhood Association v. Brown, No. C 12–3759 PJH, 2013 WL 60919 (N.D. Cal. Jan. 2, 2013), aff'd, 539 F. App'x 761 (9th Cir. 2013).

Church of the Lukumi Babalu Aye, Inc. v. City of Hialeah, 508 U.S. 520 (1993).

City of Dallas v. Stanglin, 490 U.S. 19 (1989).

City of Erie v. Pap's A.M., 529 U.S. 277 (2000).

City of Newport v. Fact Concerts, Inc., 453 U.S. 247 (1981).

City of Renton v. Playtime Theatres, Inc., 475 U.S. 41 (1986).

Clark v. Community for Creative Nonviolence, 462 U.S. 288 (1984).

Cohen v. California, 403 U.S. 15 (1971).

Cooley v. Board of Wardens, 53 U.S. 299 (1851).

Craig v. Masterpiece Cakeshop, Inc., 370 P.3d 272 (Colo. App. 2015), cert. denied, No. 15SC738, 2016 WL 1645027 (Colo. Apr. 25, 2016), petition for cert. filed, No. 16-111 (U.S. July 22, 2016).

Discount Inn, Inc. v. City of Chicago, 803 F.3d 317 (7th Cir. 2015).

Dombrowski v. Pfister, 380 U.S. 479 (1965).

Eldred v. Ashcroft, 537 U.S. 186 (2003).

Empacadora de Carnes de Fresnillo, S.A. de C.V. v. Curry, 476 F.3d 326 (5th Cir. 2007).

Erznoznik v. City of Jacksonville, 422 U.S. 305 (1975).

First Vagabonds Church of God v. City of Orlando, 610 F.3d 1274 (11th Cir. 2010).

First Vagabonds Church of God v. City of Orlando, 638 F.3d 756 (11th Cir. 2011).

Glik v. Cunniffe, 655 F.3d 78 (1st Cir. 2011).

Graham v. Connor, 490 U.S. 386 (1989).

Grayned v. City of Rockford, 408 U.S. 104 (1972).

Harper & Row, Publishers v. Nation Enterprises, 471 U.S. 538 (1985).

Heffron v. International Society for Krishna Consciousness, Inc., 452 U.S. 640 (1981).

Hill v. Colorado, 530 U.S. 703 (2000).

Hobbs v. County of Westchester, 397 F.3d 133 (2d Cir. 2005).

Holder v. Humanitarian Law Project, 561 U.S. 1 (2010).

Hurley v. Irish-American Gay, Lesbian & Bisexual Group of Boston, Inc., 515 U.S. 557 (1995).

Hustler Magazine, Inc. v. Falwell, 485 U.S. 46 (1988).

Illinois Restaurant Association v. City of Chicago, No. 06 C 7014, 2008 WL 8915042 (N.D. Ill. Aug. 7, 2008).

Jacobellis v. Ohio, 378 U.S. 184 (1964).

Jenkins v. Rumsfeld, 412 F. Supp. 1177 (E.D. Va. 1976).

Joseph Burstyn, Inc. v. Wilson, 343 U.S. 493 (1952).

Kieselstein-Cord v. Accessories by Pearl, Inc., 632 F.2d 989 (2d Cir. 1980).

Kleinman v. City of San Marcos, 597 F.3d 323 (5th Cir. 2010), *cert. denied*, 562 U.S. 837 (2010).

Kolender v. Lawson, 461 U.S. 352 (1983).

Lawrence v. Texas, 539 U.S. 558 (2003).

Leibovitz v. Paramount Pictures Corp., 137 F.3d 109 (2d Cir. 1996).

Loper v. New York City Police Department, 999 F.2d 699 (2d Cir. 1993).

Luke Records, Inc. v. Navarro, 960 F.2d 134 (11th Cir. 1992).

McCullen v. Coakley, 134 S. Ct. 2518 (2014).

Miller v. California, 413 U.S. 15 (1973).

Miller v. Civil City of South Bend, 904 F.2d 1081 (7th Cir. 1990).

Morse v. Frederick, 551 U.S. 393 (2007).

Muchmore's Café, LLC v. City of New York, No. 14-cv-05668 RRM-RER (E.D.N.Y. filed Sept. 26, 2014).

Mutual Film Corp. v. Industrial Commission of Ohio, 236 U.S. 230 (1915).

NAACP v. Button, 371 U.S. 415 (1963).

National Endowment for the Arts v. Finley, 524 U.S. 569 (1998).

Nelson v. Streeter, 16 F.3d 145 (7th Cir. 1994).

New York State Board of Elections v. Lopez Torres, 552 U.S. 196 (2008).

New York Times Co. v. Sullivan, 376 U.S. 254 (1964).

Nurre v. Whitehead, 580 F.3d 1087 (9th Cir. 2009); *cert. denied*, 559 U.S. 1025 (2010).

Park 'n Fly v. Dollar Park & Fly, 469 U.S. 189 (1985).

Piarowski v. Illinois Community College District 515, 759 F.2d 625 (7th Cir. 1985).

Police Department of Chicago v. Mosley, 408 U.S. 92 (1972).

Princeton University Press v. Michigan Document Services, 99 F.3d 1381 (6th Cir. 1996).

Public Utilities Commission v. Pollak, 343 U.S. 451 (1952).

R.A.V. v. City of St. Paul, 505 U.S. 377 (1992).

Reed v. Village of Shorewood, 704 F.2d 943 (7th Cir. 1983).

Reno v. ACLU, 521 U.S. 844 (1997).

Roberts v. United States Jaycees, 468 U.S. 609 (1984).

Roth v. United States, 354 U.S. 476 (1957).

Rumsfeld v. FAIR, 547 U.S. 47 (2006).

Schad v. Borough of Mount Ephraim, 452 U.S. 61 (1981).

SEIU v. City of Houston, 542 F. Supp. 2d 617 (S.D. Tex. 2008).

Skywalker Records, Inc. v. Navarro, 739 F. Supp. 578 (S.D. Fla. 1990).

Sorrell v. IMS Health, Inc., 564 U.S. 552 (2011).

Southeastern Promotions v. Conrad, 420 U.S. 546 (1975).

Spence v. Washington, 418 U.S. 405 (1974).

Stanley v. Georgia, 394 U.S. 557 (1969).

Stratechuk v. Board of Education, 587 F.3d 597 (3d Cir. 2009).

Texas v. Johnson, 491 U.S. 397 (1989).

Tinker v. Des Moines Independent Community School District, 393 U.S. 503 (1969).

Towne v. Eisner, 245 U.S. 418 (1918).

Turner Broadcasting System v. FCC, 512 U.S. 622 (1994).

Tyson & Brother v. Banton, 273 U.S. 418 (1927).

United States v. Alvarez, 132 S. Ct. 2537 (2012).

United States v. Davis, 353 F.2d 614 (2d Cir. 1965); cert. denied, 384 U.S. 953 (1966).

United States v. Eichman, 496 U.S. 310 (1990).

United States v. Kokinda, 497 U.S. 720 (1990).

United States v. O'Brien, 391 U.S. 367 (1968).

United States v. Stevens, 559 U.S. 460 (2010).

Universal Studios, Inc. v. Corley, 273 F.3d 429 (2d Cir. 2001).

Valentine v. Chrestensen, 316 U.S. 52 (1942).

Vance v. Judas Priest, Nos. 86–5844 & 86–3939, 1990 WL 130920, at *4 (Nev. Dist. Ct. Aug. 24, 1990).

Virginia v. Black, 538 U.S. 343 (2003).

Ward v. Rock Against Racism, 491 U.S. 781 (1989).

West Virginia State Board of Education v. Barnette, 319 U.S. 624 (1943).

Whitney v. California, 274 U.S. 357 (1927).

Winters v. New York, 333 U.S. 507 (1948).

Young v. American Mini-Theatres, 427 U.S. 50 (1976).

GOVERNMENTAL PUBLICATIONS

United Nations Educational, Scientific, and Cultural Organization and World Intellectual Property Organization. *Model Provisions for National Laws on the Protection of Expressions of Folklore against Illicit Exploitation and Other Prejudicial Actions.* 1985.

United Nations Human Rights Committee. "Wackenheim v. France." Communication No. 854/1999, July 15, 2002, CCPR/C/75/D/854/1999.

U.S. House of Representatives. *Agreement on Guidelines for Classroom Copying in Not-for-Profit Educational Institutions.* Report 94–1476. 1976.

MUSIC

Beatles, The. "Come Together." *Abbey Road.* Capitol Records, 1969.

———. "I Am the Walrus." *Magical Mystery Tour.* Capitol Records, 1967.

Beethoven, Ludwig Von. Symphony No. 5 in C Minor. 1808.

Biebl, Franz. *Ave Maria.* 1964.

Buffalo Springfield. "For What It's Worth." *Buffalo Springfield.* ATCO Records, 1967.

Cage, John. *4'33".* 1952.

Celentano, Adriano. "Prisencolinensinainciusol." *Nostalrock.* Italdisc, 1973.

Dave Brubeck Quartet, The. "Blue Rondo à La Turk." *Time Out.* Columbia Records, 1959.

Jimi Hendrix Experience, The. "Purple Haze." *Are You Experienced?* MCA, 1967.

Kingsmen, The. "Louie, Louie." *The Kingsmen in Person.* Wand Records, 1963.

Link Wray & His Wraymen. "Rumble." *Link Wray & the Wraymen.* Epic, 1960.

Mann, Barry. "Who Put the Bomp." *Who Put the Bomp.* Written by Barry Mann and Gerry Goffin. ABC-Paramount, 1961.

Prokofiev, Sergei. *Peter and the Wolf.* Op. 67. 1936.

Sachal Studios Orchestra. "Take Five." *Sachal Jazz: Interpretations of Jazz Standards & Bossa Nova.* Sachal Music, 2011.

Schuller, Gunther. *Seven Studies on Themes of Paul Klee.* 1959.

Shostakovich, Dmitri. Symphony No. 11 in G Minor. 1957.

Sibelius, Jean. *Finlandia.* Op. 26. 1899; rev. 1900.

Stravinsky, Igor. *The Rite of Spring.* 1913.

Young, La Monte. *The Well-Tuned Piano.* 1964, 1973, 1981–present.

Zappa, Frank. *Jazz from Hell.* EMI, 1986.

INDEX

ABOUT THE AUTHORS

Mark V. Tushnet is William Nelson Cromwell Professor of Law at Harvard Law School. He is the coauthor of four casebooks, including the most widely used casebook on constitutional law, and has written numerous books, including a two-volume work on the life of Justice Thurgood Marshall.

Alan K. Chen is the William M. Beaney Memorial Research Chair and Professor of Law at the University of Denver Sturm College of Law. He writes about free speech doctrine and theory, civil rights enforcement, and public interest law.

Joseph Blocher is Professor of Law at Duke University School of Law. He writes about the First and Second Amendments, property, and constitutional reasoning.